'*Wentworth* is a heartbreak and a home, a tale of hopelessness and hope. Combining an acute understanding of oral history and social theory, and writing with sensitivity, passion and respect, Ashwin Desai juxtaposes space and place to tell the story of Wentworth, a former apartheid "dormitory" for Coloureds. The space is polluted by petrochemical refineries and pathologised by violent gangs, drugs, overcrowding, internal conflicts and a dearth of opportunity; the place is a community of skilled artisans, small business operators, religious faithfuls, musicians, writers and, above all, soccer devotees, bound by friendship, neighbourliness, generosity and philanthropy. Desai brings the complexities, nuances and paradoxes of Wentworth to life.'
— **Douglas Booth**, professor and dean of the Faculty of Adventure, Culinary Arts and Tourism at Thompson Rivers University, and author of *The Race Game: Sport and Politics in South Africa*

'Ashwin Desai has written an extraordinary book! *Wentworth: The Beautiful Game and the Making of Place* reconstructs the "hidden" histories of a struggling Coloured community in Durban and its beloved Leeds United Football Club. Drawing on evocative interviews, Desai's highly readable prose presents contextualised stories of pleasure, suffering, self-making, togetherness, exclusion, continuity and change. It demonstrates how soccer enabled ordinary men and women to make their own history, despite the debilitating effects of urban apartheid and pollution from a nearby oil refinery. Reading *Wentworth* will transform your understanding of South African sport and society.'
— **Peter Alegi**, professor of History, Michigan State University, and author of *Laduma! Soccer, Politics and Society in South Africa*

Wentworth

Wentworth
The Beautiful Game and the Making of Place

Ashwin Desai

UNIVERSITY OF KWAZULU-NATAL PRESS

Published in 2019 by University of KwaZulu-Natal Press
Private Bag X01
Scottsville, 3201
Pietermaritzburg
South Africa
Email: books@ukzn.ac.za
Website: www.ukznpress.co.za

© 2019 Ashwin Desai

All rights reserved. No part of this publication may be reproduced or transmitted in any form or by electrical or mechanical means, including information storage and retrieval systems, without prior permission in writing from the publishers.

ISBN: 978 1 86914 446 3
e-ISBN: 978 1 86914 447 0

Editor: Sally Hines
Layout: Patricia Comrie
Proofreader: Judith Shier
Indexer: Christopher Merrett
Cover design: Artworks
Cover photo: Soccer grounds in Wentworth with petrochemical industry in the background (Cedric Nunn)

Printed and bound in South Africa by Pinetown Printers

For my father, who once drove two hours to watch me play.
We lost 6-1. I scored . . . an own goal . . .

Contents

Foreword by Trevor Ngwane xi
Preface xvii
Acknowledgements xxi

1 How to Tell a Story 1
2 The Ground In-Between 28
3 The Art of Friendship 58
4 A Generation of Talent 91
5 The Leftover Years 132
6 Nurturing New Talent 138
7 The Field of Relations 165
8 Living History 195

References 227
Index 233

Foreword

'Give the great woman a Bells,' said one of the old timers in a toast to Ashwin Desai's mother, whose remains lay in a vase that competed for space with the glasses and bottles of drinks on the table. Desai brought his mother's ashes to the bar because the solemn, boozy commotion that ensued revealed a tenderness that was characteristic of the deep, strong social bonds that tied the people around the table, some going back more than 50 years.

On a different day, he had promised his occasional drinking *bras* (mates) to write a history of their favourite soccer team from the old days, Leeds United of Wentworth. In this book, he has kept his promise and the story he tells of this local football club, which rose and fell in the 1970s and 1980s, is told with that same old tenderness that made the club possible in the first place.

It is a story of more than the beautiful game as played by Wentonians in their 'Cabbage Patch' grounds in a township called Wentworth, once a barracks for white soldiers, which the apartheid state declared a Coloured area before the 1960s. In telling the history of the football club, Desai decided to go 'beyond the immediate team sheets' of Leeds United and broaden his and the reader's focus on the social, cultural, economic and political conditions that made the team possible and meaningful for Wentonians, and for those who were not there but are interested and touched by the story.

It is not only 'his story', it is also 'her story'. Desai's broad canvass includes women and girls who were part of the Leeds United story, some as football players, others as soccer managers, organisers of the Supporters' Club, mothers, sisters, wives and lovers of the players, including those who were part of the community and bore witness to the sports phenomenon called Leeds: the best soccer team to come out of Wentworth.

At the heart of the story is how the exploited and oppressed make a life and create hope and joy despite the ineffaceable evil of harsh regimes, whose machinations were designed to engender pain, suffering and despair. In the face of apartheid, in and through their beloved Leeds United, the Wentonians created a space where there was more hope than despair, more joy than sorrow, more sharing than isolation, more solidarity than individualism, more trust than mistrust.

The poverty and squalor, the crime and social dislocation are problems that all working-class townships have to contend with in South Africa and in many parts of the world, some worse than others. Hapless Wentonians have to face and suffer the additional life-threatening daily exposure to the deadly fumes and smoke from the oil refineries, which are located a stone's throw from their township, not disregarding that some of them work there, especially during the few shutdown weeks when additional cheap labour is required by Engen for machine maintenance. Everyone's lungs are affected, everyone must live with the acrid stench of sulphur in the evenings, and many die of cancer and other pollution-related diseases. School kids pack asthma pumps with their lunch boxes. As Desai puts it: '[T]he violence is slower, longer, normalised into the very landscape.'

Wentworth was born of the violence of racism when apartheid's Group Areas Act was brutally imposed on communities, in the process dislocating and disorienting them. Racial classification and race-based identity politics is a vexed question in South Africa a quarter of a century after the defeat of apartheid, and 43 years after the death of Stephen Bantu Biko. He had persuasively called for the unity of so-called Indians, Coloureds and Africans under the banner of Black Consciousness – 'we are all blacks'. This unity is coming under great strain in the light of post-apartheid's competitive individualism and scuffles for resources and positions. Desai provides a unique and illuminating treatment of the subject through the lens of love and support for a football club. Without a clear understanding, all attempts to address the question of unity amount to groping in the dark.

Race and racial politics are social constructs. As such, it is important to locate the deployment and operation of these concepts, taking into account the specific socio-economic and political contexts that give rise to, shape and change them over time. Apartheid's intention, building upon and elaborating the *divide et impera* methods of imperialism and colonialism, was to divide the exploited and unite the exploiters using white supremacy and *baaskap* (paternalism) as the central anchor. As Desai points out, with Coloureds, the overriding concern was to draw a sharp line between the superior white race and the inferior 'non-whites' when confronted with miscegenation. Thus did the apartheid masters create a 'Coloured nation', which they themselves admitted did not exist, and in the process threw communities, families and individuals into an identity crisis as this harsh and categorical classification and separation tore them apart. As one Wentonian, among the many fascinating life histories in the book, tried to define himself to Desai: 'My father was Mauritian. My granny is Mauritian. My mom is actually Coloured. My dad's dad is also Mauritian – all of them from that side. Our roots are Malaysia. I identify as Coloured, but my blood is Mauritian.'

This confusion and loss of identity due to apartheid's ideologically driven racial discourse had a profound impact on Wentonians as a community. They were now defined as Coloured and treated as such by the state in ways that determined and circumscribed their life chances. They could not access housing in non-Coloured areas, and many had to move out of Clairwood and other areas in Durban that were designated as Indian. Many left the former Transkei, a Xhosa Bantustan 400 kilometres away, to live in Wentworth, 'where they belonged'. It was not only in Durban that the apartheid authorities dragged their feet in providing housing for Coloureds. Desai suggests that this was because of the vagueness of this racial category, which, though later engendering 'a hazy Coloured and Wentworth identity', was a constraint on political mobilisation that would have demanded housing and other services from the state for this social group.

In the absence of more solid grounds and discourses, these having been swept away by the apartheid ogre, the 'quest for identity had to find surrogates'. The desolate space once occupied by the military barracks had become 'Wentworth, the Coloured township', and it was necessary to turn it 'into a place, a home'. Desai quotes Lucy Lippard, who defines a place as a piece of land or 'cityscape', which, if 'seen from the inside', is 'replete with human histories and memories'. Desai's interviews and conversations with Wentonians from all walks of life reveal that to focus on the abuses and attacks on the people's way of life and living standards wrought by apartheid 'is to read one half of the page. Wentworth was also turning into a strong network of friendship and support.' Various aspects of community life suggest this process, such as friendships, marriages, the music scene, organised cultural activities, including gardening and garden competitions, and the church. This book is about the indisputable and important role that a soccer team played in humanising Wentworth.

It is about Leeds United's great players, memorable goals scored, matches won and lost, life outside the pitch, the Leeds style of play, the strategy to win matches, the commitment and discipline of training, and the boundless passion of the team and fans. Desai's brilliant method of presentation is to allow the protagonists to tell their story in their own words as much as possible. This, combined with Desai's lucid prose and light touch, makes the book so gripping that those with little interest in soccer might wish to watch a soccer match after reading it. Those who do love soccer might be more inclined to attend matches by local clubs in their neighbourhoods instead of confining themselves to watching professional teams on TV. Indeed, some of us feed our soccer bug by watching the British Premier League, Manchester United and Liverpool, rather than watching South African teams, such as Orlando Pirates and Lamontville Golden Arrows.

Desai has succeeded in meeting Njabulo Ndebele's challenge to 'move beyond the spectacular contest between the powerless and the powerful' and to zero in onto 'the nooks and crannies', 'the c(r)ooks and grannies', and to grasp 'the essential drama in the lives of ordinary people'. What is amazing is that in documenting the everyday lives of ordinary people – the working class and the poor – at every turn we are led to confront the structural source of their daily struggles, whether it is a struggle to get water or electricity, or a struggle to have a decent sports ground so that the youngsters can play. C. Wright Mills famously wrote about how private troubles are ultimately public issues. Desai quotes Pierre Bourdieu, where he suggests 'that *the most personal is the most impersonal*' in so far as the roots of the suffering of ordinary people lie 'in the objective contradictions, constraints and double binds inscribed in the structures of the labour and housing markets'.

The passion with which Bennie Whitby, the founder and manager of Leeds United, built and sacrificed for the club suggests a quest for something much bigger than winning football matches and tournaments. Indeed, it was exactly when Leeds entered the professional leagues at the highest level that Whitby's guiding hand began to falter. The great Gary Goldstone, the player who would go berserk when Leeds lost a match, could and did play well in bigger teams (as did some of his teammates) but he will tell you that his best moments were when he played for Leeds. Throughout the book, Desai suggests that there is more to soccer than meets the eye, hence his decision to use a broader lens that goes beyond the immediate activities and issues of Leeds. Contemporary left sportswriters, such as Dave Zirin, have written about and argued for the overlap between sport and politics. Sociologists, such as John Hargreaves, have noted the social functions of sports, suggesting that 'sports can be made to map national struggles'. Desai adds that it can also 'tell us much about local struggles' and how one endeavours to position oneself 'in the imposed racial hierarchy of the apartheid city'.

Zirin has famously criticised the corrosive role of corporate finance in US sports, accusing it of promoting a toxic masculinity, militarism and racism. One of Whitby's downfalls as manager of Leeds is arguably related to his hatred of corporate sponsorship and his reliance on community self-funding. As Leeds went up the lower football leagues and made it into the first division, he refused to relent: 'I hate sponsorship. If someone sponsors me with a hundred rand; they are going to want to tell me how to spend that hundred rand.' He argued that the big corporates give you very little in relation to the huge profits they make, yet, still, 'they then control you. I don't want to be controlled by anyone. This is my team.' Desai himself is ambivalent about this, noting the demise of Leeds but uncertain about 'success' in professional, corporate-funded and corporate-controlled sports.

The redemptive part of the Leeds story is that although the club is gone, it somehow lives on in Wentworth, not least in the memories of those who experienced the team at its best. Today, for example, there is a new promising team, the Young Cavaliers, which is managed by Lorna Petersen, sister to the Leeds star player Dennis Petersen. She was the former chairperson of the Leeds Supporters' Club. She takes care of the young players' needs, treating them like family, including feeding and providing shelter to those in need, just as it was done at Leeds. Desai argues: 'The historic and inspirational links with Leeds are as clear as a footpath through the veld. The path is a bit overgrown through lack of everyday use but indelible still.' Nevertheless, in the very last sentence of his book, Desai asks: 'The eternal question haunts: will Young Cavaliers escape the lower leagues and finally arrive? And if they do, will they lose their *place*?'

My answer is: capitalism works in the day and in the night. It also works through sport, as Zirin and others have suggested. But, as Desai argues, this is only half the story. At every point, the working class and its allies have to fight and struggle to survive, be it for basic services or for recreational services. That is the nature of the system. It is important to note that in the course of this daily struggle, creativity, compassion, intellectual life and humane relations are there every day, all the time. Desai's story about Leeds United is an appreciation and reflection of these qualities inherent in the people who have to fight in order to survive. It is a story about sacrifice, solidarity, decency and vision. It is a story not so much about identity but about ending the everyday alienation of capitalist existence; of developing a different and more humane way of relating to each other: sharing, caring and collective solidarity.

Leeds United provided a space where this vision, this dream, became an everyday reality. Ordinary working-class people are always on the lookout for such spaces of hope. Just as it is with workers who produce the material necessities of modern life, it is workers who themselves create such spaces. These are spaces of refuge away from the ravages of capitalist existence, including tensions among people due to overcrowding, poverty, competition and crime. Some workers in Wentworth carved out such a space in the beautiful game, in the form of a football club they called Leeds. Through Leeds, they saw a glimpse of a different way of relating to each other, indeed of a different community, a different Wentworth. Those who saw it cannot unsee it, they will not surrender it, they will protect its memory, they will die talking about it. In the football club, they became the best that they could be. Desai ensures that their story, their dream and their Leeds will live for generations to come in Wentworth and beyond. He is giving back what belongs to them. Give him a Bells!

Trevor Ngwane
President of the South African Sociological Association
Senior lecturer in the Department of Sociology,
University of Johannesburg

Preface

> Through the multiple acts of playing, organising, watching and following, people have defined and expressed who they think they and their neighbours are. And all for what? Because football matches do not change social structures. Because no victory, however comprehensive, can shift the real balance of power, or change the actual distribution of wealth and status. It is for winning, and winning in style . . . Because, when it came to it on the pitch, when the whistle blew and money, power, status, reputation and history were all sent to the bench, you wanted it more.
>
> — Goldblatt, *The Ball is Round*

It was December 2015. I sat in my usual spot at my old local in Durban. It is the last of the old-style 'non-white' bars that proliferated in the 1960s and 70s across the city. Dark and dank with wooden seats, worn-in, around a semi-circular oak bar. The chatter all gets washed down with rounds of beer and whisky called from over-receding hairlines and collected between the press of pot bellies. Food can suddenly emerge from the nether reaches of the backroom, 'on the house'. Trotters and beans, tripe biryani, mince and peas eaten with buttered bread. Maybe a vinegar chilli. Food from bygone times. To step into this bar is to step into the past. But the debates and prejudices of old are melded into the present. Sometimes, I wonder what I am doing in this den of political impropriety where every one of my views is loathed. It is for the *braskap*. Friendship? No. That is an inadequate translation. You see, when I walk into the bar, the first question they ask me is, 'How's your mum?' They had never met her. But they know that this is what brought me back to Durban. When she died in December 2017, her ashes stood on the bar as we said a toast; 'give the great woman a Bells' one of the pot bellies, once a centre-half of note, wobbled.

Many a time I have left the bar promising never to return. But deep down, I know I will be back. In this loud, smoke-filled pit, between the macho posturing, there is tenderness. During December 2016, the festive cheer was in full swing. As the drinks flowed and jocular, manly teasing increased, I asked two of the regulars, who were immersed in soccer in the 1970s and early 80s, where the best soccer talent in Durban came from. They both instinctively called out Wentworth and the best team to emerge from the area was Leeds United. They regaled me with player names and team exploits and challenged me to record this history.

I said I would. Bar-room promises are taken more seriously in my world than those made in the boardroom. It can make or break a reputation, if not your head.

Of course, I was also attracted by my own love of the game. As a teenager, I had watched professional games at Curries Fountain in the 1970s and writing the book now gave me the chance to break bread with boyhood heroes. I played a little in my university days in Grahamstown for a team called United Teenagers and then for the Kwazakhele Soccer Board (KWASBO).

Kwazakhele Soccer Board: me (bottom row, third from left), c.1984.

A centre-half, I earned the nickname 'Die Boom' (The Tree). I thought it was because of my strength in tackling and sturdiness in the face of adversity, but I soon learnt it was because of my inability to turn with grace and pace; 'slower than the Titanic'. Nicknames can be as cruel as revealing in soccer.

The journey of this book begins in the second half of the 1960s, just as apartheid's planners took a knife to Durban's geography, slicing places into racial group areas. In this quest, I allowed myself to drift into stories beyond the immediate team sheet, to talk to people who hung out on street corners, who peeped through slightly parted curtains of two-bedroom flats as I knocked on the neighbour's door, and those who marched behind placards.

Wentworth flats overlooking the oil refinery.

In many senses, this book is to take up Njabulo Ndebele's challenge to move beyond the spectacular contest between the powerless and the powerful, to focus on 'the nooks and crannies', the c(r)ooks and grannies, to hone in on 'the essential drama in the lives of ordinary people' (2006: 49–51).

And so as it unfolds, this book is also the story of place, how it was and what it is, guided by the idea that 'to understand and judge a society, one has to penetrate its basic structure to the human bond upon which it is built' (Merleau-Ponty 1969: xiv).

Acknowledgements

The debts I have incurred through the writing of this book are enormous. It would be remiss to start naming people because the list is lengthy. My closest friends in Durban played a huge part in editing, pointing me in new directions and scouring for potential sources of information. To the people of Wentworth, who took me into their hearts and lounges with tea and snowballs always on offer, I owe a huge gratitude. Thank you also for the patience in what became a five-year journey.

1

How to Tell a Story

> There is no doubt that the emotional, time-consuming and expressive connection with a football club may be a manifestation of a class, social or geographical position in which the identification with a certain club is, so to speak, taken in with the mother's milk ... There is some scientific support for stating that among dedicated supporters in particular, there are strong senses of local pride and identification within particular cities and locations, and that the local football team becomes an important catalyst for, and a manifestation of, these identifications.
> — Porsfelt, 'Supporter Rock in Sweden'

In South Africa of the 1960s, at the exact time that so many neighbourhoods were being destroyed under mass relocation programmes, quest for identity had to find surrogates. Soccer. Clubs were formed. Patches of turf were secured as a bleak landscape was turned into expressions of skill and desire to win trophies as well as developing the talents of a new generation. All this took sacrifice, a sense of mission, and for some at least, a commitment to the long haul of turning Wentworth, an apartheid-imposed Coloured township into a place, a home. Perhaps that is also why the friendships borne in hardship and want are the most powerful.

Dolores Hayden warns that 'place is one of the trickiest words in the English language, a suitcase so overfilled one can never shut the lid' (1995: 15). Once I opened the lid on the history of soccer in Wentworth, I could not stop looking. Photographs, trophies, beautiful memories, deep wounds that refuse to heal. Every time I tried to shut this suitcase, it burst open with the force of a suppressed memory suddenly recalled on the psychologist's couch. It is what makes oral history exciting and challenging as one deals with deep emotions as much as fading and selective memories.

I battled initially with the way in which the story that pivots around the pre-eminent team in Wentworth of the 1970s, Leeds United, should be represented. One obvious way was to present it as a narrative unfolding like a single game of soccer, with me as referee deciding what was in and what was to be red-carded. But that had the potential to hem in a project designed to be 'about real people and their actions, about all their diversity, freedom, richness and unpredictable accidents' (Sardica 2013: 385). I settled on the approach influenced by the idea of group biography whose major benefit

> . . . is that it avoids the artificial isolation which inevitably accompanies an intense focus on a single individual in which all others become secondary to the main figure under discussion . . . Group biography . . . takes as its primary subject the relationships between a group of people: their importance for each other, whether emotional or intellectual, becomes the primary issue for discussion . . . biographies of groups of friends and of networks also allow for the sustained analysis of how people are linked to each other and of the importance of the changing nature of those links over time (Caine 2010: 61).

Group biography does not mean that individual life trajectories get subsumed. As Caroline Knowles points out:

> The living and telling of life as stories highlights the individual choices unique to each biography, in which individual life trajectories are as significant as the broader (social) spatial and policy contexts in which they are cast (2000: 10).

Neither does group biography mean that there is a coherent collective script (Sangster 1998: 90). There are sometimes different interpretations to events, as one will discern, for example, in the reasons afforded for the demise of Leeds United. The challenge is to ensure that the opinions of those whose histories are still raw are recorded and therefore open to renewed challenge.

This book is not simply about bygone times but seeks to explore its impact on a whole new generation of soccer players in 'an era of intense collective experience of the past' that is fast fading (Frisch 1998: 33). As one interview with a player led to another with a supporter, as the past and present blurred and widened, the power of 'biographies of groups of friends and of networks' became increasingly apparent.[1] Soccer was born as Wentworth was emerging as a racialised Coloured group area. In the early 1960s, those pioneering soccer in Wentworth were crossing over into places such as Mayville and Cato Manor to scout for players. And when youngsters like Gary Goldstone and Dennis Petersen were forcibly moved to Wentworth, their talents were already known. Their own friendship leant on their families' historic proximity in Cato Manor and remained firmly in place for over half a century. Friendship, that unexplored terrain in the social sciences in South Africa, is also an important part of this book.[2]

This is not to idealise or romanticise community (Guijt and Shah 1998). As these pages show, communities are replete with exclusions, territorialisation and hierarchies. But alongside this, some of the earliest residents of Wentworth bonded, and 50 years later, they still stay in touch, deeply connected with one another's lives.

'I identify as Coloured, but my blood is Mauritian'

> Landscapes can be deceptive/Sometimes a landscape can be less a setting/for the life of its inhabitants than a curtain behind which their struggles, achievements and accidents take place.
> — Berger, *A Fortunate Man*

While this book has its genesis in a place that apartheid sought to racially congeal, my approach is not to take race thinking as a given. Rather, I approach race as a social construct (what else could Colouredness be, given its confrontation with fixedness? - there were seven sub-groups for Coloured, ranging from Malay to Griqua to Chinese), while being sensitive to the impulses of everyday life that give race thinking and

---

1. This book is based on a series of interviews, informal conversations and on hanging around the watering holes of former players and administrators.
2. For a notable exception, see Walsh and Soske (2016).

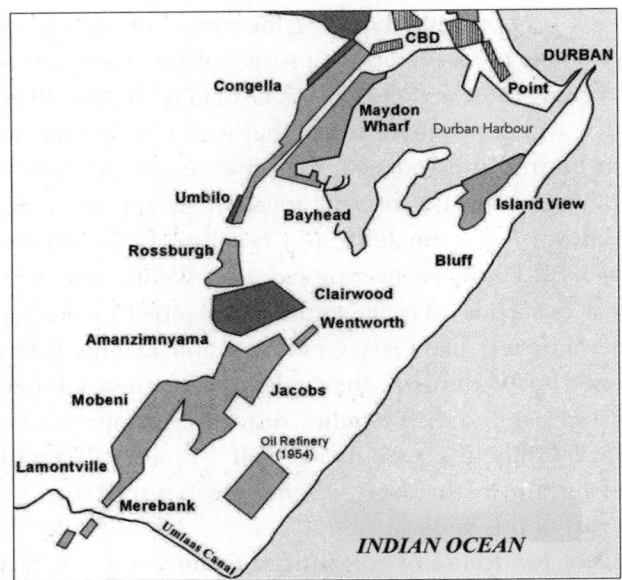

Wentworth: hemmed in by oil refineries and the industrial area of Jacobs.

belonging to place such resilience (Erasmus 2013: 47; for an historical overview of Durban Coloureds see Fynn 1991).

As Knowles puts it, while

> ... racial categories are social and political constructs, they are also effective in the making of who we are in the world and what we do in it. They operate in the manufacture of identities and in activities composing human agency ... They don't have a force in human biology, but that is a different point. They have a *meaning in social and political organisation and human action* (2003: 29–30; original emphasis).

Throughout the 1960s, tens of thousands of residents in Durban were put on the move as city authorities sought to ensure racially fixed group areas. While there was resistance, it was never powerful enough to stop the apartheid juggernaut. By the mid-1970s, one could clearly discern distinct racial geographies. To the south of the city centre, lying in a valley below the Bluff, Wentworth began to earn its reputation as a bleak and rough Coloured area:

> The main approach was up Quality Street, past the Girassol Café and at the crest of the hill the very first and only hotel owned by Coloured businessmen, Palm Springs Hotel. The sandy roads were rutted and uneven, often strewn with building rubble and household rubbish, and after a sudden tropical downpour the craters in the road would form small lakes. Packs of dogs roamed the streets and children played in the open storm drains. The houses were mostly cramped, identical redbrick units, or mean corrugated-iron shanties, with dusty backyards piled high with discarded tyres, rusty fridges and disused car parts . . . At night the Mobil Oil Refinery glowed with a thousand pinpricks of light . . . By day the oil refinery emitted a constant plume of greyish white smoke and sometimes by evening a sulphurous stench hung over Wentworth. It was a cloying, acrid smell that bit deep into the lungs . . . (Rostron 1991: 24–5).

Communal washing areas in Wentworth, 1972.

Across and above are the Indian areas of Merebank and the white highlands of the Bluff, which hang over the Indian Ocean and look down upon Wentworth. Snuck in-between is a small enclave called Treasure Beach, designed as a preserve for middle-class Coloureds.

If you stood on the ridge that cuts across these areas in the late 1970s, you would see a few soccer fields stretched out alongside the smoking chimneys of petrochemical refineries. For that is partly why Wentworth was laid out exactly there, so that Coloured artisans could be close to their 'natural' calling: kitted out in blue overalls, welding, fitting, turning, plumbing and grinding for a living. There was not nearly enough work for everyone, but the belching refineries of South Durban would never lack labour. One local soccer legend whose life we will return to later, Gary Goldstone, recalls how the Group Areas Act fundamentally damaged people's lives.

> We were forced to come live in this place here – Wentworth. Our parents were forced from their homes. Sometimes I think about how we survived. I still blame apartheid for my mother not living a full/true, long life. At 49 she died. The state of how some of the people had to live here. My mother never saw 50. I went off my head. She had a brain haemorrhage.

At the time, everything was on the move. Trucks flowed out of Wentworth transporting fuel to the Highveld. Cars and buses passed through, carrying commuters in and out of Merebank. Through the late 1970s into the 80s, many male Wentonians made the steady trek to the Sasol Industrial plant in the former Transvaal Province, only to return on pay weekends and the Christmas break to show off new cars, splash money around and pick up a new generation of recruits. A steady trickle of Coloureds from the former Transkei (Eastern Cape), escaping the Bantustan's 'independence', made it their home.

In telling the story of Leeds and the making of Wentworth, I was guided by Lucy Lippard's idea of place as

> . . . a portion of land/town/cityscape seen from the inside, the resonance of a specific location that is known and familiar . . .

> A layered location replete with human histories and memories, place has width as well as depth. It is about connections, what surrounds it, what formed it, what happened there, what will happen there (1997: 7).

As space turned into a place called Wentworth, it never stood still. It was full of energy and sacrifice as people built places of worship, sports clubs and networks of solidarity and support. Starting from the oil refineries, Wentworth was about five blocks up a slight rise and then ten blocks down the other side under the N2 highway.

By the second half of the 1970s, 'Wentworth had become a tougher, more unruly place. A whole generation had grown up in the converted military barracks' (Rostron 1991: 36-7). Gangs proliferated.

> Some of the gang members were as young as ten years old. The gangs themselves had also become more vicious; territorial wars were fought with guns, knives, stones and broken bottles . . . Occasionally a knifing would take place in broad daylight; some had their stomachs slit open or organs sliced off, and late one afternoon in front of a large crowd the Woodstock Vultures burned a rival alive. The Trucks and the Vultures were the biggest gangs and the most hostile rivals, the dividing line between them being Austerville Drive, the main road through Wentworth . . . The Trucks controlled the Drake and Frobisher districts, the Heartbreakers ruled in Ogle Road, while between Alabama and Dromedaris Road . . . the F-section held sway [while in nearby Reiger Road the Destroyers flourished with the Drain Rats in control in Assegai and the Zanzibaris ruled in Happy Valley] . . . Nearby, on the other side of Fairvale High School and just along from the Mobil Oil Refinery [in Duranta Road], the 88s lorded it over the most dismal area in Wentworth – long squat rows of concrete coops with flat asbestos roofs . . . known by everyone as 'Rainbow Chicken', after a well-known Natal battery farm (Rostron 1991: 37).

Marking gang territory.

A dwelling in Happy Valley was described in a local newspaper as 'a rickety, two-bedroomed shack, the "garden" a windswept waste... Wentworth's Happy Valley – probably the most inappropriately named Coloured settlement in South Africa' (*Daily News*, 4 November 1971).

Happy Valley: family of eight sharing a two-bedroom shack.

But to read Bryan Rostron and newspaper reports is to read one half of the page. Wentworth was also turning into a strong network of friendship and support. Lloyd Keshwar was born in Wentworth in 1959 and was to play an important part in the area's sporting history. He remembers the early years with fondness:

> My father and mother, when they married, lived in Sydenham. They used to live in Foreman Road. Then my father bought a plot – in 1953 in Wentworth and built a house in Elm Avenue. Where I grew up was a beautiful place. It was known as Happy Valley; a place that was really and truly a happy valley. It was a place where everybody loved and supported each other. People never chased you away. Back in the day, values were in people – not in your motor car or your fancy house. That's what Happy Valley taught a lot of us. If you talk to anybody from Happy Valley who came from that era of the fifties and sixties, they will tell you exactly what I'm saying. They will tell you it was a place where everyone respected each other; people lived; people helped each other. Where I used to live, there were wood and iron houses around us and no electricity in those houses. We lived in a brick house and there weren't many brick houses around. And those were the only houses that had electricity. So the majority of neighbours lived in wood and iron homes. They lived by candlelight. I recall my father bought a special fridge and made it available for the neighbours. People used this as cold storage for poultry, fish meat, etc. . . . I still live in Happy Valley now. A lot of people say that I will never leave, and I guess when I leave, it will be in a box of some sort or the other.

Housing, as Keshwar alludes to, was, and remains to this day, a constant problem. It has a particular historical backdrop.

Through the first part of the twentieth century, the white city council did not make provision for Coloured housing. The category's vagueness and the lack of mobilisation from those defining themselves as Coloured allowed the city to simply ignore the issue. Voices of protest about the lack of housing were raised in the 1930s from a mixed bag that ranged from Mauritians to Malays and St Helenians who complained about overcrowding and demanded housing from the city (Department of

Economics 1952). Wentworth, which was a military barracks for whites, was first mooted as a Coloured area in the late 1930s. It was only two decades later in the late 1950s that Coloureds started to move into Wentworth in significant numbers. As much as this had to do with the push from below, it also had to do with the apartheid government's determination

> ... to create a Coloured nation they admitted did not exist in order to buttress 'White Afrikanerdom' from the fluid ways in which passing for White miscegenation continued to occur. In order to accomplish the feat the meaning of Colouredness had to be asserted. The regime hoped that a harsh system of racial categorisation and separation would achieve these ends by foreclosing other options for those identified as Coloured (Johnson 2017: 15).

Long-time resident of Wentworth Kevin Alexander tells me:

> My father was Mauritian. My granny is Mauritian. My mom is actually Coloured. My dad's dad is also Mauritian – all of them from that side. Our roots are Malaysia. I identify as Coloured, but my blood is Mauritian.

It is a persistent refrain in Wentworth; people with varied bloodlines congeal into race and place.

In the 1970s, as the former Transkei consolidated its status as 'independent' Bantustan many newly married couples moved from the area to Wentworth. A woman in her early seventies, let's call her Helen Kelly, who lives in one of the houses opposite the flats in Alabama Road made her way in the mid-1970s from Mount Frere in the Transkei to Wentworth. She had to form new friendships and she was initially made aware that she was an outsider:

> Coming from the Transkei I sounded different. People always asked me where I came from when they heard me speak. Wentworth people expected you to know Afrikaans. There are quite a few people in Wentworth who were very Afrikaans. At the same time, you can pinpoint who is from the Transkei. The

Iris Murray (née Knock) and Patrick Murray, April 1969.

way they dress. Common, shabby dressing. The way they speak. Their attitude to life. Grown people wearing pyjamas to the shop.

The Murrays were some of those Transkeians who made their way to Wentworth. Patrick came first in 1969, making a weekly trip back 'home' to the Transkei. A couple of years later, Iris was to follow. Moving through the years from a tin house to a flat, they then got lucky and acquired a home of their own. They have never left Wentworth although family links with the Transkei remain strong into the fiftieth year since Patrick Murray first made his way to Durban.

Into the present, there are those who move back and forth between Wentworth and the Transkei and back and forth with their identities. Rodney Roskruge is 29 years old. A poet and entrepreneur, he was born in the notorious flatlands of Hime Street, commonly referred to as 'Crime Street'.

> I spent some time in Wentworth before going to the Eastern Cape – because my mother is Mpondo. Mpondo is a nation in the Eastern Cape. So I was between Wentworth and the Eastern Cape. I came back to do my primary school at Austerville school – until I did my Grade 7 – and then I returned to the Eastern Cape to do my matric. I actually went back to learn isiXhosa.

Hime Street flats, 1984.

Rodney has spent time tracing his lineage:

> My father is a Roskruge. Cornelius Roskruge. My mother is a Thembela Mbunjutwa from the Eastern Cape in Libode near Mthatha. The Roskruges, funny enough, come from a shipwreck in 1782 in the Eastern Cape. I think the captain miscalculated the distance between the sea and the shoreline by 300 metres or something and they were shipwrecked on 4 August. From 1782, one of our ancient ancestors of the Roskruges who survived is a Frederick Roskruge, who 'did the things' with the Msukude, which is a clan name. And from there you've got the Roskruge lineage until here in Hime Street and across the world. They were travelling back from India. And that accident has me sitting here with you today.

Residents who had moved into the area in the 1960s needed more space for growing families, but there was none available. Coloureds from areas like the Transkei, attracted by urban possibilities and alienated by the machinations of Bantustan politics, vied for housing and added to the pressure. A constant refrain is that people from the Transkei who left after the apartheid government declared it an independent Bantustan were given priority. Leeds United legend Elijah Adams, for example, argues that

> ... precedence was given to Coloureds who left the Transkei ... they also had the money to buy houses in Wentworth ... There were also problems of classification ... My father Albert Nxumalo was classified African. My mother was Coloured – Julia Adams. I took my mother's surname. Even my children – Durban Coloureds – were not known as Coloureds. We were known as other Coloureds. Just by the look. By looking at you they could say you look more like a Coloured or you look like an African, so you can fall into that category and you fall into this category.

Elijah Adams (right).

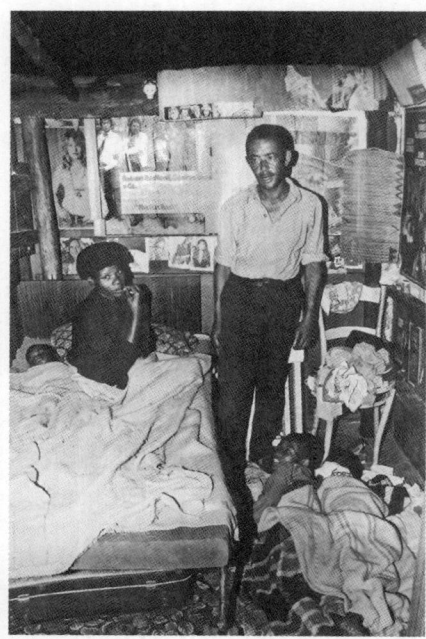

Paul Smith and his family share a tin shack in Ladysmith, 1973.

Added to the pull of Wentworth was the lack of housing for Coloureds in the rural areas of KwaZulu-Natal. The media in the late 1960s were replete with stories of the plight of Coloured housing woes. Part of the issue lay with the fact that as apartheid boundaries were more tightly drawn so not much provision was made for the category Coloured. A typical story is that of Paul Smith and his family that was highlighted in the media in December 1973. They squeezed into a single-room tin shack in Ladysmith and used family networks to move to newly designated Coloured areas like Wentworth.

Tensions were most overtly witnessed in the emergence of gangs. A politics arose of both resistance to and collaboration with apartheid. Churches were built and congregations cemented.

However, alongside the tensions came attempts to build ways to entertain and express musical and sporting talents. With the first generation of Wentonians calling it home, bands started to make an impact, many inspired by The Flames, which had their origins with the Fataar brothers of Sydenham.

The Flames.

Seth Robert 'Sonny' Pretorius, born in 1931, is one of the earliest exponents of the saxophone in Wentworth. He grew up in Clairwood and then made the trek like so many to Wentworth in the 1960s. Sonny remembers how people in Assegai slowly became like family. His father bought him his first sax. Entertainment revolved around the

> . . . community hall in Wentworth. At that time, the top, leading band was The Big Four. When they weren't available, they would tell us to fill in. They were tops. Four guys. A drummer, bass guitarist, rhythm guitarist and a lead guitarist. And they sang. They sang beautifully. They tried to copy The Shadows. Errol Shoes was the rhythm guitarist and he used to sing. Peter Oliver was the drummer – and he played for us in the end. I loved living in Wentworth. You could sit in your yard. It was beautiful in those days. The environment was nice. And the girls used to wear their frocks that puffed out and we used to wear bow ties. A tie is the main thing. Neat. You always wore a tie.

Sonny remembers how in the late 1960s and early 70s he got involved in beautifying the garden in the family home.

> It was something different from living in Clairwood... the house was nice – garden in the back and front. And I love a garden. Out of my father's sons, I loved the garden. I made a patch, I dug, put in hen and chicken plants. Then I put my flowers. Beautiful.

Sonny intensified his efforts when the city council inaugurated a competition to encourage people to beautify their gardens.

> And there were going to be prizes. First, second and third prize. So I got stuck into it. I told my dad, 'Buy me a mower.' The one that you push. The grass was high. They even put the date there. They give you about six months to pull your garden up. I worked on it. They came to check.
>
> So I treated it and I mowed it nicely. On this patch I was going to do this and on that patch I was going to do that. I cut it like that. And I had to dig it up with a spade. My father said, 'What are you doing? You're messing the garden up. You're messing the grass up.' I said, 'Wait, Papa. You keep quiet. Give me money.' By that time you could buy flowers in little plastic packet with sand. I bought them and put them in like that. I was proud of it... A flower garden. Ha! Third prize.

These 'little' stories that get lost in the narrative of gangs, drugs and the alienation of the new are as important in understanding the making of place. In similar vein to Pretorius, a local youth group took to turning rubbish dumps into gardens in the late 1970s.

Music and dance groups were starting up. School teacher and one of Wentworth's soccer legends Patrick Moodley remembers the group Kiss:

> Kiss was all about dancing. Hell, there was a span [lot] of entertainers from Wentworth. Fantasy was another top music group from the seventies – and they lasted for *long*. A top, top group... the Eaton Brothers. They were big in the seventies and eighties. They were singers with a band – all instruments. Top group. Ernie Smith is connected to the Eaton Brothers.

Two children stand over a rubbish dump turned into a garden, April 1979.

He wasn't fully into singing then as he is now. But, he's from that family; the Eaton and Smith family. Benjamin Ball - he's also from here. He died a couple of weeks ago . . . 'Flashlight, Flashlight . . . Oh No, No, No, No' - that was his number. His number was 'Just a Flashlight' - a one-off number and we never, ever heard him again. Totally *mal* [crazy] thing. The Moollens . . . They were hot those *laaities* [youngsters] . . . They went gospel.

There were the Coon Carnival bands, referred to as the 'nigga bands'.

But these carnivals fell into disrepute as it was seen as reinforcing apartheid stereotypes.

The gap was filled with a plethora of dance groups, none more pioneering than that started by Terrence Smith in the early 1980s. Terrence was still in primary school:

Quinton Smith, three-year-old member of the Philadelphian Moonshiners, 1980.

When I saw the first breakdancers on TV (a TV in our flat that only I knew how to operate), I formed the Reckless Breakdancers dance group. We went into town with our cardboards – you know, for us to spin on – and put them down at the market in Warwick Triangle. From there we made our way down to the beachfront, street by street, performing for money. There were seven members of the group and we made R250 a day and we split it among ourselves. We took the money and bought red and white tracksuits. It was like a performance uniform. You could tell we were a dance group – a team.

Terrence dropped out of school in Standard 8:

The next year I really got into dancing. That was in 1991. In 1992, a guy from Malawi comes to South Africa. I meet him in Xanadu Night Club – 'Xanies' in the city centre. I never paid to get into the club. I offered to dance in place of me paying the door charge.

Terrence Smith: the street-dancing years.

It was me and Bradley Jackson that time. This Malawian guy – his name was Tapuwe 'Taps' Bandawe – tells me he wanted me to dance in his music videos. This guy, Taps, was under David Gresham's music label. Remember he had that music show called 'Pop Shop' on TV in the 1980s.

We were the first Coloureds on TV. The show went out at 5 pm. After the show, when we went outside, the people went wild when they recognised us. We then named our dance group Taps, after him. Taps then became the frontman. He sang. We then did a music video with Dr Victor and the Rasta Rebels. We filmed all the music videos in Auckland Park at the SABC studios. They flew us up to Joburg. The way I see it, I feel like I paved the way for Coloured people in general – in terms of breaking into the music industry. They felt good about themselves. They saw the first Coloured boy on TV. Somewhere in their minds, they thought maybe they could appear on TV too – and dance and perform professionally in music videos. It was a possibility. This is what many people don't know. I wish I had those tapes from the SABC.

Occasionally, Wentworth offered people a chance to reinvent themselves by taking advantage of the relocations wrought by apartheid's planners. Terrence, who was born in Richards Bay, remembers:

My father worked on those Indian buses, taking people around town. My parents met on a bus. My mother was Gladys Joan Smith (formerly Singh) and my father was John Cele. My mother moved to Mayville in the late 1960s. My father stayed in Richards Bay. My mother wanted a better life. When we first moved to Wentworth, the road was just a dust road. Nothing. No tar. Because my mother wanted to be considered for a flat in Wentworth, she made up a new name for herself. She gave herself the surname Smith because she thought they wouldn't give her a flat if they knew she was Indian. So, our Smith surname is completely made up. The same goes for Cele. She didn't want to use that name because she thought that if they saw her as black – you know, African – she wouldn't get a flat based on that. Besides, my father never married my mother. But they had children together. First was my brother Theo, then came Adolfius, next my sister Jackie, then Anthony, Elaine, then it's me. When I was born, we got a 'new dad'.

At exactly the time the apartheid regime was seeking to freeze racial boundaries, Gladys Joan Smith was freeing herself from them, brazenly adopting an identity that would give her a fresh chance in life.

* * *

In my initial forays into the field, I concentrated on the pioneering efforts to build the game in Wentworth. In this quest, I went in search of players, managers, coaches and fans. This is the story of that club through the biographies of its iconic players. But this could not, did not, cut me off from stories beyond the gaze of my central focus, as contemporary struggles to make a life in Wentworth forced their way into the script. There are stories in this book of housing battles, gangs, sexuality and the looming presence of petrochemical companies that at once provide jobs and make the area the most polluted in Durban. This is a tale, as you will witness in the pages ahead, that broadens into a whole cast of other players, supporters and teams. In the process, they also speak of Wentworth, a place they sought to make as *their* world, as much as they were made by it.

The passing game

> On club level . . . mixed team will not or cannot exist. Precisely the same applies on the provincial level, and so, too, on the national level. However, there is the exception . . . [such as] . . . the South African Games. You will then read on the scoreboard . . . 'A South African representative team', which consists of whites only, which plays against a South African representative Coloured team consisting solely of Coloureds. The South African representative white team will be able to play against Indians in an Indian team consisting solely of Indians and it will also, if our policy is carried to its logical conclusion, be able to play against a South African representative Zulu team, a South African representative Xhosa team and against a South African representative Tswana team, etc.
> — Piet Koornhof quoted in Booth, *The Race Game*

The history of soccer in South Africa was haunted by racial divisions. In the 1950s, there was an attempt to bring Africans, Coloureds and Indians under one umbrella body, the South African Soccer Federation (SASF). In many ways, this challenged apartheid's logic of racial separation. But the attempt had its limitations, with the three 'non-white' groups playing inter-race matches that as much as it crossed racial boundaries also reinforced racial division (Ngidi 2014: 328). Learning from these experiences and that of the broader anti-apartheid political environment, officials linked to the SASF formed a professional league, the South African Soccer League (SASL), which saw its goal as

> . . . challenging racism in sport. The SASL encouraged those athletes classified by the apartheid regime as African, Indian or

> Coloured to compete in racially mixed teams. SASL's principled and unwavering commitment to non-racialism, a stance motivated by a combination of moral principle, political consciousness, and market-driven interests, represented a direct challenge to Pretoria's master plan of separate development (Alegi 2004: 119).

However, the early gains made in integrating soccer throughout the 1950s and early 1960s was dealt a blow during the 1970s as the apartheid government imposed its multinational policy on sport:

> The 1970's witnessed the white regime's coercive re-imposition of strict racial segregation on the pitch . . . The white soccer establishment and its political allies in 1970 ordered the South African Bantu Football Association to expel Coloureds and Indians from African clubs. Faced with a false choice of either abandoning or accepting this racist ultimatum, virtually every township capitulated (Alegi 2004: 138).

In Durban, this resulted in a regrouping under the banner of the SASF with a professional wing called the Federation Professional League (FPL). These leagues consisted overwhelmingly of Indians and Coloureds. Meanwhile, the apartheid city was taking shape. As the government imposed segregation from above, the new racially defined group areas also stimulated a sense of place and belonging. As we will see in the story of soccer, both a hazy Coloured and Wentworth identity were incubated by the players, administrators and fans.

In the 1970s, no other team from Wentworth, one might even venture to say from the SASF in Durban, called forth such a deep sense of place and identity as Leeds United. This was not least because of excellence on the pitch, but also due to a sense of alienation from the 'imposing' groups of majority black Africans, Indians who were considered 'one step up the ladder' and racist whites. For a moment, in the first half of the 1970s, Leeds United came to stand for Wentworth's collective sense of self.

It may do well to recount that in the madness of apartheid classification, Coloured came to be defined by what you were not. According to the Population Registration Act of 1950: 'A coloured person is a person who is not a white person or a native' (Union of South Africa 1950). In

1983, Marike de Klerk, wife of the future president of the country, F.W. de Klerk, put her own particular take on this definition: 'You know the Coloureds are a negative group. The definition of a Coloured in the population register is someone that is not black, and is not white and not Indian. In other words, a non-person. They are leftovers' (Rostron 1991: 31).

Those Coloureds who sought entrance into a white world were rudely rebuffed. Wentworth resident Robert McBride, an uMkhonto we Sizwe soldier of the African National Congress (ANC), remembers his experiences playing for a white rugby club in the early 1980s:

> . . . Robert became aware of some of his own team-mates casting sly aspersions behind his back. He ignored them. But the strain between the two worlds – the gaunt reality of Wentworth and the white figment of his hopes – could not be reconciled . . . He might be a member but that did not mean acceptance . . . all he saw in the mirror . . . was that he was not white. So he became the opposite. There was a decisive moment for this conversion. It came when he was finally picked for the A team. In the changing room Robert overheard another player commiserating with the dejected lock forward who had been dropped to make way for him. 'Gary, don't worry about it,' said one white sportsman to the other, 'Robert is just a bushie' (Rostron 1991: 66).

McBride famously threw himself into the role of a revolutionary, plotting the overthrow of the apartheid state and spending years on death row. In doing so, he embraced the broader identity of black. However, his assumed black identity and joining of the armed struggle did not mean that McBride could simply rise above apartheid-imposed categories:

> There was a kind of different expectation from me because I am a different colour. And my approach was that I'm committed to non-racism, and other people must see me as equal to them. And I make sure people see me like that. So, it's interpreted as arrogance on my part. But I have never doubted that my commitment to the liberation struggle was the same as anybody else, no matter what colour they are (Houston 2006).

There were others who attempted to pass themselves off as white. As Lloyd Keshwar attests, if this was successful, a permanent move to the white side of the apartheid fence beckoned:

> In my family there's whites, there's Coloureds, there's Indians. One of my father's brothers was a *wit ou* [white guy] – and he went across the colour line – because he looked like a white, had them blue eyes and the works. He went that side . . . he had a better opportunity. Those days to work as a white you got paid more money. So he got this opportunity to go work as a white man. Of course, he took it. He didn't ask them to classify him as white – and he didn't classify himself as white. He went to go do a job as a welder, so they classified him as white. But now he had to play white. He couldn't show them that he wasn't a *wit ou*, because if they found out that, they were gonna cut his salary or possibly dismiss him. So he just sort of stayed his distance because he didn't want to be identified. It was a fear of losing the job/money. Then, of course, he pushed the boundaries . . . met this pretty white lady and married his sweetheart. They lived in Redhill on the white side. And he's got two children who carry the Keshwar name but were classified as white, not by their own choice one must add. So, he became a *wit ou*, but I recall he did come to visit us on a few occasions. After all, he was my father's biological brother.

Papa (Phillip Gordon) Stokes, whose story we shall pick up later, was one of the pioneers of soccer in Wentworth in the 1960s. His son Casper (Arthur Cyril), born in 1952, says that his father claimed he

> . . . was an only child. He said they were seven boys, but six died. All the babies died. I don't know how he survived. Sometimes I think that what happened is that in the apartheid days, they all became white – and he is the only one who became Coloured. I remember when I wanted to buy a car in 1978/79 . . . I went into Smith Street. I met a white guy there – Neville Stokes. And we got talking. 'Where you got this surname from?' And I explained to him where my dad was from. He said, 'My dad was also from

there.' But that's the only information we both knew: that my dad was from there. His dad was from there. My dad's brothers were all dead. His dad's brothers are all dead. And we were supposed to meet again, but we never got the chance. I thought maybe I was speaking to my own brother. But he was a white man. But I was also white-skinned and fair with white/blonde hair as a baby. Then we bumped into a black guy at Natraj Shopping Complex in Merebank and he married a Stokes and knows all the Stokes from Port St John's. He is from there and he is now staying in Wentworth. When it comes to blood there are no straight lines.

There were those who went the more formal route to get themselves reclassified. In the initial years of classification,

> . . . a person's race could be changed, if the individuals who so desired, for reasons of access to better life resources or because of love and personal affiliations, were willing to go through the degrading process of appeal against their existing classification and could bear refusal (Maré 2014: 38).

Faced with a hostile world, Wentonians increasingly developed an identity that revolved around place. It served as protective armour that, for some, turned anger inwards onto the body (alcohol and drugs) and outwards towards gangs. Beyond these pathologies, there was the making of a life. Church was an integral part of the community, with older established churches, especially the Catholic Church being an influential local institution (Fynn 1991). There was pride in skilled artisanal work. There cannot be many other towns in South Africa whose husbands and sons were as sought after as fitters and turners, electricians, millwrights, boilermakers and arc welders. And there was sport, soccer in particular. If Wentworth was a cauldron of internal conflicts, of values and ways of behaving, it also created a deep sense of insiders and outsiders, us and them, a community as Fredric Jameson would put it 'by way of a kind of secession: it must always, in other words . . . posit an enemy' (2003).

The storm water drain was a playground in Wentworth, 1982.

Historically, Coloureds were a minority within a minority in Durban, in the sense that they were a much smaller group numerically than Indians. They were also smaller in other respects. The Indian community was more visible in the media. Three newspapers in the 1970s – *The Graphic*, *The Leader* and *The Post* – were dedicated to mainly Indian news. Indians had a merchant class that was largely absent in the Coloured community. Coloureds dominated the largely intermittent occupations of welder, fitter and turner, bricklayer, boilermaker, panel beater and plumber. Coloured were one above the black African but one below the more mercantile Indian, who, especially in the 1970s, exploded in terms of a class of university-educated professionals holding down permanent jobs. The Coloured population was also starting to take on some class pretentions of its own. Parts of Sydenham and Greenwood Park (other Coloured areas of Durban), particularly with the rapid increase of teachers coming out of teacher training colleges and high-school graduates pushing on to university, began to assume the trappings of a middle-class lifestyle, one step away from the traditional labour niche markets that Coloureds occupied in the construction and petrochemical industries. Wentonians then tended to have a lower, more precarious position in the class and racial hierarchy.

But Indians and Coloureds were bound together in the Durban milieu. They lived in close proximity to each other, shared the same nightclubs and cinemas, and intermarriage was common. The 'boundedness' produced its own stereotypes, divisions and contests.

One of the ways in which this played out was on the soccer field. Twenty, thirty years later, in a Durban pub, these contests are still remembered, albeit by ageing men, in jocular, mocking prose. As John Hargreaves (2000: 13) reminds us, 'the contest element in sport is especially significant because it allows opposition, conflict and struggle to be experienced and represented in extremely dramatic and spectacular ways, whereby sports can be made to map national struggles'. To this must be added that sport can tell us much about local struggles, as performances both on the field and in the stands become a way to confirm and contest one's status and position in the imposed racial hierarchy of the apartheid city.

There are two anecdotal stories that tell of the power of Leeds United to capture the imagination of an economically distressed community, haunted by enforced removals and beset by gang violence and petty crime. One is that when Leeds United played at Curries Fountain (the Mecca of non-racial sport), a stadium 15 kilometres away in the city centre, the number of house burglaries in Wentworth increased, for the crooks knew that the place had emptied out and the houses could be too. The second is that warring Wentworth gangs, known for their deadly attacks on each other, united in support whenever Leeds played. Like a church could be a sanctuary within which the mafia would not commit any violence, so, too, were soccer grounds during a Leeds United match.

While this narrative is about soccer, it is also about what was happening beyond the immediate field of play and tells a story about the making of place.

2

The Ground In-Between

> I play therefore I am: a style of play is a way of being that reveals the unique profile of each community and affirms its right to be different. Tell me how you play and I will tell you who you are.
> — Galeano, *Soccer in Sun and Shadow*

In the 1950s, a number of Coloured soccer clubs had made a mark. There was the redoubtable Yorkshire Football Club that had among its squad Blondie Campbell.

They swept all before them until challenged by high-school students from Bechet in Sydenham who had formed a team called Rialto. One of the star players for Rialto was Edward 'Ettie' Abrahams. He was to go on to play for Fulham in England – a story he recounts with style and humour in a booklet entitled '*Eddy of Time: Rialto FC: 1958–1961*':

> On first arriving in the United Kingdom on my first ever plane trip, I was completely overcome by nerves as I tried to grapple with the cultural shock . . . Imagine going from segregated Sparks Estate in Sydenham one day to a salubrious state in the woodlands of Wimbledon the next . . . I was on a learning curve as never before, the most exhilarating being signing autographs for worshipping kids and travelling to away matches in a magnificent luxury coach – a far cry from the 'green mamba' [the municipal buses]. It was like being in a vortex of new values (Abrahams 2009: 13–14).

The consolidating of the apartheid city in the early 1960s had an immediate impact on many of the clubs that trained and played on the

Top row (left to right): C. Hulley, N. Stainbank, S. Bonhomme, L. Isaacs.
Middle row (left to right): B. Thompson, H. Stalls, C. Sanders, L. Barnes, E. Deane, C. Davenhill, W. Campbell.
Bottom row (left to right): F. Egelhof, A. Johannes, J. Jaffer, A. Johnson, V. Campbell, H. Chockrane, J. McAllister.

The incredibly gifted Durban player Ettie Abrahams (right) meeting Leeds star Gerry Francis in the United Kingdom in 1961.

edges of the city centre. Families and friends went their separate ways and clubs were destroyed. Abrahams's much-heralded Rialto, for example, had folded by 1964.

In the newly designated areas, such as Wentworth, the slow process of rebuilding began with people like Papa Stokes and Bernard 'Bennie' Whitby making tremendous sacrifices to build a soccer-playing culture.

By the early 1970s, a number of soccer clubs had emerged in Wentworth. A long-time resident of Wentworth, Whitby, was one of the people who recruited the best local players into Leeds United. The origins of the team's name are contested. For Gary Goldstone, his wife Ursula and Lloyd Keshwar, it came from a street name in nearby Congella. As Keshwar remembers:

> Leeds originated and was conceived while sitting at the old Outspan Hotel, near the old Sunblest Bakery. Just before Flamingo Court, there was a bakery. Now, just before that bakery, a lot of Coloured and Indian men would meet at the Outspan Hotel. That was the time – you go grab a chow and a dop [drink]. It was during one of those days that Bennie Whitby and a few other soccer fanatics were sitting there. There was a road called 'Leeds Place' – in Umbilo/Congella. So, it was in this time, as Bennie was sitting with a couple of the guys and he told them that he was going to form a team someday and he would call it Leeds.

For others, whatever the origins, the name reflected an obsession with English soccer, born out of the English club's success under Don Revie and through a South African connection. In the late 1960s, Bernard 'Dancing Shoes' Hartze famously had a trial with Leeds and was on course to join the club but found life there difficult and returned home (Alegi 2004: 187). Gerry Francis went from shoe repairer in Johannesburg to sign for Leeds as a professional in 1957. He was followed by Albert 'Hurry Hurry' Johanneson, who also made it into the first team of Leeds after joining in 1961, and by the end of the decade, had achieved legendary status, earning the nickname 'Black Flash' from Leeds fans. When both players were selected against Stoke City in 1961, they made history as the first two black players to play together in the same team. It was hauntingly ironic that both would never be able to play against their white countrymen. All three, Francis, Hartze and Johanneson, were, in South African parlance, Coloured, and one can see how the name of the club resonated locally. Giving credence to the 'English' connection for the origin of the name Leeds was that other top clubs in the area, Chelsea and Everton, also took their names from the island where the game was born. Motherwell from Scotland toured South Africa in the early 1930s and Wentworth, too, was to have a Motherwell in the 1970s (Alegi 2004: 58).

Motherwell Football Club.

There could also be a Catholic connection. In the 1960s, Catholicism was the denomination of choice in Wentworth. One can see this in the name of Everton and also Leeds's green and white kit, which was inspired by Glasgow Celtic. With one essential difference. According to Keshwar, 'Bennie Whitby did not fancy the hoops of Celtic so hence Leeds adopted the green and white stripes rather.'

Keshwar remembers Leeds as a breakaway club from Railway Swallows (formerly known as the Brazilians):

> Wentworth resident Papa Stokes had a team called Railway Swallows. Railway Swallows was formed back in the day in the mid-sixties. Where they got that name was from when we used to have the sleeper trains and a lot of the lads from this section here worked as pageboys on those trains. Papa Stokes was one of the attendants who worked there. He got work for the young boys on the train. They got jobs carrying luggage for the white people, making beds, and some of them would have been waiters. In the evenings they would serve drinks. This was in the early to mid-sixties. Bennie Whitby also played for Railway Swallows. This was before Leeds - Bennie Whitby, Ronnie Roach - these were all ex-Swallows guys. So, it was a breakaway that formed the team Leeds. That's the background. Leeds came from Railway Swallows. A lot of soccer players don't like it when they don't get game time. That is the primary reason for new clubs forming. That's a fact. Unfortunately, only eleven can take the field.

Papa Stokes's passion for the game is still spoken about with some awe. His son Arthur remembers how his family moved to Durban from Port St Johns in the former Transkei:

> My father was already working in Durban before the whole family moved here. He first came alone in the 1940s after the war, started to work, and lived in a place called Second River - Durban North side. For years, he lived there, and then moved to White City, Wentworth. He joined the Allied troops in Egypt as part of the ambulance corp. He didn't want to tell us much about it because they were always picking up dead bodies, arms, and body parts all over the show and they didn't know who those parts belonged to. They just had to collect and put them on the trucks and keep collecting. That was his job in the war. There are big differences in the ages of my sisters Daphne and Maureen because of the war. Daphne was born before the war and Maureen was born when my father came back. The rest of us are all born two years apart.

There were Coloured soldiers from Durban, Cape Town, Joburg. Lots of them. Fighting against the Germans.

As the Coloured corps returned to Durban and renewed attempts were made to harden the racial boundaries of job segregation, which were often blurred during the war, the government offered Coloured men jobs working for South African Railways as 'bedding boys'. Papa Stokes was one who took up the opportunity, criss-crossing the country. When Arthur turned fifteen, he joined his father during school holidays:

> We used to look after the trains, keep the trains clean and, at night, make beds for the people to sleep on. Pull the bunks down. Take out the blankets and pull it out – make beds out of them. As bedding boys, we wore a khaki uniform with a black tie. Black shoes. And a khaki cap. And we wore a red badge on the front of the cap with the South African Railways emblem. You trained at the base – at the bedding store – just off Umgeni Road; the place they used to call Lords Grounds. Near Alice Street.

Working on the railways offered Papa Stokes job security and a chance for him to organise part-time work for his sons. He worked on the railways for 48 years. Apartheid job segregation was strictly in force:

> My father just stayed at the level of bedding boy. Only white people could be foremen and all that. Right up until he retired, there was never a 'non-white' foreman or a train driver. There was no other race that worked as bedding boys besides Coloureds. Africans used to clean the stations and help the passengers with their luggage. This was at the height of apartheid. It was at its peak then in the sixties and seventies. The bedding boys came from all different places, but eventually they all moved into White City. Because all of us four Stokes brothers worked on the railways, we knew what went on. They paid us R28 a month. But it kept us busy and out of trouble. You had pocket money and it all came home to Mother. She used to buy our clothes and give us what we needed. At that time, that was money. A rand was worth a rand at that time.

Papa Stokes with wife Gertrude (extreme left) at daughter Maureen's wedding.

The Stokes family also kept expanding:

> My dad had three stepchildren on the outside. They even came and stayed with us in Wentworth. Maybe there are more, but we haven't met them. We heard there were seven in total, but we only know three of them. And my mother took them in. When I was six, seven, eight or so, we stopped at Estcourt station. There was a woman waiting there on the platform and she said, 'Here's your child. Take it.' And my dad brought her home. We were just told, 'That's your brother. This is your sister.' In those days, the train was much cheaper than anything else, so Coloureds and Africans used to travel by train. They must have met all these women on the trains. Maybe at every railway station they had a girlfriend. My father brought all his children home. My mother accepted them. We never slept hungry. She always made a plan. Always.

Mr Alexander was the founder of Railway Swallows but when he became too old to run the team, Papa Stokes took over. Arthur remembers him as soccer crazy.

> He never played. But, as our manager, he used to do everything for the team. Buy jerseys. Boots. Whatever the guys needed. My dad bought anything for them. The South African Railways bought us soccer jerseys for a short while. Afterwards, when my dad took over, he started buying us jerseys. The Whitbys were with us from White City. When we first moved in here, they broke away from our team and formed Leeds Football Club. Mr Whitby Senior went away from Railway Swallows and created Leeds – and Railway Swallows remained the same. When Leeds was formed, we had to get new players to replace them. And we had a lot of players in the area. We just went for younger guys.

Papa Stokes was more than a manager: he was their guardian:

> My father loved his players. He used to give them all the food that was cooked for us in the house. He was not worried about us. My mother had to re-cook. He used to feed his players. Entertain them. Train them. There were also other players who used to help with the training. Much of the time he was away on the train. But he used to try to make sure he was here on Sundays. Watch the games. Be there for the players.

The newly formed Leeds hit the ground running. More people were arriving in Wentworth and so the market for players was increasing and enthusiasm growing, as were particular streets marked out and identified with newly sprouting soccer clubs.

Wellington Meth, one of the pioneers of Wentworth soccer, recalls that the game was played on

> the Cabbage Patch, so-called because the grounds were so small. Then it was getting full there and we were running out of space, so the municipality gave us the area where Wentworth High School is. The crowds there were fantastic. People used to leave home in the morning and not go home for lunch because they didn't want to miss a match. I think Father Carey from the Catholic Church chased us away because the balls used to go over the wall and he used to pop them. And then the people, instead of going

to church, they used to just hear the noises and turn in there. It was fun. From there, they decided to build Ogle Road grounds.

The first years of Leeds's history were a revelation. Affiliating to Durban South Football Association, Leeds made a clean sweep of all eleven trophies that they competed for. Managed by brothers Bennie and Ignatius Whitby, they also won the prize for the best-dressed team. Bennie Whitby remembers how he used to go to Reg Wright Sports shop in the city centre and buy jerseys. Every second week a new set was ordered.

> ... Different outfits for various occasions. We weren't a team that just wore one outfit. And what was clever about this whole thing was fashion. We had white jerseys and green shorts. Those were our colours – green and white. The following week, we would change the same thing into a different outfit altogether by just changing the top and keeping the green shorts. It was fashion. And people say, 'Look at how nice he looks.'

Early photo of Leeds. Top row (left to right): Pinky Marais, Marshall Justine, Colin Paul, Martin Swartz, Bernard Whitby.
Front row (left to right): Duncan King, Paul Peters, Ronald Meth, Dingaan Marais, George van Niekerk.

But for Bennie Whitby, it meant more than that:

> It's how you control yourself – your outfits and how you put it all together. It's about style. Seeing all that, the guys used to dress smart. Leeds was the best-dressed team in the whole of Natal. Our tracksuits were mind-boggling. At a game, we would play the first half in this set of jerseys – and the other half in another set. For every jersey, we had different tracksuits. We were posh. We were the first team – even compared with Berea and Aces or any pro team; we were amateur – we went in with different coloured jerseys; we were playing Spearman Lads – and in the second half, came with a different outfit altogether. People used to think, 'These guys got money.' It wasn't money. We never had sponsors. Everything about us was just to be ahead of everyone.

There was no attempt to get sponsorship, rather money was raised through self-organisation:

> To raise funds, we used to have Games Evenings. If we needed R1 000 for five balls, we just got together, have drinks – sell drinks . . . You just come with your bottle and put it there. There's about five bottles. Cool drinks also. And then we have games. Cards. You can make R2 000. Easy. And back then R2 000 was a lot of money.

But it was not simply the dress sense of Leeds that denoted change. It was Whitby's thinking around the game. He was keen to develop a 'squad' of players and using the players on the field in new and innovative ways:

> Leeds . . . was the only team – even including professional teams – that had three goalkeepers. And top goalkeepers. We had three centre-halves. Three strikers. From there, we could work around. Push this player here. Push this player there. But the player must be capable of doing it. If he can only play in one position, I don't want him. I was ruthless. Phillip Peters used to play left wing for Ixopo Wolves. Great player. He wasn't an all-round player. When he came to Leeds, we pushed him into left-half and then left-back. We even played him centre-half. You've got to make them

diversify. Even Gary Goldstone. Gary was a left-winger, but Gary ended up playing centre-half. Gary could even play in the goal.

The very first team included the likes of Colin Paul, who earned the nickname 'Stormy', Wilfred Phillips 'Kaapie' and Marshall Justine 'Psycho'. The following year saw the inclusion of Lesley 'Fishy' Titus, Ronnie Roach and Geoff Petersen. In 1969, Eddie McKnight, a solid and dependable goalkeeper, joined. Other clubs, such as Aralian Lads, Cavaliers and Aston Callies, were also developing strong squads. Aralian Lads saw a lot of its players migrate to Leeds, acting almost akin to a feeder club.

Aralian Lads: manager Albert George (third from left), the legendary Colin Paul (extreme right) and (to his immediate left) James Ullbricht.

In an ironic twist, Leeds, given its own ability to attract the very best of Wentworth, had its downside. In 1970, professional clubs came headhunting. Pivotal players, such as the Peters brothers, went to Berea, and Ronnie Roach, Colin Paul and Wilfred Phillips went to Aces United. But this seemed to have little impact as Wentworth kept producing talented players keen to make their mark with Leeds. As a sign of their continuing ability to perform at the highest level, Leeds began winning tournament after tournament.

The emerging powerhouse, Leeds 1972.

Leeds played in the Grand Challenge League. Some of the province's most powerful teams, such as Spearman Lads, Durban Suburbs, Motherwell, Dimes United, Santos, Young Springboks, Port Shepstone United, Young Aces and Chatsworth Royals, were part of this league. It was also the year that the dynamic trio of Dennis Petersen, Keith Bezuidenhout and Obed Petersen signed up for the club. The following year, arguably Leeds's most iconic player, Gary Goldstone, entered the dressing room. No other player of this Leeds generation wanted to win more than Goldstone. He focused his energy on outrunning the opposition, chasing a referee, Keith Nelson, into the stands and turning on one of his own players, giving him a hard clout across the face for missing a goal. 'It's only a game,' as Goldstone would probably say, 'but it's the only game' (DeLillo 2004: 15) Forty years later, these stories are still relayed with an instinctive reflexive comment: 'Don't tell Gary I said it.' In 2018 and despite a couple of strokes, Goldstone still manages to evoke awe and fear.

Leeds United turned professional in the early 1980s, and their coach at the time was Blondie Campbell. From the mid-1950s, Campbell was involved in the game with Yorkshire Football Club and then made a name playing for Avalon Athletics in the early 1960s. This was the radical breakthrough of non-racial soccer and Blondie was part of the pioneering group of players that was both playing the game at the highest level and confronting the logic of apartheid's obsession with racial separateness.

Avalon Athletics. From left: Reginald Gcabashe, Selby Wand, Talfran Nkabinde, Cedric 'Sugar Ray' Xulu, Victor 'Blondie' Campbell, Kenneth Gama, Dharam Mohan, Hector Fynn, Denzil Easthorpe, Moses Strydom, George Francis, Maniraj Singh.

It was this kind of visual presentation of playing non-racial soccer that exposed white soccer in South Africa, which into the early 1960s enjoyed international affiliation. Despite support from bigwigs in the International Federation of Association Football (FIFA), South Africa was eventually expelled in 1964 and these groundbreaking soccer players of the late 1950s and early 1960s, who confronted the imposed categories of apartheid on the field, were as important as the activists who spoke in their name.

The big names of the era slip quickly off the tongue and people can point out the houses where players lived or still live. Dennis Petersen, born in 1950, and still living in Wentworth, was known as the hat-trick man. He played on both wings but could also be a very effective striker. Gary Goldstone was a left-winger but could play in all positions, including goalkeeper. If Petersen and Goldstone were knitted together at the hip, swinging between left and right wing, only to meet up at centre-forward, their approach to life was played out at opposite ends of the pitch. Goldstone was always on the edge of being enveloped by drugs, fighting and gangs. On many occasions, he got into scrapes that led him to court and then jail. Petersen, a man of quieter disposition, lives with his extended family in the same road in Wentworth in which he first donned a Leeds jersey.

They still come together to talk about the old days. Before playing for Leeds, Goldstone played for Barracuda soccer team, owned by Roberts Construction. Every site they worked on had a name. Barracuda was their site, so they just took the name. This was in the late 1960s.

Goldstone recalls the moment in 1969 when his life fundamentally changed.

> You know in our Coloured homes, the mother is the one who holds everything together. So when my mother died, I went madly off the tracks. From about 1969, I went mad. It was when I got a job at Roberts Construction. The minute I got a job, I found out they wanted footballers to play in the year-end tournament. You get a job as an assistant – assistant to a boilermaker, assistant to a welder: today, you will say a 'labourer' or 'operator'. That's what we were there [at Roberts Construction]. I was seventeen years old. In those days we were legal.

While working there, he remembers, nearly 50 years later, how two guys from England unbeknownst came to check out the locals' soccer skills.

> I go back to Roberts Construction, Bob Grey and Roy Carrelle ... These guys came from the UK ... they used to allow us to train two days a week, from two o'clock to five. They must have thought, we will take these Coloureds and see if they can kick a ball. The construction site was where Mondi is now. And we used Badullah Road grounds to train and practise, so it's very close. They used to actually let us train – and we'd get paid for it. Come on. During working hours. That was up to the bosses. No one could tell us nothing. When they saw us train ... All of us as a team – and a lot of us came from different places, because there were some Africans who could play and some Indians who could play – we did well. We were all in this Barracuda side. As a unit, we did well.

What Goldstone did not know was that Roy Carrelle and Bob Grey were filming them, editing and sending the tapes to Leicester City Football Club in England:

> It was in September of 1969 that they came with this offer. It was usually in September we had that long weekend. One day I was running off and trying to make a *skyf* [a dagga smoke]. We saw this bunch of white helmets coming toward us. This one boilermaker said, 'Ja, but Gary, what did you do now?' These people were coming straight for us. I said, 'I did nothing.' And he was a smoker, too. He reckoned, 'You didn't get caught?' I said, 'No. I did nothing wrong.' And, these people came right to us. So, Roy Carrelle called me, 'Gary, come down here.' I was on the ladder. And as I was coming down . . . And I'm a little *laaitie*. I'm shaking! Because we needed the jobs. Nice money, too. Roy says, 'Come here. Mr Grey wants to talk to you.' Mr Grey was one of the site managers. They asked me where I learnt football. I said we learnt in the streets. They told the boilermaker, 'Gary is not coming back here anymore.' The boilermaker probably thought, this *laaitie* is probably fired.

But Bob Grey had put Goldstone in charge of the storeroom:

> He just put a couple of angle-grinders for me to give out to workers in the morning and see that they come back in the afternoon. And the whole day I had to read these books about football – to read them and go through them and look into the game. To me it was really like, 'This is what I'm gonna be. This is what I'm gonna be.'

And then out the blue, Roy and Bob came to the store and handed Gary a contract for Leicester City:

> One day he showed me the contract and he said, 'Take this. Show your parents.' And I still remember thinking, my father doesn't really worry about me . . . My father had already chased me out

> the house. But people said to take it and show it to Cora [sister], so I showed Cora and Shirley [sister], but Shirley is the one who really went through the papers. I was always fighting. We had friends who were big gangsters and we grew up with heavy peer pressure. My brother-in-law was a guy who sold this and that on the black market. My manager also ran the whole district those years . . . So, let me put it this way, when Dennis and I were that age, we could do just about anything and get away with it. You couldn't touch us. Even the police. We played for the police. The police would come pick us up, next thing we're gone, we play, we win. Then the 'exhibit' drink will come out for us. But for me this was the big breakthrough.

Soon after the offer, Goldstone went into the main office. For a Coloured to be in charge of the store was unheard of and it created problems with his fellow workers.

> Baker and all the Indian clerks – I went in there, and you know how they are . . . Jealous. They said to me, 'Hey, Bushman, you got it made now, hah?' Because they heard how I got a little store, a few machines, and I got all this colourful paraphernalia for what goes on in soccer, what it's like. And, I had to go to the store one day. So, they're saying, 'Ja, Bushman, you've got it made.' And me, instead of saying, 'Ja, you clevers.' From the upbringing and how we grew up, everything is about anger. I took the ashtray and I threw it at him, and I walked off the site, and I walked out of the gate and forgot about my money and never went back. And I lost the opportunity to go overseas.

In a twist of supreme irony, which reveals the depths of apartheid's social psychosis, the racial tormentors who cost Goldstone his big break in life were not white. They were, like him, also consigned to a ghetto, albeit one reserved for those of a slightly different hue. *Divide et impera* worked its spell even in a forgotten storeroom where a young man stood on the cusp of personal triumph but was pulled back down to his allotted station in life. The missed chance to play for Leicester City didn't stop Goldstone's hunger though. Even then, he admired his local team, Leeds United. He remembers:

> No matter which amateur team we played for, Leeds was always the strongest opposition – and, I would say, at that time, the most well-run side . . . Whenever we came up against Leeds it was always a tough game because those guys were seasoned players – not professional, but they all had the potential to be professional. Some of them did go pro – like Bennie Whitby. Bennie played for Aces United. A lot of them at that time could have been professionals because they had some brilliant players. When you talk about Butch Harvey, Robbie Small, goalkeeper Eddie McKnight, they were all good players and they all ended up staying with Leeds United. In addition, you had Fishy Titus, Bony van Niekerk, Colin Paul, Ronnie Roach – all outstanding players. So, they weren't just a side with a big name. They had good players. What made them so good is that they were united.

When Petersen and Goldstone joined Leeds United in 1975, it was to prove to be two golden years for the club, and they quickly became one of the most successful amateur sides of the 1970s. Goldstone recalls their nickname, 'the Green Mambas. Somebody had given us that name. They said we strike like a mamba.' For Keshwar:

> The mamba was also classified as someone good at doing something. You say, 'That *ou*'s [guy's] a mamba!' So 'mamba' was associated with greatness or a skill of sorts. But, because of their green kit and they were a great soccer team, they became known as the Green Mambas, which was also relevant to the serpent in the form of strike, because when they struck, they had a deadly strike. So the name Green Mambas was synonymous with who they really were. The name Green Mamba was actually the right name for them. They grew into that name. Those guys are the real McCoys. Everyone wanted to play for that team.

The Green Mambas. Back row (left to right): J.R. Williams (manager), C. Smith (of Spar – sponsor); R. Mentor, C. Bezuidenhout, G. Birch, B. Fynn, N. Steenkamp, G. Jonathan, A. Green, S. Mayisa, H. Wagner, B. Campbell
Front row (left to right): W. Marais, B. Robertson, C. Tucker, S. Warren, H. Tucker, E. Singh, E. Africa, K. Green.

Playing for Leeds also meant you were given some protection from the violent gangs that were marking their territory, as Bennie Whitby remembers: 'At that time you could walk around at five o'clock in the morning if you played for Leeds or were associated with it. You could walk anywhere – the ganglands of Austerville, Assegai, anywhere in Wentworth – and no one would touch you.'

Alongside a powerful squad of players, Whitby was keen to build a family atmosphere:

> You never found the wives and partners of players drunk. All the ladies used to mix and they had self-respect. So the kids were picking up on all this. I'm talking about those kids – not the kids now. After a game, we used to get together, a couple of guys with the wives and open up bottles and drink – because the game is over now – but it was always contained and controlled. It never got out of hand. And it was about three or four different families – it wasn't you going home on your own, hitting your wife . . .

And this was the power of the game; to give people a sense of togetherness, pride even in a completely new environment forced upon them by apartheid's obsession with creating racially pure spaces of living. Men such as Whitby, jersey by jersey, sought not only to build a soccer club, but a way of being in a hostile world.

A big man with big ideas

> Is not anyone who has lived a life . . . worthy of biography – the failures as well as the successes, the humble as well as the illustrious? And what is greatness? And what smallness?
>
> — Woolf, 'Virginia Woolf'

By the early 1980s, the club was ailing. As Dennis Petersen remembers, while Whitby gave a lot to the team, the glory days of the mid-1970s could not be rekindled. A takeover by rich business person Errol Hughes loomed. Some hoped his money would stem the leak of Leeds players to clubs that could pay salaries and offer some security to players. For the first time, Whitby's control of the club was under pressure.

Roll back the years. Bennie Whitby is the almost mythical figure of Wentworth's soccer history. The founder of Leeds. More than that. The inspiration behind so many greats who played during the early 1960s. Born on 16 December 1948, his commitment to nurturing soccer in Wentworth bordered on the fanatical. Whitby was of that era of big men who ran clubs, threw their own resources into the game and brooked little interference.

The early period of Leeds in 1966 saw the likes of George van Niekerk, Patrick Hutchinson, Pinky Marais, Derrick Dunn, Dingaan Marais, Neville Peters, Luffy Pretorius and Ignatius Whitby at centre-half. But it was really in the following year that the team began to take off. As Bennie Whitby remembers, lots of players were let go:

> The following year, half those guys went. They had to go out of the team. The story of Leeds starts here. It was all family and friends. But, I had to get rid of them because I was making this dream team of mine. Leeds was a dream team, not only for me, but for the whole of Natal. South Africa. Wentworth. So we

only wanted the best. We won nothing in that first year. Only the following year, when the players came in – players like Colin Paul – slowly we were building a team . . .

Whitby's early years were spent in Stanger where his father worked for a sugar company. They then moved to Mayville and were once more put on the move to Wentworth. Whitby's father went to work for the railways: 'He worked as a bedding boy. They came and made the beds in the morning. It was nice. They would go to Cape Town for about a week and come back. It was cool for them.'

Whitby was determined to make a home in Wentworth. In any case, as apartheid's boundaries consolidated, the options were limited. He began to play for a few clubs. The clubs began to emerge as the township grew, with friendships formed at work often inspiring a coming together on the field:

> I played for Young Cavaliers. Young Cavies was one of the best amateur Coloured teams in Durban. They had great players. We used to play in Springfield Park. And at that time, we were all Coloureds. We all met each other while working at Motor Assemblies. Ninety per cent of the Coloured guys worked at Motor Assemblies. That's where I went after Standard 9. That was my first job – as a trimmer. I lasted there quite a while. There was no building trade, welding and all that for Coloureds back then. They used to go in to work for Motor Assemblies and then come in and join the building trade. That's when they started opening up the building trade – and welding.

In 1965, Whitby was playing for Railway Swallows when he decided that he wanted to form his own team. He was just seventeen!

> When I was fifteen, I started playing for Railway Swallows. I already had my soccer skills. Railway Swallows was old school for me. It wasn't soccer. It was what you did instead of drinking on the weekends. You play and versus so-and-so. Like youngsters. Like when they used to go play for a crate of Cokes. It was a

similar type of thing. That is why I formed Leeds. My brain was working already. I can't be playing with old men. So I played for Swallows for one year. While I was playing for Swallows in 1965, I took five guys from Swallows. These five guys were the youngest of the team. The rest were old men. I took the young bucks. The whole five came with me because everything I did in life, people used to follow me. I was a leader and they had faith in me. That's how we formed that team. I had a vision. My vision was to make this Coloured team the best team in South Africa. I couldn't let anyone down. That's why no one will fight with me in Wentworth – even in Sydenham – all those places . . . Wherever I went, I was known. In Wentworth, every mother, child and youngster knew me. They all wanted to be involved in this Leeds. That's how it started and it just grew from strength to strength. My Leeds years were 1966 to 1980. Fourteen years of commitment and dedication.

Using Railway Swallows as a base, Whitby began to search for talent:

The five players I brought from Railway Swallows were just to start this thing. The following year, half of them, the elderly ones were let go. In addition, I brought in another five people. From there I would take them along the journey when they were ready. To me, we had some good players, but they weren't great players. Some of them were my friends and family. Now friends and family, you go along with them, but at some point, you have got to let go. They become like baggage to you. They are heavy. As the years go by, you will find that half those guys go, and another lot come in. But it's not ten or eleven – it's just like five or six. Always. Every year you are changing because you want to maintain the standard.

Whitby gave up his own soccer-playing ambitions to build the Leeds team:

I retired from soccer at the age of 24. I had so much pressure of playing, recruiting, coaching, signing players, meetings, getting jerseys, getting balls, kit and all that. And we were the first team that even had floodlights. We used to train at night. We put in the floodlights on Christ the King grounds. We took electricity from people's houses with an extension cable and we paid them for the costs. It was not like just for nothing. Other teams could not train at night. My vision was that nothing must hold this train back. This train must just go one way and if I was to be the driver of this train, then I could not also play.

While Whitby wanted to build a top Coloured team that could exemplify the talent emerging out of Wentworth, he was not averse to bringing in players from other 'racial' groups. He recruited from the Zanzibari area at the top end of the Bluff, including a rollicking Indian centre-half named Adam Essop.

I brought him to Leeds and he used to play in the same position as me, but I brought him in because I saw he had potential. He wasn't a good centre-half, but I thought, hey, this is a guy that I can teach. That is when I retired – when I put him in my position. And I used to teach him every week.

Leeds became family, figuratively and literally:

... You will see inter-marriage in Leeds. Colin Paul and Eddie McKnight both played for Leeds and they were brothers-in-law. A lot of the players ended up having developing relationships with fellow player's families ... Peters playing for Leeds was going out with my sister. That's why Leeds was more of a family thing. It was always family, children, no gangsters. When we went to go play in Sydenham, the people would go with their baskets. It was like an outing.

But, the game was eating into Whitby's family life:

My late wife June Davids loved soccer. The children loved soccer. But she couldn't take it anymore because she couldn't have me.

Leeds (left to right): Gerald Cockrane (manager), James Ullbricht, Graham Harvey, Robbie Small (with trophy), Bennie Whitby (obscured), Colin Paul (with trophy), Pinky Marais (front with trophy), Eddie McKnight.

> Soccer took me away from her. From my family. Everything. I was committed and invested. That's the thing. You either go for perfection or just go on a Sunday and make as if you are playing soccer. That wasn't me. There was no anger. I didn't leave Leeds in anger. The few players that I had a meeting with, I told them, 'I am getting out of Leeds.' Time out. I didn't want to leave. The arrogant trash that I recruited . . . Instead of saying, 'Let's go talk to the wife . . .' No. They had a bigger picture in mind: money.

The pulling power of Leeds and its successes on the field of play dazzled those seeking to cash in:

> Leeds was a money machine. If it was run the proper way. I took it to a stage where I could have sat back and started making money out of this team. But I'm not that type of person. I didn't form this team so that I could become a multimillionaire. No, no, no.

> Leeds was more family than anything else. I could have made it a money-spinner if I wanted to. That's what the guys did after I left. In life, you learn to see a smirk on a person's face. You learn to see a thug and a crook. When they have a smirk on their faces that says, 'Go. Carry on. We can do without you.' And I told them, 'You know something? The day I leave Leeds, y'll never ever make it.' A couple of years after that, the same guys – like Pat Bilham, as an example – I said, 'Hey, bru, what happened? Remember when I told you all what would happen if I left this team?' They were not capable of running this thing. They don't know meetings. They don't know recruiting. Maintenance. Training. Coaching. Management. Sustainability. You can have ten other guys there with you, but you're not going to make it work. They didn't have what it takes. I was doing the job of ten people rolled into one. Everything. I didn't delegate. I'm a wonderful person, but I am arrogant. I don't like it if I give you a position in the Leeds team, and you come to me tomorrow and say, 'Why are you signing Peter?' I'm gonna say, 'Hey. You're questioning me?' I didn't want to recruit guys to help me out because they were gonna ask questions.

For Whitby, it was the attention to detail and total commitment that was at the root of his success:

> Every player that played for Leeds during my time, I signed them. I brought them in. You could never get into Leeds without going through me. You could have been Messi or Ronaldo, but if I didn't want you, you would never have got in. I evaluated and assessed everybody until I let go of it. Then Leeds took a dive when I left. You can't control this thing. It's not to say that it's too big. It's the work that you've got to go through. It took sixteen years of my life that I devoted to Leeds. And you think you can just step in . . . It will run away with you. It's too big a thing.

Whitby was more than manager, coach and recruiter in chief; he was also a social worker:

> If a player was fighting with his wife, the next day I was there by his house. I would say, 'What's happening?' – not ignore it. 'You are a man. How can you do this here?' I used to be like a counsellor. To try and put the couple back together . . . Because it interferes with the team. This guy . . . his wife is divorcing him, now he can't play. You must take your bags and go. You are holding up progress.

Wentworth was a young township. Old bonds nurtured in the Transkei and Mayville were suddenly torn asunder as the Group Areas Act put people on the move and corralled them into Wentworth. In talking to people like Whitby you begin to realise how a space became a place, stitched together by sacrifice, vision and a bit of old-style, top-down leadership.

After Whitby left, he cut himself off completely:

> The guys who played for Leeds from the time we formed until I left, even those guys don't know about Leeds because they played for about two years and then they were gone. I was the one constant. After I left, I never, ever went to a soccer game when Leeds played. After I retired . . . I never wanted to watch what became of it. You could pay me to go watch. Never. It never got better. It deteriorated. It's like the ANC. When Zuma took over, there was only money and greed in mind. It was the same with Leeds. I made sacrifices. But people don't do that today.

In places in which the biographies of people like Whitby are woven into the very landscape, the wounds are deep. Some 30 years later, Whitby remains bitter despite his protestations, and when invited to a Leeds reunion in 2013, he did not pitch. As Lloyd Keshwar remembers:

> We sent him an invitation. We kept a table for him and his late wife. We had his jersey for him. He didn't come. And then the proceeds from the dance, we bought KFC – about 80 packs – and took them to John Dunn [home for the aged]. And then we asked him to come – Bennie – and he came. He came for that.

But he wasn't happy about what transpired. Now I can't make sense of what's he's saying. There was a takeover . . . He was going nowhere with the team.

Whitby's values about how the game should be played is a curious mixture of far-sighted tactics and strategies, such as building a strong squad with versatile players, while being militantly against things such as sponsorship:

> I hate sponsorship. If someone sponsors me with a hundred rand; they are going to want to tell me how to spend that hundred rand. That is sponsorship. Number one, they will want their logos on the jerseys. And it's so simple. The easiest game in the world to play is soccer – when you know how to play it. And people don't realise that. Take Chiefs, Pirates and Sundowns – the three biggest clubs – talking about sponsorship. Say Chiefs has 100 000 supporters. If each supporter puts in R2 each week . . . Not mega bucks. Just R2 times 100 000. That's 200 000 every week. They don't need a sponsor. The money rolls in. Take Clover milk or Coca-Cola . . . How many people are buying Coke and milk? . . . The sponsorship that they are giving is nothing compared to how much they are making. They then control you. I don't want to be controlled by anyone. This is my team. I didn't sleep at night. Then a sponsor must come and tell me how to do things. It is not that you do not get anything. You get jerseys. Guys like Ronaldo and Messi get BMWs and Porsches. That's good for them. But they tell you what to do. They can even tell you which players to sign. Sign this player. Sign that player. It goes very deep.

Keshwar's comments might have some resonance as the game became professionalised and Leeds stretched beyond place and family ties, but they also lack a sensitivity about people like Whitby who were trying to build more than a club, to forge a way of living that could inspire a community that was getting made and broken at the same time.

Whitby does not suffer fools gladly:

> I don't go to functions. I do go sometimes, but the moment people start talking about soccer, I get up and I walk out because they don't know what they are talking about. It happened in Australia now – when I was visiting my daughters. There were guys sitting around. Anyway, the topic started about soccer. I'm sitting in their company. 'Spearman Lads . . . These were the greatest players.' And this one guys says, 'What about Leeds? Leeds was nothing.' And I am listening to this idiot. I got up and I walked away. I went to smoke.

In 2013, Whitby's wife died.

> I never remarried. All my girls say, 'Dad, you must meet someone nice and get on with your life. But don't ever come here with a 16-Valve. Come with a mature lady, not a young one.' They said, 'If you come with a 16-Valve, we will chase you and her.' But at least I've got my licence now. My girls are angels.

When asked about the best of Leeds's players, Whitby pronounces:

> The best Leeds team ever was – from 1966 right until now – was: Eddie McKnight, Martin Swartz, Wilfred Peters, Keith Bezuidenhout, Graham Harvey, Dennis Petersen, Ronnie Roach, Gary Goldstone, Colin Paul, Pat Bilham, Phillip Peters and me.

For Whitby, the reasons for the sacrifices made were clear: 'It's not a money thing. I was trying to uplift Coloureds. I wanted to uplift Wentworth into something to be proud of. To not only build a soccer team but nurture families and inspire the generations to come.'

Bennie Whitby is a special kind of person – old school, who brought innovations to the field of play, built a squad rather than just a team of eleven and creating a spectacle with a dress sense that evoked pride and envy.

The penchant for innovations, from the uniforms of supporters to a real, live mascot, was one line of march that did not stop with Whitby.

The mascot

> A dog's tool of perception includes the capacity to hear ranges of sound far exceeding humans. Reflective lenses amplify available light, equipping them with a high degree of night vision. But most significant is a dog's sense of smell . . . Where we observe the shape, colour and function of a thing, invisible scent signatures that we're blind to speak volumes to a dog's nuanced nose . . . So armed, a dog can access dimensions of experience we can't fathom.
>
> — Sousanis, *Unflattening*

Leeds supporters were always bringing something new to the ground. There were Leeds cushions. And then there was the Leeds mascot, courtesy of Skiddo Joseph and his sister Lorna Petersen, chairperson of the Supporters' Club. Almost three decades later, she remembers:

> We had a dog. His name was Rex, who we took with us to the games. He was our mascot. We gave him a green outfit that went over his back. He ran on the field before the team, carrying a Leeds flag in his mouth. He led the team onto the field at Curries Fountain. He was so disciplined. He would then politely run off and take his place with one of my family members.

Given Wentworth's reputation as a rough place, in which gangs dominated the streets, Rex exuded a completely different aura, as Lorna attests:

> He was a very well-trained dog. My brother Skiddo trained Rex. He was very passionate. Rex was even a scout and had a full scout uniform. At the games, he wore a green jacket with 'Leeds' on it. Rex lived for many years. He died of old age. He was a cross between a ridgeback and a boerboel and had a tan coat. Rex would do anything Skiddo taught him to do. He was a very intelligent dog. We used to even send Rex to the shop. We would send him with a list in his mouth – and the basket, with the money. The shopkeeper would take this list and give Rex what he wanted, and give him change. Believe it or not, if there were cigarettes on that list, with his mouth, he would take them out the basket and

give them to my mother. He knew that the cigarettes belonged to my mother. A basket, money, and a list – and nobody dared take it away from him, or tried to. And Wentworth was at its peak of violence then. Rex was a lovely dog, but don't push Rex. Don't try to rob him of his duty. He'll sort you out.

Rex's notoriety grew when he was arrested:

> Rex went to court and eventually ended up in jail. He was locked up with my brother for stealing from some residents from nearby Merebank. How they identified him was, 'That guy that owns that big brown dog.' Rex went to court with my brother to be identified – because they used him to scare the people so my younger brother could rob them. And the minute the victim described the perpetrator as 'the guy with the big brown dog', the police knew immediately exactly who it was. They were quite familiar with this dog and his owner.
> Skiddo was naughty. He would just rob them for their 50 cents or their rand that they had. He thought it was very, very amusing. For him it wasn't a criminal activity. It was more a prank.

All the time, apartheid was closing in. The last remnants of Coloureds were pushed out of Durban's mixed racial areas, joined by Coloureds from the Transkei and the rural areas of Natal, into Wentworth and the newly proclaimed Newlands East. In Wentworth, new social relations were forged as musical groups made their mark at local nightspots, gangs marked territory, churches solidified and soccer became the sport of choice and a chance to rise above. In talking to old players and supporters, one gets a deep sense of Leeds as a magnet and aspiration. In thinking through the ways in which Leeds United and their supporters responded to apartheid and their social location in the city, one is reminded of Pierre Bourdieu's

> art of living, a wisdom taught by necessity, suffering and humiliation and deposited in an inherited language, dense in its stereotypes, a sense of revelry and festivity, of self-expression

and practical solidarity with others . . . in short, everything that is engendered by the realistic (but not resigned hedonism) and sceptical (but not cynical) materialism which constitute both a form of adaptation to the conditions of existence and a defense against them (1984: 394–5).

And when things deteriorated in Wentworth (jobs drying up in the petrochemical firm of Sasol in the Transvaal and local textile factories, families disintegrating, gang violence and drugs, middle-class exodus), soccer became a major resource. Jordi Pujol's words, president of the Catalan government, speaking about the Barcelona football team in the immediate aftermath of fascist dictator Francisco Franco, are prescient: 'Barça is like other folkloric manifestations of our people – a reserve we can draw on when other sources dry out, when the doors of normality are closed to us' (in Burns 2012: 245).

As the abnormality of apartheid seeped in, men such as Bennie Whitby were opening doors of opportunity, turning the curse of forced removals into a resource to recruit new players and inspire ways of living that fought back against the gangs and myriad pathologies that were enveloping the flatlands of Wentworth.

3

The Art of Friendship

> Engagement in friendship takes time, it gives time, for it carries beyond the present moment and keeps memory as much as it anticipates. It gives and takes time, for it survives the living present.
> — Derrida, *The Politics of Friendship*

Dennis Petersen and Gary Goldstone grew up alongside each other in Mayville. Dennis's family produced a number of soccer players, none better known than Basil Petersen. Goldstone takes up the story:

> I was born in Mayville. Dennis Petersen's grandmother and his family lived next door. From that time – ever since I can remember, Dennis was my friend. We grew up there and in 1962/63 we were forcibly removed and came to Wentworth. My mother [Dorothy] was a housewife. My father [Christopher] was a slaughterer at the abattoir in Dalton – right by the Wharf, under the bridge at Federated Meat Industries. They were the main suppliers to most of the butchers in the province. In those days, they didn't have all these machines. He was the top guy with the gun that was used to shoot the animals.

From the age of eleven, both Dennis and Gary started playing for Cerro in a league in Sydenham:

> Dennis's grandfather and my grandfather [Harry] were very big friends. They used to play Thunee (card game) every Saturday afternoon. In those days, you had those wrap-around verandahs. They used to ask us not, 'Did y'll win?', but 'How many goals y'll scored?' It became ingrained in Dennis and I. We also watched

The fabulously talented Basil Petersen (standing, extreme left) playing for the all-conquering, five-a-side team NGI Lads in the 1950s.

> Dennis's uncle, Basil Petersen, who was a legend. Dennis was right-winger, me on the left. Playing for Cerro, our main rivals were Wanderers from Sydenham, Checkers Juniors, Northern Suburbs, Rialto. This was our little under-12 league in Sydenham. It was the first football ever played in Sydenham. The former Berea centre-back, Goofy Fredericks's father, was in charge of the grounds – not in a big-money way, but his input into those grounds for the Coloured community was the start of football there, in Tills Crescent.

Dennis's and Gary's (soccer) education was also helped by watching games at Westridge Park Stadium:

> Many of the legends like Pat Blair, Basil Petersen were there. Dennis and I, as far as coaching is concerned, we may not have had top professional coaching, but we had the best telling us what

to do and how to play – every day. Westridge Park was a place where most of the good players met. We had that extra advantage. People talking football all the time to us.

Goldstone and his six sisters, two brothers and parents were forced by the Group Areas Act to move to Wentworth:

My eldest sister was one of the first residents of Wentworth in late 1959/60. They lived in Dunbar Road area. The first place we moved to in Wentworth was K1 Section when I was about eleven/twelve years old.

Luckily for Goldstone, he had some experience of Wentworth visiting his sister as a ten-year-old. Once installed in Wentworth, he began playing soccer at the Durban East School grounds in the under-14 league for a team called Rangers, and then he and Dennis went to play for Avalon Athletic Colts. Wellington Meth, who was heavily involved with developing Wentworth soccer at the time, watched him play:

We played the immediate curtain-raiser before the big games for Avalon Athletic Colts. They used to get huge crowds. Orlando Pirates was playing there. This was between 1962 and '64. I was about fourteen. I was in Standard 7. And Wellington came to our house and said, 'Mrs Goldstone, please let Gary come play for us.' She said, 'Is this the same under 21? Do you want to kill my son?' Wellington said, 'I'll look after him. Don't worry.'

At the tender age of fourteen, Goldstone began playing with much older players:

I played for about three or four months for the under 21s – Young Cavaliers. Wellington used to come for me at half past six/ quarter to seven on a Sunday morning. I had to go to church on Saturday night for that to happen. St Gabriel's Anglican Church. He used to take me to pick up all the guys. If he couldn't find some of the guys and he could not make a starting eleven, then I played. In that year, I played more than three games for the seniors, which meant that I couldn't go back to the under 21s. Throughout that year I was playing tournaments. I played left wing. When the year was finished, I became their regular left-winger – because they had a left-winger, Roley [Roland] King. If he hadn't broken his leg, then I wouldn't have been given the chance. He was much older than us. I was still only fourteen years old. Then I became a regular and I was scoring goals. We scored a lot of goals.

Goldstone laughs at the memory of a wisp of a boy playing with the big *ous*:

From the very first game I played . . . I came up against a guy – and he was a man. A big man – a centre-back. Growing up in those Mayville years and getting hit by defenders, and you've got the ball at your feet, and its close, then you're gonna get kicked. Dennis and I both knew this from young. I was a timid cry-baby. Dennis was short and sporty. As we grew, we got a bit more speed and a bit cleverer. The games used to be fast. So, this big-sized guy got me a few times but I beat him many more times. From that day, I knew I was an out and out left-winger.

Soccer was becoming more and more popular and more organised in Wentworth, as Goldstone remembers: 'In 1967/68, it was teams like Leeds, Aralian Lads, Young Ones, Railway Swallows, All Blacks. It was the Preston and Chelsea era. They were old teams.'

Goldstone's home life was strict:

You would get shouted at for the simplest of things. So I became a timid person. I was also spoilt in that I was the first boy – after five girls. And I was a little mollycoddled. That's why in the beginning of my football, I was a cry-baby. They used to whack me. I was a thin little *laaitie* with so much speed and control. So these big men now – double my size – and the boots we played with in those years, you could get hurt. I used to cry on the field. Then I got the schooling of the street from my brother-in-law and his mates. At that age, I could run a gambling school with big men. My job was also to watch out for the police. Big men, I could tell them, 'Keep quiet. That's not your bet.' At that age. I knew all that but I didn't implement it. I knew no one will touch me. I could also fight. I would also pull a knife. And I would also shoot. I had a gun. I had unnatural strength. My father was also unnaturally strong.

Despite this immersion in the 'underworld' of Wentworth, Goldstone kept playing soccer:

> From Young Cavies, I went to play for Preston – for Ronnie Matthews, the nephew of Zoot Henry who was the manager of the All Blacks. Wellington at that time couldn't carry on with the club and went to play professional football for Golden Arrows. Our main rivals at Preston were Leeds, and later the All Blacks. All Blacks was practically formed in my brother-in-law's home. Leeds was always our enemy.
>
> It became monotonous. Young Aces was a top side. I ended playing for Young Aces. We won the league. We were brought into the professional ranks. Aces United ended up at the bottom of the league. Within the next two weeks, Dennis, my old mate, came. And Jerry Singh, Enver Ali . . . We didn't have the best of sides and we were all inexperienced. We weren't professionals. Coming up against experienced players. But Dennis and I still made a mark. A big mark in the pro ranks from 1971 to 1974.

When they played together, Gary on the left wing and Dennis on the right, they switched and swayed and bamboozled their way as if they were joined at the hip. But they were not 'birds of a feather', as Goldstone puts it. Firm friends off the field, Dennis the Menace stayed close to home, while Gary ventured widely, wildly. Still, the bond between Gary and Dennis has lasted over five decades.

> Today, when we talk football, and I go to meetings with the Federation, Legends, and they talk about football and this guy

Dennis Petersen (right).

and that guy, then they say, 'Gary, what you think?' And I say, 'Y'll not gonna agree with me, but this is what I know to be the truth: I've never met another player that could make goal-scoring look easy.' And they say, 'Who?' And I say, 'Dennis Petersen.' If ever there was a person who made goal-scoring look easy and make the goalkeeper look like a stupid, it was Dennis Petersen. And I never saw Dennis miss a goal one-on-one with the goalkeeper. What I see today on the field, I've never! Dennis would make that goalie look like an utter fool and actually go by the line with the ball and stand on the ball. He's actually got the right name – Dennis the Menace. That's his nickname. You get some guys call him Rocky, but we know him as Dennis the Menace. I'll tell you something . . . We were young and we used to duck church to go to the grounds. And we would go early now, to go pass Etna Lane to Curries Fountain to wait for the players to come in. Then the minute they come in, they knew we were with Basil Petersen (Dennis's uncle), we would go inside with them. We'd just carry the bag. But when we used to pass Etna Lane – now that's the Dasheen gang side – there were all these big gangsters and they used to shout, 'Dennis the Menace!' He was so naughty. I got into so much trouble through Dennis as a friend, I tell you.

Petersen remembers that they were inseparable at the time. Their lives were spent traversing the city in the name of soccer.

> There is a team, also from Wentworth – a team called the All Blacks. Me and Gary played for them in 1970 and can you believe it, there's only four of us that's alive. There's only two of us that played for Leeds here. The only time that we split . . . The only time that me and Gary didn't play on the same team is when I played for Verulam Suburbs and Gary went to Berea.

Petersen, with a half-smile, explains why they parted ways for a while:

> You know, there's a guy that played for Berea – and he liked a girl that I used to always talk to from Sydenham. He thought I was going out with her, and I wasn't. My best friend, Ashley Oakley, was going out with her. Her name was Lynette Riley from Barnes Road. I was in Mayflower Road. Every time he came there, we thought he was going out with her, but he wasn't. He was trying to get there. He saw me as a rival . . . They wanted me to play for Berea. But, I couldn't play for Berea because that guy was playing for Berea – because we were enemies in his mind. I left Verulam Suburbs to go to Leeds.

The 1975 Leeds side were at the peak of their game. Petersen remembers them playing the glamorous professional side of Berea:

> We played Berea twice, and we beat them twice. Berea was a professional club and Leeds was amateur. It just shows you what a team Leeds was. We worked hard. We trained hard. And we were serious about things. We wanted to prove things. We wanted to do well – and progress. We had a good coach. Blondie Campbell. He was very shrewd.

He recalls how the team travelled the country

playing tournaments – and winning tournaments. It was every youngster's ambition to play for Leeds. It was every . . . Coloured person's ambition to play for Leeds.

In fact, as Goldstone attests, the trophies they accumulated throughout this period showed their prowess.

The Leeds of 1975 and 1976, I would say was one of the best sides I've played for. In 1975 we won the league, the Coca-Cola Cup, the Clover Cup, and we represented Durban South and we won the inter-district tournament. The whole Leeds team, they represented Durban South . . . We were practically unbeatable. We won the league in '75. We won cups in '75. The Clover Cup in 1976.

Leeds winning the 1976 Clover Cup.

Sometimes however, Goldstone's antics off the field got him into trouble. Petersen remembers: 'One year we were waiting and waiting for Gary . . . I think we were going to Cape Town . . . He was locked up . . . we couldn't get Gary out of jail, so we had to go minus Gary.'

The many lives of Gary Goldstone

> I, for one, was a personal admirer of Gary Goldstone. I used to love watching him play soccer. I thought he was the greatest. Even today, if you ask me, 'Who was the greatest soccer player that came out of Wentworth?' I'll tell you, 'Gary Goldstone.' Some people may differ with that, but everyone has their point of view. That's my personal point of view that Gary Goldstone was the best soccer player. Elvis Singh and Dennis Petersen. Those two were the greatest strikers that came out of Wentworth for me. *Klaar* [Finish]. If we went for goalkeeping, I would go for Eddie McKnight. The best.
>
> — Lloyd Keshwar

From the age of seventeen, life for Goldstone became a roller coaster. His mother, who kept things together and also kept a beady eye on him, died. It sent him on a downward spiral.

> I had some naughty friends, but I couldn't be with them because my mother was strict. When she died, that's when I really went. I was seventeen. At the same time, I was still playing top football. When my mother died, it affected me a lot. It was like I had a nervous breakdown. For about a week or two, I didn't know what was going on. I had to get treatment for that. I was still very angry. I was a cry-baby. Quick to cry. And then I became quick to fight. Because I could fight. In late 1969, if you were sixteen years old, you were a baby. Even though you had to work, you were a baby. I worked for the first earthmoving company in Durban. After my mother died, our home broke up. Finish and *klaar*. Six months later, my father brought a new woman into the house – my stepmother.

Suddenly, Gary was out of the place he called home:

> My father had a new wife – and one day I came home late. At about nine o'clock. He told me, 'Take all your fucken things. Go by your friends.' I said, 'I got no friends that I can go to in their homes.' And he said to me, 'And I don't want to catch you by one of my daughters' houses. Don't put your foot there.' That's all

my sisters. So I used to sleep in the bathrooms. We had public/communal toilets and bathrooms at that time. I had naughty friends – Charlie Peppers and Goofy Fynn – we used to sleep in the bathrooms. They had big boilers that were warm and we kicked the door down to sleep where it's warm. I started getting sick with bronchial pneumonia. But, at that time, because I grew up being a clean person, there was hot water there; there was no need to be dirty. My sister used to live across the road. She used to wash my clothes and iron my clothes. When it was cold, and you found a car, you steal the car, start it up and drive it around to get warm. You sleep in the car until 2 am when you are shivering. You drive it the whole morning until the petrol gets *klaar*.

The area was rough:

In K1 flats you had to be tough. I saw people die in front of me – long before the gang fights. At the same time, you still had to be a good football player. I always think how I did it. And I think it's because I didn't know how good I was or how bad I was. For instance, one young guy in Umhlanga in about 2015 – *wit laaitie* [white youngster] – and there's a 50 metre drop where you can fall and die. He is tottering on the edge. Now, I'm the ops manager. I call him. So he gets off. He walks past me and he says, 'If you're not living on the edge, you're taking up breathing space.' I said, 'Don't walk away when you make a statement like that. Come here. Let me respond to that.' He came and I said to him, 'Listen carefully. Did you ever live in the township? Then you don't know what's living on the edge.'

And Goldstone was always standing on the edge of a precipice. No. He was hanging on by his fingertips:

The last time I went there [rehab] I was finished on drugs – Mandrax. I got any amount of Mandrax that you could think of. I could go smoke the whole day. I could go smoke the whole night. And I could smoke the next day. Any amount. I had access to it. I used to get it for R2. I was the kind of person when, even

Sydney and Michael Abrahams outside their home, which was attacked by gangsters, 1982.

in company, even with the family, they would leave me alone. I didn't like to take photos. It's only now that I'm in a lot of photos.

It spurs me to ask if there are any wedding photographs. Goldstone's wife Ursula sadly reveals:

Our wedding photos were taken to OK Bazaars for developing by a lady who lost the slip. And they would never give them to me, so we never had our wedding photos.

There was a time in which Goldstone was pursuing Ursula and he had to cross gang territory to visit her:

You had to carry a knife at that time. I was quick. I would run from K1 to Assegai and while I'm running I'm watching. When people poke, it's to stab you dead. There's no couple of hits and kicks. And the next route is on the main road – Tara Road, where Engen garage is. One day when I hit the Engen garage, there this

The gullies and narrow pathways that Gary Goldstone ran through.

ou jumps in front of me – Henry McAlister. And this was a big *ou* in years. In those times reputation played a big part. He was going to work but was determined to sort me out. By the time he put his lunch down, I had my knife out and stabbed him. He charged me. I came off this charge because he grabbed me first. I told the truth. I also did a lot of illegal stuff – but not from the house.

Ursula backs this up:

He never ever, ever did anything illegal from our home – to such extremes that our small boy was in Grade 11 already and then he only found out about their father. He did everything in the gullies. I used to go to work. At Adams & Griggs. And then I was transferred to Victoria Street to the school books. So, for example, one Sunday somebody came and knocked on the door and said, 'Auntie Ursula, your husband shot somebody.' I said, 'What nonsense.' I carried on baking. He had shot somebody. But when he came inside he acted innocent.

Ursula laughs and recounts that despite living rough and running through 'enemy' territory, Gary 'was very smart. He was always clean. He used to come to our gate and take his hanky out and dust his shoes before he comes through the door. I used to be watching through the lounge window. He used to tuck in his shirt.'

Ursula is warming to the conversation and asks rhetorically, 'do you know how Gary got to me?'

> We were going to church. Gary was already waiting in Durban East School for me. He was always very clean. There was no love yet. So, I don't end up at church, I end up sitting with him on the school grounds. His story was that he is very sick and that he is going to die when he is 21. I felt so sorry for him and he was now becoming my best friend. Anyway, eventually at eleven o'clock we were walking through the grounds and these ladies were waving at him, 'Gary, Gary, Gary . . .' – in one of the old army houses. I didn't know who they were so I waved back. I didn't think much about this guy. So we went past and he said, 'You see that double-storey house there? That's my father's house.' I said, 'Oh, that's nice. Y'll come from a well-to-do family.' We are just ordinary people from town and we are six in the family. He said, 'We are nine in the family.' That army house was his house and those were all his sisters waving at us, which I found out after I was in love with this guy who was critically ill, but played soccer like a master. The sisters were very receptive and my father-in-law adored me. He said, 'Gary got a nice girlfriend. His children will be good looking. She's fair.' By the time I found out all the truth about him, I was already in love . . . He asked me one day, 'What is it that you like about me?' I said, 'Your legs and your bum.' The way he started building up those legs and that bum.

Gary Goldstone was a driving force of a gang called the Trucks. He does not talk much about it. But Graham Birch, who captained Leeds for a while, is more forthcoming:

> Initially we weren't called the Trucks. We were called the Sinners. Then it was Club 7. Then the youngsters grew up and they

became the Trucks gang. I was sixteen when I was in Sinners. Gary was there, too. First it was through being influenced by the older guys and then we started doing dagga and that created its own bonds.

They hung around Adams shop in Austerville.

That was our spot. Gary, me, Desmond Leslie, Bernard Samuel. That was our clique. We worked now and again, but mostly we were unemployed. I was eighteen. We got odd jobs like at Token Toys. After that was a little bit of engineering, some painting – whatever came around the area of Durban. In the late seventies/early eighties, Wentworth was bad. Lots of people lost their lives. Some from us. Some *ous* in the area . . . my friend Bernard Samuel got killed. We were together the night before. They killed him the next day. We were in Briardene near Greenwood Park. Then in the morning I heard he was shot dead. He was with his son when they attacked. His son was four years old. They pushed his son under the car. They offloaded about ten shots on him. And they poked him after they shot him, just to make sure. This guy. Wiped him out. Completely. When they buried him in the church, he started bleeding from the nose because he had been left out for too long. Then it seemed overnight they couldn't come over to our side. We couldn't go over to their side. That's how this whole thing started.

For Birch, it was soccer that saved his life:

I was five years into my marriage already. Still moving this way and that way. I used to go out on a Friday. My wife used to stay in Newlands East. I used to only rock up back on a Tuesday. One time, I didn't even know where the house was. It was a terrible life. What kept me sane was the soccer. If it wasn't for the soccer, I don't think I would be around today to talk. Life was just meaningless in a sense. But I was committed to the soccer. Training. Every day. Very fit. We used to start training at six o'clock in the evening. We used to finish training at half past eight

Graham Birch with the coveted Clover Cup.

> at night. But I would only reach home at half past eleven. I must detour along the way . . . Austerville. Have a smoke. Eventually get home. That was the lifestyle. The one good thing that I thank God for is that my children don't know that lifestyle. They were all small. They only hear from the people. 'Yes, Graham was a rascal, but he could play wonderful ball.'

According to Gary, life on the street did not hurt his soccer but actually helped it:

> Through all the hits, I became a tough player. I don't ever remember being carried off injured from the field. Never, ever. Yes, I got a cramp sometimes. It would get me so bad that I couldn't complete the game.

It was a far cry from the mollycoddled, cry-baby days of the sixteen-year-old.

The Legendary Walla Homiel.

Goldstone's mentor was Walla Homiel, a soccer legend in his own right, who lectured him, not exactly in the Queen's English, about fitness:

> One day I got hurt playing for Aces United. And Walla Homiel came into the change room just after half-time. He always used to look after me. When it came time to tell me off, he did not hold back: 'It's because you're not fucken fit that this happened.' From that day I became one of the fittest guys on the field. I trained every day. I played football every day. And I started dropping back into positions like left-half, centre-midfield – just behind the forwards and the strikers – sometimes centre-back. I could be playing midfield and we could be three up or two up – and something happens with our keeper, I can get in there. And you click into gear. That was something inbuilt in me – where I can perform in the goal and it was like I never played centre-forward. If something happened when I was playing left wing and Blondie said, 'Gary, how about you drop back to left-back', I could click on and go to left-back just like that. I could go to central-midfield and in the next game I could play in the inside right position, not so bad being a left-footed player.

As the cups rolled in, the only blemish for the team was not winning the Mainstay Cup in the mid-1970s. Goldstone recalls that there was an important reason for this.

> I know we didn't win the Mainstay Cup because that Saturday night Adam Essop, our centre-half and captain got knocked and killed in a hit-and-run. So, a lot of us were up practically the whole night. And we still asked for the game against this one club to be postponed, and they refused. Just to think, the night before, your guy has an accident. Half the team was with him when it happened. A guy hits him off the pavement and drags him, and he dies, and they expect us to play. So we just let the game go. That team beat us 6-0. I'll never forget. But we weren't even worried. No one was even interested. I don't think I played that day. Many of the guys didn't play that day. That year we didn't win the Mainstay Cup.

It was 1976 and the year in which Gary's son, Gary Junior was born. He was to have a successful career as a professional footballer in an era when apartheid had collapsed. He started off playing for those old Leeds rivals Cherrians, but as there was no professional soccer in Wentworth, he had to go on the road linking up with his father's old club Manning Rangers, then moving on to the Johannesburg-based glamour club Kaizer Chiefs and ending his playing days with Bloemfontein Celtic.

What was the secret to winning, I ask Goldstone?

> We had a top coach – Blondie Campbell. We had a good trainer – Harold van der Berg. Blondie played you where you were supposed to play. Not like coaches today. Blondie was a person who did not raise his voice. We trained at Tara Road grounds. Pat Bilham was one of the best amateur players. He never went professional. He played midfield – box to box – you don't get them like that anymore. We had a good side. Guys like Keith Bezuidenhout, Elijah Adams. We won the leagues. The leagues used to finish at the end of November here. We didn't play during summer. We had the off-season. Now the league ends in

Leeds coach Blondie Campbell (centre).

October. In 1975 and 1976, that was some of the best football. Not one pro club ever beat us in a friendly in those two years. The guys could play and they knew the game.

Technically, Leeds had a jump-start on many other teams. The knack of this game is to make space. About seven or eight players in Leeds had the ability to beat one player. That's what made Leeds a top side. That side was the best Leeds side, period.

Graham Birch remembers the period as one in which there was a lack of discipline:

Before we got into professional, there were two camps in Leeds. It was one team, but you had the smokers and the drinkers – two camps. That was the discord. Eventually it worked its way out. It didn't last long. But we were all together in the parties. At the grounds it became a little bit ugly. It was also mostly among the supporters, too. Drugs and drinkers. Two camps. Eventually they used to drink at the manager's house and come from the disco late. I was a smoker. With smoking it can still work out for you. You can function. Very well. With alcohol, you can party the whole night and go sleep in the morning, but when you start – and your game is at 1 or 2 or 3 pm, when the sun is on, you will have a problem. The second half. That's when they used to kill us. The other teams knew that's when we run out of steam. They knew our guys liked good times. Those were some of the mishaps. I don't want to make it sound glamorous.

In Don Delillo's *End Zone* he tells us:

Football players [US gridiron] are simple folk. Whatever complexities, whatever dark politics of the human mind, the heart – these are noted only within the chalked borders of the playing field. At times strange visions ripple across that turf; madness leaks out. But wherever else he goes, the football player travels the straightest of lines. His thoughts are wholesomely commonplace, his actions uncomplicated by history, enigma, holocaust or dream (2004: 2-3).

This was certainly not the divide of the Goldstones and Birches. In the times in which they lived, the city's 'non-white' nightlife emerging, access to fast cars and drink and drugs, meant that the madness of the field was carried into all spheres of life.

Still, the emergence of more structure and the fanaticism of the supporters worked; Goldstone's wife Ursula attests to the fact

... that Leeds had a good structure. They always got the wives involved. And the families. And they had a following. They had to hire two buses on a Sunday for the supporters. They were also making a change in people's train of thought in Wentworth. There was no entertainment. Now suddenly they had a place to go where they could enjoy the game and watch the guys from Wentworth. That was the era of Rex – the mascot dog – with his hat.

Leeds supporters on the bus en route to Curries Fountain.

Blondie Campbell was key both on and off the field. Abdul Kader Adams, the Leeds keeper between 1980 and 1983, also attests to Blondie Campbell's influence; always thinking of new coaching methods and always on the lookout for new talent. Blondie was part of the coaching team when D'Alberton Callies won the premier amateur tournament at the Clover Cup in 1979. Adams was the goalkeeper and Blondie was instrumental in luring him to Leeds. For Adams, Blondie was an outstanding coach because

> . . . he coached from the heart, he was a fatherly figure, but he also understood the game and he focused on individuals, working on their weaknesses to improve them. The players would have given their lives for him.

Lloyd Keshwar remembers how they used to get to Curries Fountain:

> There was a ballie [older person] that lived here in Dromedaris Road - Mr Oliver - and that ballie had a big truck. He used to give people free rides to the grounds. But he had it covered. It

Joyce Petersen (middle).

was like a construction type of a truck. Everyone who was anyone would run and jump on that 'bus'. The ballie used to charge a small fee, but when the ballie wasn't looking you just dive in the back and you got a free ride. If he came to the robot, and he stopped, you just dive in while he's not looking. Mr Oliver was much cheaper than buses. That ballie used to take everyone to the soccer. Uncle Willy was his name. There were plenty of buses going to Curries Fountain. Some of us would go with cars. This was now in the eighties when Leeds was playing professional football. They used to also hire a bus for the fans. I think Joyce Petersen and her daughter Lorna were the chief organisers. They were big soccer fans. Lorna's mother, Joyce, used to pack the buses. Joyce was the key Leeds supporter. The whole Petersen family. For years. The only thing she didn't do was pick the team.

For many Leeds supporters, when Leeds played at Curries Fountain, Sunday mornings would start with church; the Holy Communion with

God. And just after lunch, the buses, vans and private cars would make their way to the stadium. As they filled the stadium tightly bunched, one gets a sense of the notion of communitas, which, as Edward Casey points out, 'is not just a matter of banding together but of *bonding together*' (1998: xiv; original emphasis).

Currie's Fountain was also the scene of some hair-raising moments, as Lloyd Keshwar remembers:

> I remember one day when Leeds was playing at Curries Fountain. We came down to the grounds. I told my *vrou* [wife] . . . My second daughter Tanya was just born then – my second youngest. My *vrou* was carrying her. Now, you know us, how we carry our drinks onto the grounds. You're not allowed to take it in, but we all sneak it in. I said to the wife, 'I'm gonna drop you outside. Wait there. Don't go inside. Let me go park the car.' Because she's got the kid. Now, the plan was, I was gonna let her carry the bag with the dop in it and I will carry the kid in because they won't search her. Those days they didn't search ladies. So, anyway, I go park the car.

Leeds in the final of the D'Alberton Callies tournament at a packed Curries Fountain, early 1970s.

With the baby's nappies and drinks at the bottom of the bag, Keshwar, much to his horror, saw that his wife had already passed through the turnstiles:

> So now I've got to walk through the security with the bag of alcohol. Of course, they search the bag. The cop – a white cop – says to me, 'What's inside this bag?' I say, 'It's just the baby's napkins and bottles and all that.' So he feels the bag. Then he says, 'So does your baby drink cold bottles?' If ever I needed a cold one it was then. Anyway, they opened the bag. They see the bottles of vodka and beers. They arrested me. Now I'm pissed off with her. I'm saying to her, 'It's through you, now.' They took me upstairs to the room to charge me. Now, they want to lock me up. Out of fear, I started telling lies. I gave them wrong names. Plus, I told them I was from Pietermaritzburg. I didn't have my ID on me. Now I'm hitting a plea deal. I'm saying, 'Give a man a break.' And they are like, 'You bloody Bushmen, y'll always . . .' So I'm insisting I'm from Maritzburg and I have to get home this evening with my wife and children. You can't lock me up. Lies! This is all happening in the charge office at Curries Fountain stadium.

Suddenly the office was filled with shouting and screaming. Enter

> a guy called Speedy. Speedy was a big Berea supporter. Speedy was an animal of note. He was Dasheen. He was king of the Dasheens. They arrested Speedy for dop or some offence or the other too.
>
> They bring him into the charge room. But now Speedy was a big, strong man. I was like, 'Yoh!' Two *wit* [white] cops got him there. By now the cops had all my drinks out on the table. The evidence is all there – lined up. Ay! The next thing, these cops started fluking. The one cop punched him. Then he never played with them. He rolled with them. He hit those five cops there. It was chaos in that charge office. He's a *maljan*. This is not he-said-she-said. I watched him attack those *wit ous*. The *wit ous* were struggling to contain him and restrain him. As all that was happening, I was like, 'Toss this!' I take all of my drinks, put it in

The iconic Curries Fountain (photo: Ranjith Kally).

> my bag, and kick it out of there. I even took some extra drinks for good measure that wasn't mine. I said, 'Done'. Then I was into the crowd. By the time they finish fighting with Speedy, they must have realised that I was gone. Obviously I took my jersey off. I'm sitting there in the crowd, watching the game, and the cops are walking up and down looking for me. I'm sitting with the *bras* [mates] here. I'm watching the game. I put on a cap and glasses. They were walking past me. But, I didn't go sit where my *vrou* is, because they would have made her out. So I didn't park where she was ... they couldn't find me ... after the game I sneaked out.

Many of the players and supporters remember the fact that Leeds's discerning quality came down to playing with passion, as if their lives depended on it. Losing was taken incredibly hard. In the words of Gary Goldstone:

> You know one day I was so angry, because we were beaten by some team and when I came home ... I was a very sore loser. I *hated* losing. I came home. I took all my miniatures out. With the amount of trophies we won. I smashed every single trophy. I

smashed them all. That's the person I was. No one would come near me to say, 'Gary... Don't...' because they would be in big, big trouble.

A fellow Leeds player remembers how sometimes things could get really out of hand:

> When Gary plays, he plays with the heart. He plays with passion. All those young players got hidings from Gary. Yoh! At the training... We know he's mad. We know when he don't take his tablets. In and out the mad house. Escaping from jail... We know Gary. Oh, Gary. On the field... Passion, commitment. On the field, second to none. His off-field antics. Whoa! He was going off his head... How many times we had to go fetch him from the *mal* [mad] house... We had to keep him because he was good on the field... You play shit... Whoaaa... Gary's onto you. And he will tell that player, 'You cost us the game!' In the change rooms, he's all, 'I wanna fucken dig my heart out!' Say we lose 3-2, and maybe he scored a goal or scored two goals... He goes off. He says, 'I want my fucken two goals back!' Where you gonna get your two goals back? We lost the game! You're fucked up in your head! But no one could tell him that because, well...

Another of those who played with Goldstone, somewhat earlier, and who ran with him in the Trucks gangs, reveals:

> Even when he's playing... If he doesn't get his way, he used to even hit the youngsters – at training. Gary was too hot. He was a no-nonsense guy. Very short-tempered. Gary was a perfectionist. When he passes to you, he will pass directly to you. He was that type of a player. And so they would always ask me to go talk to him to calm him down a bit. He was a very, very good player. Sometimes, though, he would sacrifice the team. That's the danger. Sometimes he would be playing and he would upset the team. Then you will end up playing with eight or seven players because the team is upset and not able to function on the field.

> Even at training they would go sit down because he would manhandle them. Even the coaches and the managers couldn't tell him not to smoke.

Goldstone was volatile by his own admission, always on the edge of losing it.

> I ended up in Townhill in 1978. I was playing for Berea. I had a fight one day – and it ended up in knives. They had me locked up. Then my father came. He immediately took me out of that cell. At Berea, I had some top games there, and yet it was my worst period as a football player. I was a K1 Truck [gang]. In Austerville, not many people talk. You don't just talk to cops. Today it's different. In those days, don't talk too long to cops. At that time I was volatile. I was in Townhill for some time. I had some good psychologists who even allowed me to go home. I was even allowed to smoke my zol [dagga]. But not to ever touch a drop of alcohol. Nobody could do anything. They took me to a hospital, Fort Napier, and let me drink a glass of alcohol, big, neat. And that was up my alley because I hadn't had a drink. After about an hour or so, they took me in a room and put all the machines on me and asked me questions. They found out that this is definitely not good for me – alcohol. I was like a raging wild animal. Six guys couldn't hold me down.[3]

Between the years 1976 and 1978, Gary was at the height of his ball-playing powers and at the lowest point in his life. But there was incredible support, as Ursula recounts:

> They [Berea] brought a busload to Townhill Hospital to visit him. It was so beautiful – all the people that came to visit him. Manna Govender, the manager, got the bus and they brought some of the supporters and all the management. Everybody came. Fortunately God has given me the ability to be a very strong

---

3. Townhill and Fort Napier are specialised psychiatric hospitals in Pietermaritzburg.

person and I was able to stand with him. He broke down. It was a build-up of a lot of anger and hurt. His mother's death. Being rejected by his family. And Gary didn't know how to deal with that because he had no mother now. He never used to talk. That was his main problem. The psychologist said to me, 'You have to come for counselling.' And when we had the meeting she told me, 'Don't think about leaving Gary because he already told us he will kill himself' – and kill me if I tried to leave him. I was like his crutch. I said to her that I had never thought about leaving him, otherwise I wouldn't have come this far for him to get better.

Ursula was not prepared to leave Gary:

We are from the old school. You stay married and you bring up your children with a mother and father. We are not from that school where you can just get divorced and hop with the next one. In any case, I wasn't a hopper. And in this I had everything – a drinker, gambler, fighter, lover man. He still played soccer. It never interfered with his soccer. Once later, he went for another two weeks. The thing is we never once threw that in Gary's face. We never said once, 'You are in the madhouse' – like people normally do. We never, ever went down that avenue. He went for help there. And it was beneficial to him. He actually came to me and said, 'Put me back there.'

But Gary Goldstone was a man of superlative talent. For Keshwar,

Gary was still the greatest soccer player for me – not from a goal-scoring point of view, but as a man that controlled the game; a creative guy who made things happen on the field. He could make openings and he could create openings for you to win the game. He was an *intelligent* player. I've got my detractors. When I say, 'Gary Goldstone', a lot of people say, 'What about Colin Paul?' – this one and that one. And, yes, they were all good players in their own right. That's not taking anything away from them . . . Gary's craziness is part of what made him a great player.

As a teammate at Berea remembers: 'The only thing Gary Goldstone's left foot couldn't do was talk.'

Petersen and Goldstone were some of the last footballers to play for the Coloureds against Indians and Africans. It was here that Goldstone proved his versatility. He played as goalkeeper!

> I was such an accomplished goalkeeper that I represented South African Coloureds in goal in the first multinational tournament in this country in 1969 – just after my mother died. Both our goalkeepers got hurt at the build-up. We were selected for Southern Natal – and in those days there were just four provinces. When we got to Joburg there was a big problem between the *bruin ous* (Coloureds). The Indian *ous* had their side mixed from all the provinces. We played a little round-robin thing and some of their guys didn't get picked. And then they protested. So both goalkeepers were buggered up from Durban – Eddie McKnight and Philly Brooks – and we needed a goalkeeper from Joburg and he refused to play. A lot of the big guys said, 'Gary, go in the goals.' So I played in the goals – and I played well.

The 1970s saw a movement led by the South African Council on Sport (SACOS).

> As the sports wing of the internal liberation movement in the 1970s and 1980s, SACOS contributed to the understanding of apartheid's effect on sport. SACOS showed that every aspect of apartheid adversely touched sport. For most people, this was a revelation given sport's status as a sacrosanct social practice and it helped clarify the objectives of the sports boycott. While African states had viewed the sports boycott as a struggle against apartheid since the mid-1960s, the principal objective of the international sports community was to integrate South African sport. SACOS's input was critical to turning the boycott into a strategy against apartheid *per se* (Booth 1988: 110).

On home turf, SACOS confronted apartheid's racial divisions in sport by insisting on the principle of non-racialism. In this vein, the South African Soccer Federation sought to drop references to apartheid racial categories and build a non-racial culture. It is debatable how much of this ideological offensive filtered down to the players, but, for Gary Goldstone, it was part of his political education:

> I played in the South African Soccer Federation. It took me a couple of years to realise why I was playing there. Because in that time I had an offer – when I went to Berea, I had an offer to go to Durban City. Then I was called on by the late Mr Norman Middleton and the late Mr Archie Hulley and Samba Ramsamy.[4]
>
> And they said to me, 'Gary, this is the reason why you are playing in the Federation. You are playing here and you are helping fight apartheid through sport.' So I wanted to know why and how come? Here I could earn nice money and get a job selling cars. You know the *wit ous* all sold cars, no *bruin ous*. So they said to me, 'Look. You're gonna play for Durban City. But, your parents wanna come and watch you, they have a segregated area in the hot sun. That's where they gonna sit. They won't be able to come into the change rooms and wish you and greet you or whatever. You go in the change rooms. You're gonna shower with these guys, everything. The moment you leave the grounds, you won't be able to sit in the same restaurant as them. But, you can play football with them.' So how can you play normal sport in an abnormal society? From that day, I took more of a radical stand when I played. I'm very pro-black. When I say black, I mean, Coloured, Indian, everything . . . all blacks.

Goldstone and Petersen did cross over the racial boundaries and played in the African townships:

---

4. Norman Middleton was a trade unionist and activist for non-racial sport, later becoming president of SACOS and a member of parliament at the age of 78. He died in 2015. Archie Hulley lived in Wentworth and was a pioneering member of SACOS. Ramsamy was appointed to Aces United in 1970. He subsequently went into exile and became one of the leading figures in calling for a sports boycott of apartheid South Africa (Ramsamy 2004).

Federation league stalwarts Norman Middleton (facing the camera) and Charles Pillay (with dark jacket to the rear).

When I played in the township in those days, you had to get a permit. We just gave ourselves or were given African names and managed to get around the legal rubbish. But we played mainly betting soccer where these lahnees [wealthy people] would come and pick me and Dennis up. By half-time we had scored five goals just between us . . . we come off, get in the car and they take us home.

Goldstone also got to play against Durban City soon after rebuffing them. Forty years later, he remembers the story as if it was yesterday:

At the end of 1976, one of the highlights of our five-a-side tournaments and our seven-a-side tournaments was meeting Durban City. Durban City were the so-called white league team. In their seven-a-side, they had players who played for the Springboks, the national team. We had met them in the final of one of the biggest seven-a-side tournaments in Natal – on Brickfield Road. And, we won that game: 3-1. But we taught them a football lesson. These same so-called Springboks . . . Lawrence Chelin, Chicken Price, Neil Roberts, Dennis Wicks, Alan Watts, Dougie Coetzee . . . Springboks . . . We gave them a hiding. And to prove a point, a few weeks later we met them in Chatsworth at a five-a-side and we beat them again: 2-1. This is playing as Leeds. And some of them today, when we meet at functions, they never forget it. They still say, 'Gary! We thought we knew this game until we played against you guys.'

From the vantage point of 2019, these moments might not seem like much. But at the height of apartheid, when white privilege and a sense of superiority was at its zenith, these singular moments when five played five, when the ball did the talking, to prevail was a form of vindication like no other. It was these fleeting moments in which white footballers 'are stripped of their traditional head starts and privileges, and in which they have to face the challenge of others with only the resources of their own bodies to secure ascendancy' (Mills 2005: 1).

Goldstone. To write a life is to have a sense of a timeline that is linear. But when you listen to Keshwar and a myriad others describe Gary on the field, you realise there were no straight lines. He was all body, spontaneous and fluid, dominating the midfield, always on the edge of fury. But why then is he talked about with such tenderness? In all this, you see, there was a vulnerability, hovering on the precipice of self-destruction, a sadness even.

Goldstone embodied the spirit of the times. Wentworth. The 1970s. Soccer players trained in grounds next to petrochemical firms that spewed black smoke into the air 24 hours, 365 days of the year. Schoolchildren packed asthma pumps alongside their lunch boxes. Cancer rates rose. Coffins of the young were lowered. Men left home to seek work in the Highveld. No matter how long you worked at the local chemical plants, you were always temporary, always on contract. The horizons for a top soccer player were limited to a pittance as a part-time professional. Gangs and drugs, like Jehovah's Witnesses, always came knocking. To keep going at the top of your game, to pull others along with you, to remain competitive, to be a leader as Goldstone was, permanently poised, with a mad love of the round ball and a desire to win, meant a heavy dose of craziness, irrationality even. When you talk to those who shared a

Gary Goldstone (left) in action at Curries Fountain.

change room, who watched him play, it is these qualities that make Gary Goldstone so revered. Then. And now. But there is also something else. A shock, a suspicion even that Goldstone survived. When many fell. Like his dominance of the midfield, he pulled it back together and made a life.

Goldstone recalls the moment in which the short fuse that was his life took a Damascus turn:

> Half past six in the morning in Natraj Centre outside the fruit and veg shop. Kevin Cross, a little runt owed me money. And there he was. I asked him if he had my money. He was like, 'Hey, Brown . . . [my nickname].' Well, I smashed him. I wounded him. He tried to fight back. People phoned the police. The police came. I said 'Charge me'. I told him, 'If I don't get my money, wherever I see you, I'm gonna hit you.' It was the nineties. I was still doing my business. I was going there because my cigarettes were all there. My bread and everything. The next day, same thing. I go pick whatever they leave for me there at the Rivera

> shop. I told them to get my order ready and went to go buy some fruit and some samoosas, vedas . . . As I'm walking past the fruit and veg shop – that lady is a Christian lady – there was this song playing: 'I Sing Praises To Him/To Your Name, The Lord'. It's still my favourite gospel chorus. Something happened. I stopped. Then I went in the shop. Yesterday I was fighting, today I'm coming in. I said to her, 'I want to ask you something.' And I was pointing and going towards the radio. Well, she was scared. I said I wanted to know what station that was. She said it was Radio Highway – 101.5. And then I started reading the Bible. I couldn't understand anything there.

For Goldstone there was no turning back as he attended Bible College daily for six months, to learn.

> It was a good experience. It opened my brain. Every Christian person, after matric, should go to Bible College during their gap year. Then they must go to university – once they know and understand God. Life is complicated, but I know the answer is there.

I listen without trying to butt in with another question or seek some clarity. Goldstone is not a man to stop when he is in full flow.

Later, as an aside, I ask Dennis Petersen what makes Gary Goldstone a figure that endures through the generations. Dennis is a simple man of simple tastes and a life spent within three, maybe four square kilometres. But his reply intrigued me; 'Gary lived against lies that we were nothing, because despite everything that was thrown at us, he felt we always had to prevail on and off the field; he was unstoppable but vulnerable. He still is.'

I was reminded of the words of Jacques Derrida who wrote of the person who lived as 'the friend of truth – but a mad truth, the mad friend of truth' (2005: 45).

And it was a round ball that held the line between Goldstone's genius and madness; between falling into an abyss or shallow grave and today tending his garden with the air of a man who refused to die, born-again.

4

A Generation of Talent

> This journey has been hard. It has been up and down. It has been hard. Then it became even harder when the personal pain piled up – until I had to make it easy for myself, find Him and me.
> — Patrick Wiseman

Patrick 'Boa' Wiseman lives in a small house in Wentworth. I arrive there on a Friday in June 2018. Sixty-three years old, he has penetrating grey eyes and an easy smile. Born in Mayville, the family was forced out after the land was claimed for the construction of a freeway. The year was 1971 and the Wiseman family of seven siblings and mother Audrey (his father had died in 1970) moved to Wentworth.

> We were supposed to come here in 1969. Then in 70, they said now y'll have to move. We were one of the first persons here in the flats. There was hardly anyone. It was empty. There were a few families only. The flats were all done. They were ready for occupation.

Wiseman had already acquired a reputation as a soccer player in Mayville. At the age of sixteen, some guys spotted him juggling a tennis ball with his feet. They were members of a team called Lags X1 and he joined them.

> We used to always stand by the rank where buses came to turn and go back to town. That's where they spotted me juggling the ball and fooling around. So they invited me to come and play at Tills Crescent. At that time I used to play in the schools. I was a goalkeeper in the Sydenham schools.

At Lags he used his speed and trickery upfront. His stay was short. Wiseman was recruited to play for a well-known team in the Mayville area, Rangers. It was to be the story of his career; making a name for himself and then quickly moving on to the next club.

Life in Wentworth did not have the same networks and old friendships that Wiseman had got used to in Mayville – a place in which there were friendships handed through the generations and networks stretched across into nearby Sydenham:

> In Wentworth there was nothing much to do. The only thing I used to do was to play ball. I joined a team called Carlton Athletic. I was a striker. We played in a Wentworth league. That was 1973/74. We played against Chelsea, Leeds, Aralian Lads. [The top teams at that time were Leeds and Preston North End, later renamed Motherwell.] We used to train in Highbury and Ogle Road grounds.

Soccer took Wiseman across the province in the manager Lenny Linderboom's kombi:

> Now and then there were parties we got invited to – but mostly tournaments. We used to go for seven-a-sides and five-a-sides – all over; Tongaat, Verulam, Ixopo. We travelled by kombi. Linderboom was a welder and worked in Maydon Wharf. He did a lot for us. Anything we asked him for. He knew about the game – the organising and administering. Above all, he cared for us, transporting the team and always on the lookout to ensure we had a job.

Wiseman secured a job in Swaziland in 1979. Part of the rationale for the move was that he had met a woman, Sharon Sharpley, and they were to be married later in the year. Wiseman was desperate to earn a bit of cash for the wedding and to set up a home. He worked there for a year and a half, often coming to Wentworth over weekends. It was the life of many Wentonians who took their skills across the country, working especially at Sasol in the former Transvaal:

We had three children. One passed away. My son Warren got stabbed in 2008. He was 27. Marice and Chanel. One works for Sage in Umhlanga Rocks. The other is a nurse at King Edward Hospital. I'm living with my daughter, the nurse, now. My wife, who suffered from schizophrenia, died in 2009.

Soccer, his passion from the time he juggled a soccer ball at the bus rank, continued to be part of his life. Into his twenties, Wiseman's reputation grew and people came knocking on his door. The soccer-mad Martins family ran the Young Ones Football Club and Wiseman was enticed to leave Carlton for them:

> I changed because there was an internal squabble. The players weren't happy with Carlton. Someone stole something from another player. That's how we ended up splitting. At Young Ones, there was one game where I scored four goals when we played the highly rated Villa Park from Sydenham at the Boardmill grounds in Greenwood Park. That ground was so small, but it was very wide. That's how I like it for it gave me space to hang on the wing and cut inside.

It was during this time that he earned the name 'Boa'; 'like the snake, I was always hungry for goals and slippery'. In 1976, Wiseman's big chance came to join Leeds United, now a powerful team in the province and the pre-eminent team in Wentworth. Leeds was desperate for an out-and-out striker:

> I was feeling like I was on top now – playing higher division. That's where I wanted to be. The manager was John 'Cocoon' Williams. Blondie Campbell was the coach. That first season at Leeds was exciting. We came to a lot of semi-finals. Durban Heights was there. Spearman Lads. Young Aces. It was good times that time – under Southern Natal. That's the year I got selected for Southern Natal. We went to Cape Town. We stayed in a Holiday Inn in Bellville. We lost in the finals. Western Province was too strong.

For the first time, Wiseman saw himself as something more than just the club:

> We gave Leeds everything because of the township we came from. We had to give it all. We tried to bring some kind of professional soccer into Wentworth. And we did. We met Witbank Black Aces, a professional side. We played in Wentworth. It was the Mainstay Cup in 1985. We lost because of a penalty shootout. Sometimes you take it like a sportsman. But it lingered a whole week. That was the first time Leeds went on TV.

While Wiseman had good times at Leeds, men with big promises came knocking and Wiseman was willing:

> ... another team wanted me. So I went to Durban Suburbs. Godfrey 'Zulu' Fynn's team. I was the only Wentworth guy. That was a good year for me. I think I was like the best player there. Everyone was just always around me. I never had problems. Nothing.

Like many a family in Wentworth, soccer skill ran through the bloodlines. Patrick's younger brother, Gregory, was also making a name for himself at local side Everton. As Gregory's reputation grew, he was recruited to play for Cherrians. But then tragedy struck. 'He died in 2008. Just after my son. A heart attack killed him.' Patrick meanwhile was on the move:

> I spent one year at Suburbs. Then I ended up at Berea. As we came back from Cape Town for Southern Natal, Don Moodley, the manager of Berea, and his henchmen were waiting for me at the airport – so I had to go with them. Later on I realised I made a mistake because Suburbs was very disciplined. Legends like Pat Blair and Dudu Moonsamy were playing for Berea. When I first came there I was sitting on the bench. As soon as the winger James George got hurt, I took his place. That's when I started playing on the wing. Our main rivals were Cape Town Spurs, Glenville, Blue Bells, Swaraj, but mostly Cape Town Spurs. We

beat them in Cape Town. We played them in a cup game and beat them 1-0. That game was very important. The formation we played against them was key . . . because we knew they had such good ball players, we were on them the minute they got the ball. I think they call it the high press these days. Well, we did it in those days.

While Wiseman might have lit up the pitch and was playing for the glamour side Berea, the wages were meagre as the Federation had little sponsorship and clubs were run through largesse and a few individuals. Wiseman kept picking up jobs as a carpenter to supplement his income. As times got hard, a major club from the National Professional Soccer League (NPSL) came knocking. The NPSL was formed in the early 1960s. It received a fillip after South African Soccer Federation (SASF) teams were hounded out of municipal grounds because of their refusal to bow down to demands by the apartheid government that they do not play teams consisting of all races. In 1985, the NPSL was torn apart with the formation of the National Soccer League (NSL), but in the early 1980s they attracted huge crowds and lucrative sponsorships (Nauright 1997: 119). The team wanting to sign Wiseman was the mighty AmaZulu.

It was a big change. The big league. We were playing against Kaizer Chiefs. All the top teams. The crowd loved me. My nickname was Aeroplane – because on the wings I used to fly. That was the early 1980s.

At AmaZulu the money was better. The soccer was stronger. We were playing against big teams. Plus big crowds. And the support was passionate and intense. In the Federation the ball was too weak as many top players simply gave the game up as it did not pay anything and they had to travel long hours for games. The second time I went, I took Vish Govender and Paul Bishop with me. Paul was a general – centre-half. They liked him. Vish, too, when he started, they liked him.

Playing in a predominantly African side meant there were cultural challenges, but Wiseman was a 'happy-go-lucky guy', as he put it:

> They used *muti* there. But I never believed it. Me and Paul Bishop and Vish never worried so much. We just put it on, but not believing in it. We just carried on. For us, we knew our game. Maybe for them it must have worked. It's a mind thing. It's only a mind thing and not something that causes miracles. Some of it smells when it's enclosed. If we were changing in a room and they burn all those things. We just washed our toes in it and then put our socks on. Otherwise, sometimes when we were coming out in our kits, then they would throw us with the smelling stuff so that the opposition won't mark you close. That's how they do it.

At the height of their game, Wiseman and Trevor 'Cheesa' Baptist were offered a trial at Chelsea in 1981:

> We couldn't go. We were banned by FIFA. I enjoyed it there in the big leagues. Then I went to Bushbucks in 1982. The legendary player at Bushbucks [Mlungisa] 'Professor' Ngubane recruited me. He saw me in the tournaments. They were training at SJ Smith Stadium. He invited me there. I used to just run to training from Wentworth. I was in the midfield there. Henry 'Black Cat' Cele was our coach. I stayed until Lawrence Ngubane came there. Then he started buying players from Joburg. In 1984 I left. I was there from '82 to '84. At that time I was working for a company called Stevenson as a carpenter. Then I left them and went to Umhlanga Rocks to work for Edmund Builders. I worked for them while playing professional.

Wiseman was on the move again:

> In 1985 I went back to Leeds. Errol Hughes had now bought the club and he brought it into the second division of the NPSL in '85. We had some players from Kansas City Hotspurs. Given Khumalo. Timothy Zoy. Brian 'Pondo' Robinson. Neil Blankenberg. We went to the play-offs in Mthatha. We won the league. We played against legends like Fani Madida. Shakes Mashaba. They were playing for Blackpool. Blackpool came second. Paul Bishop was coaching us. In '87 we went into the first division. The first game we played was the Olsson's Cup.

A Generation of Talent

Leeds making headlines in the early 1980s.

Against Chiefs at Ellis Park. We lost 1-0. A stupid loss. After the leagues, we played in the pros – until Errol Hughes wanted to sell the team. So I went to Black Aces, which was based in Witbank.

When I got there, I played one/two friendly games. Now Leeds didn't want to give me a clearance. They said I must wait. I stayed only for two months. I came back to Wentworth. I tried to get back to Leeds. Nothing happened. So I started just training myself. I never played professional again. I played amateur ball. I started coaching.

Wiseman teamed up with his old mate Gary Goldstone:

Me and Gary started a team – Cerro. Gary liked that name from Portugal. We were mates from Berea. We went two years with Cerro. We went into the final of the Clover Cup. We lost. Dennis Petersen was playing for us. All these old professionals were playing for us – the *ous* that couldn't play professionally. So they came here. We opened the side. That's how we started. We had Obed Petersen also playing there. Then the team went down. Then I joined a team from my neighbourhood Pascal as a coach. We went for about two years there – until the league was robbing us – and then I left them. We opened a lot of other clubs. I coached Motherwell. I coached Young Cavies. I coached Wiestham. I even coached Berea Football Club during [Nelson] Mandela's time.

As Wiseman remembers, he never stopped scoring goals:

At Young Ones I used to score two or three goals. In every game I was scoring. Even in the over-35s. When Patrick 'Putts' Moodley opened the over-35 side, called The People of the South, I was the highest goal scorer there.

Wiseman lives opposite the local school and hopes to take up a position there as a coach:

I got my C-licence in coaching and training and developing. Now they are repairing the school. Durban East School. SAFA [South African Football Association] said that in 2019 it must be compulsory that all the schools have sports. Outside, everyone wants to be a coach. In the schools you can teach properly.

Wiseman (extreme left) and Goldstone (extreme right) with a new crop of players.

Wiseman still lives in the house he moved to in 1980. He is still working:

> I work as a carpenter. I get work here in Wentworth, on the Bluff, Sydenham. I could have made it higher [with soccer] than where I ended up. But this racial thing doesn't work out. It only spoils ... Especially in development now, you'll always find it. Coloureds are sidelined.
>
> Now I am helping these youngsters with no experience – Pascal United. We revived the team. These kids were born in the nineties – when I finished my second time in the pro. With Leeds from '78 to '84. Then I came back to amateur and back to pro with Leeds again. When I talk to this team that I am coaching, I tell them that where I come from, you all are not even halfway there. You all complain about a lot of things where we never complained and never used to even get paid. We used to get a salary of R500 a month. No bonus. Nothing. Just get for training. Until we got a sponsor. Then we got R500 a month, R80 for a win, R40 for a draw. Nothing for a loss. That was our income in the seventies. I was a carpenter back then. I used to go

to work during the day and training in the afternoon. And not complain. I loved the sport.

His decision to leave Berea and play for AmaZulu still comes back to haunt him as he was seen as a defector from the ranks of the Federation Professional League (FPL) to the NPSL. The Federation has a Legends get-together for the stars of yesteryear. It fosters camaraderie for those who were incredibly talented but whose careers were always played out in the shadow of apartheid and the struggle to ensure that the regime was isolated on the world's playing fields. Many of the political divisions of the past continue to haunt the present:

> The Feds Legend is against me because of the defection. From those days. Don [Moodley] and them. I went to go play against Joburg Legends in Curries Fountain. I missed a penalty. It was a social thing. So they pulled me off. Other *ous* were playing worse than me and they still stuck around.

And despite the fall of institutionalised racism, there is always in everyday life the feeling of racial prejudice. Wiseman feels that in the Legend's camp Coloured players are marginalised:

> Gary Goldstone would see that he is the only Coloured there. It was no longer a multiracial thing. When we had a meeting in Curries Fountain, Ashwin Trikamjee came and said that this thing must be multiracial. But you must see the jersey they gave us – 'South African Non-Racial Soccer Academy'. Why did they put that? Now you can see. It should have just said 'South African Soccer Academy'. Finished.

For Wiseman, 'non-racial' still implies the Federation. The irony is that Wiseman left the Federation, which was almost exclusively Indian and Coloured to play in the NPSL, which was almost exclusively African. In many ways, as he himself attests, he was breaking racial barriers but somehow he is seen as transgressing the FPL commitment to non-racialism. The Federation's real resonance, of course, came in adopting the adage 'no normal sport in an abnormal society' as a way to support the global sports movement in boycotting apartheid South Africa, its own inability to break into African areas notwithstanding. There were persistent tensions between the FPL and the South African Council on Sport (SACOS), with the latter often insensitive to the FPL's need for sponsorship and making other compromises to keep certain clubs afloat. SACOS accused the FPL of flouting its double-standards rule, which began as a way to instil 'internal discipline' but quickly 'became a tactic of political purification' that eschewed 'alternative strategies' (Booth 1998: 151–2; for fascinating details on this policy see Venter 2018).

As I probe Wiseman on his family, his voice lowers as he remembers bad times. Like many in Wentworth, it is of a life cut short and in Wiseman's case it is the stabbing to death of his son:

> My son was good with his fingers and hands. He was like an electrician. He could fix stoves, TVs, irons, DVDs, kettles, things like that. So he was fixing up this DVD and the one lady in Quality Street told him he could have it. That was a Saturday afternoon. He went there with his friend. They were thinking of going to sell it. So there in Quality Street by the garage, he came across three African guys. They asked him if he wanted to sell it. I don't know what was going on there. This guy said he wanted to buy it. He said, 'Come to the garage there is an ATM there. We'll get the money there and we'll give [it to] you.' I don't know how much. When they took the money out and they gave [it to] him, maybe there was some argument over the payment or something like that. While they were arguing, the security guy there in the garage chased them and told them to go across the road – that side. 'Go argue there. Don't argue here. You're causing it.'

Wiseman remembers:

> The call came here Sunday morning at about two o'clock. Knocking at the window. I opened the door. They said, 'Hey, your *laaitie*'s there.' I said, 'How y'll know? What is he doing there?' They said he was coming from the jol [party] and they came past and saw the silver paper. Then they wanted to go see who it was. When he opened, he checked the face – and said he

knows this face, but he didn't know where he stays, so he went to Pascal Road. And there in Pascal they told him that I am the father and I stay here. So they came here. In the morning, I jumped in the car and went there with my daughter. We went to go view the body. I saw it was him. My daughter couldn't take it. My wife, too, couldn't take it. I think that's what killed my wife. My son passed away in November 2008. In January 2009, she passed away. My brother passed away also in this period. It came all one time. It was just good that I was with the Lord. He gave me the strength to take all this. Imagine if I was in the world. I was gonna be dopping [drinking] and causing a lot of things.

I ask Wiseman for photographs. He says most of them were torn up by his wife. There is one stuck away; Wiseman on the shoulders of AmaZulu supporters. It is 1980. He had scored a hat-trick against Durban City in a friendly. There are a couple of others scattered around. Before giving me a few photographs to scan, Wiseman takes a good hard look at them.

Wiseman carried aloft after his hat-trick.

He walks us to the gate. I can see the boy in him juggling a tennis ball on the fringes of the bus rank, the boy who became an Aeroplane that kept taking off as he landed.

'Show Me Your Number' and the 'Wentworth Takeaway'

> Never . . . do words have more meaning than when they describe the nexus between the game and society in all its horror, in all its glory.
>
> — Young, 'The Lexicon of Love'

Leeds legend Patrick 'Putts' Moodley was born in 1959, six years after Goldstone. But he still got to play alongside the two stars, Goldstone and Petersen. Coming from a family of thirteen children, Moodley was the only boy:

> My mother was Coloured – Emily – maiden surname, Hendricks. My father was Indian, but he was more of a Coloured. Steven 'Crimes' Moodley. He was wild. My mother was from Kimberley

Patrick's father, Steven 'Crimes' Moodley.

Patrick Moodley (left) playing for Leeds against Vereeniging Old Boys.

and fluent in five languages. She spoke Portuguese, English, Afrikaans, Zulu and she learnt Hindi from my father's people . . . My ballie [father] was a skelm [crook] . . . He was involved in everything. Drugs. Guns. Murder. I had a gangster for a father. He was in and out of jail . . . He was convicted of three murders . . . He was always with Coloured people . . . My mother worked in the textile factories in Mayville. She was a machinist . . . My mother died of a heart attack in January 1978. My dad died in June of 1979.

In 1979, at the age of twenty, Moodley got married to

Helen Booysen from Reiger Road – a la-di-dah family. She was a nurse – a top sister, becoming a matron – at Entabeni Hospital. Including outside my marriage, I've got five children altogether . . . my wife died in November 2010 at the age of 49. During the World Cup, four foreigners fell ill and came in with swine flu. Within seven weeks my wife was gone. It was total devastation.

In the years 1979-81, Moodley became a fixture in the Leeds team. In 1979, Leeds won promotion to the FPL. The following year, Gary Goldstone and once prolific centre-forward Elvis Singh returned from Berea to Leeds. They acquired a new goalkeeper, Buddy Govender, as well as Barry Duschene and Greg Gillot. Moodley was at the peak of his game, and like Goldstone and Petersen, rates beating the all-conquering Cape Town Spurs on their home ground as an indication that Leeds could take on all comers and beat them.

In 1978, while studying at Bechet Teacher Training College, Moodley was approached by NPSL side AmaZulu with a lucrative offer: R30 000 signing-on fee and R6 000 a game. Moodley spent eight years at the club. For Moodley, the experience was a revelation: 'Although playing in front of 15 000 fans at Curries was a fantastic feeling, performing in front of around 80 000 fans when we played Kaizer Chiefs was electric . . .' (*The Post*, 16 May 2007). It was also a time when games were televised and besides 'Siga-bopha' (Cutting through the defence; catching them), he also earned the nickname

> 'Show Me Your Number'. What it means is that after you score a goal or make a hot move on the field, you must turn around for the TV cameras so viewers can see your jersey number and they show it on the TV screens. Blacks are fanatical about soccer. You pick up names for anything. 'Siga-bopha' and 'Show Me Your Number' used to tie me in knots.

Moodley moved on to African Wanderers for three years and then to Bushbucks as player/coach. Moodley divides opinion in Wentworth. Some see him as a big mouth, 'always after the crown (money)', as an old teammate puts it. Others see him as a superbly talented footballer, who could mix it on the streets and was always keen to take soccer in Wentworth to the national stage. Some of this is generational of course; older guys contemptuous of smart alecs like Putts. Still, Putts Moodley is a ubiquitous figure in Wentworth – a persistent reminder of how gifted he and many of his generation were and the major role they played in giving Wentworth the reputation of producing players that could grace soccer fields at the highest level across the country. We will return to Putts's journey later for it is an opportune moment to introduce a player and person who is universally respected.

Gregory Baptist. A prolific striker, in 1980 he made his debut for Leeds. Until then, he had been shadowing Elvis Singh, whose ability to put the ball in the back of the net tormented opponents and thrilled fans. As I am talking to Baptist, Elvis comes to visit. They are still mates some 30 years later. Like many of his generation, for Baptist, Gary Goldstone was the inspiration: 'Gary was my mentor. His leadership and motivation was amazing and he never failed to perk up the boys before every match' (*The Post*, 16 May 2007).

Greg Baptist (top row, third from left) at Wiestham United.

Unlike Moodley and his brother Cheesa, Gregory did not make the move to the NPSL. He joined Berea, making a lethal pairing with Boy Barends and Keith America. His loyalty was rewarded when he was chosen in 1984 for the SACOS XI.

> They held a tournament for all codes of sport in Cape Town. It was a front for a political rally ... That was when I realised how

Gregory Baptist all tied up.

strong non-racial sport was and was glad not to have made the move when Leeds joined the NPSL (*The Post*, 16 May 2007).

Gregory moved between clubs inside the Federation, seeking an outlet for his prodigious boot and to make a bit of cash. One of the highlights of Gregory's career was playing for Tongaat Crusaders, popularly known as the Cossacks:

> Playing for Crusaders will always be special for me. They had supporters who were prepared to go to war for us. Some of the supporters would even pay me R100 for every goal I scored.

After a spectacular goal against Manning Rangers, one of the supporters, in handing over R100, referred to his goal as a 'Wentworth Takeaway'.

One of the most proficient players that Wentworth produced was Gregory's brother, Cheesa Baptist. Possessing a brilliant left foot, Cheesa tormented defenders down the wing. At the age of 22, he joined African Wanderers in the NPSL. Two years later, complaining of back pains, he was admitted to hospital.

Top row (left to right): Barry Duschene (captain), Margo McKenzie, Gregory Gillot, Buddy Govender, Elvis Singh, Phillip Peters, Charlie leCour, Graham Birch. Bottom row (left to right): Patrick Moodley, Gerald Robinson, Denzil Bull, Trevor 'Cheesa' Baptist, Raymond Mentor, Tyrone Bezuidenhout.

Cancer. He was dead at 24.

For people like Lloyd Keshwar, remembering Cheesa is to bring back memories of Leeds United's most unforgettable games:

> The most memorable game was the game when we were playing Manning Rangers – in the semi-final. We were losing 2-1. And the clock was gone. I remember I was walking out. Many of the Wentworth people had already left by that time. They had resigned themselves to defeat. I was one of them. I was walking out the stadium. I hadn't left the grounds. I was walking toward the exit. As I got towards the exit, I stood, looked back, and watched. We were in the last seconds of the game and I'm already heartbroken. And Cheesa Baptist – and anyone who was at the grounds that day will tell you – if I could take it and make a movie out of it for you, I will. I can see it. Cheesa comes down the right wing with the ball and this *wit ou* comes and attacks him. His name was Eddie Mulheron – and he does a jink over him. Cheesa had this way about him. I used to play soccer with Cheesa, even at school when we were young boys. Cheesa; we used to call him

Cheesa 'Loop en Val' (Run and Fall) (right).

'Loop en Val'. He had this manner of running in such a way that was very deceptive that looked like he was going slow *and* like he was falling, yet he was moving at pace. Deceptive. And you battle to figure him on the soccer field. When I played against him as a *laaitie* he would leave us for dead. That's the skill he had.

Keshwar continues:

Anyway, on this day, he jinked in on the box, came in from the left wing and he was cutting in – just lifting the ball over them. When he got towards the outer edge of the eighteen-yard line, he let rip with a curler that flew into the roof of the Manning Rangers net. Never in my life, so long as I live, will I ever forget that. I can't. Anyone who was in stadium that day – the Elvis's, Putts Moodley, Gary Goldstone, Dennis Petersen, you name them, anyone from Wentworth – ask them to describe Cheesa's goal against Manning Rangers in the semi-final in 1981. It was round about October. Then he scored. That was the last kick of the game. He saved us from defeat. People were running back into that stadium like crazy. Even me. I was like, 'Fuck!' We scored an equaliser. The score was 2-2. We were down 2-1. He made it 2-2. Then extra time. We finished them in extra time 5-2. Left, right and centre. Leeds finished Manning Rangers. Manning Rangers was *the* professional soccer team at the time. Leeds was a new professional team. Leeds came from amateur. Now they're playing against these big guns like Berea and Rangers. They were the giants. So, for us to come there and slay the giants was phenomenal. It was unheard of. In my mind, I was only, 'Oh, God, they beat us again.' But, I promise you, when he scored that goal. A phenomenon.

Abdul Adams holds that while

> Gary Goldstone was superb, the centre-half Barry Duschene was brilliant, but the player who really stood head and shoulders above everyone was Cheesa Baptist. I think that he could have held his own on the world stage, a wonderfully balanced player,

Barry Duschene (right of goalkeeper).

a joy to watch, for those who did not see him, think Ryan Giggs, that's how good he was. His death was a big, big loss; he died very young. It was not just a loss to football but to the community as a whole because many youngsters looked up to him as a role model. He was passionate about his football, but jovial off the field, fooling around, really the life of the party.

Keshwar recalls Cheesa's funeral:

> When he died, Wentworth came to a standstill. We went to visit him in the hospital on a few occasions. It was very sad to see how he just withered away. When he died, I'm not kidding you . . . he got buried at Christ the King Church – man, that church was filled to capacity. You couldn't get near that church. The cars. The people that came. The white people. Black people. All of the soccer fraternity. He almost had like a state funeral. It was massive, massive. Father Carey was the celebrant for that service. Wentworth was locked down. You could have gone and raided Wentworth that day. If you were a rogue, you could have broken into any house.

Gregory still feels the pain. For many a year, Cheesa was everywhere. In the jersey he pulled on. In the ground he trained on. In the friends he socialised with. The street he lived on. Wentworth changed. Forever. Listening to Gregory in his home and seeing the images of Jesus Christ on the wall, one is reminded of the words of St Augustine who reflected on how his native city, Thagaste, was changed for him with the death of his childhood friend:

> My heart was now darkened by grief, and everywhere I looked I saw death. My native haunts became a scene of torture to me, and my own home a misery. Without him everything we had done together turned into excruciating ordeal. My eyes kept looking for him without finding him. I hated all the places where we used to meet, because they could no longer say to me, 'Look, here he comes,' as they once did (quoted in Tuan 2001: 140).

Despite the pain, Gregory keeps memories of the great football times he had with his brother. There is a gloomy photograph of his mother and him joined in grief over Cheesa's death that mingles with Gregory dressed in tie and jacket and kit bag and a gem of history – Gregory in one of his first soccer teams. With some trepidation he allows me to nip round the corner and scan this history.

Lloyd Keshwar: The stadium dreamer

> Stadiums are sites of unforgettable human dramas and mundane realities.
>
> — Gaffney, *Temples of the Earthbound Gods*

As you will come to realise in reading the story to follow, to this epigraph must be added that, in imagining a stadium, in building it, in naming it, a great deal is reflected about a people's social location and desire to make a life under the racial gaze of apartheid.

Tell people in Wentworth that you are researching Leeds and they will invariably tell you that you need to speak to Lloyd Keshwar. Approaching 60, Keshwar has lived in Wentworth all his life. His appetite for soccer still runs deep:

> I was five years old. And my brother took me to a game – my elder brother. He was about eleven or twelve years old. And he took me to a game of soccer. It was at a place called Hoy Park or Old Kingsmead. I know for a fact that this is something that captured my imagination. When I was in the stadium, and this noise, and the cheering, and the screaming . . . And when a goal is scored, the ecstasy. I was a little boy and I was captivated by this highly charged atmosphere. I remember that day like it was yesterday. And from that day, I loved soccer. I lived for it. It just became a part of my life. I blame my brother for it. Because if he never took me to that game, I wouldn't have been captivated. It captured me – and it built a burning passion inside me. That passion still burns inside as I sit here today.

By the time Keshwar was ready to train for a working life, Coloureds had come to monopolise the categories of boilermaker, welder, fitter and turner in Durban. Keshwar followed his dad and became a boilermaker. His mom, at least for a while

> . . . worked at Engen Oil Refinery in the canteen. My mother was a very good cook. For us, as a young boy, when my mother worked at the Engen canteen – really, for me – that was special, because on Friday it was fish and chips day. So when she came home from work on a Friday, she came with a big parcel of leftovers from the canteen – they being the cooks and whatever they were. She came with that whole thing wrapped in brown paper. You know how we used to devour that. You can ask any one of my brothers about 'fish and chips Friday'. Up until today, I love fish and chips. I love it! Every Friday, that was like a staple diet. In the morning before she went to work, I used to say, 'Ma, please don't forget to bring the fish and chips' – because sometimes she would come home with nothing, like if they ran out of it on that day.

Keshwar's hunger for fish and chips was matched by his obsession with the game of soccer. In talking to those involved in the making of soccer in Wentworth and listening to Keshwar's own reminiscences, one gets a sense of his contribution in bringing some organisation and structure to the game. When he was nine years old, Keshwar

> . . . started a soccer league in Wentworth. For Juniors. We had leagues and teams from the different roads. Ogle Road. Elm Avenue. Umbria Road. Reiger Road. And we used to come and play together. We used to have competitions. I used to buy minerals. You know, Pepsi. Two bottles for seven cents. And we used to play for litres. They used to put their money – and the winner wins the four, five or six bottles of cool drinks that we'd buy. It was a winner takes all competition. And then we'd have knockout competitions. Then I used to make a league up. I'd draw the league tables and put them up by the shops. I used to draw up the fixtures for them. They could come there and they could see who's playing who, and at what time they are playing. So I'd put the league positions up at the shops to create the interest and keep them wanting to win . . . you could see who was

on the top of the league and then you fight hard to beat them. But these were all like young boys. Juniors.

At an age when many of us were reading *Shoot* magazine and making up fantasy games, Keshwar was making things happen on the ground. And incredibly, out of a patch of land, Keshwar built a stadium:

> We made a little soccer ground here. It was a patch of grass that we cleared out in Quality Street – where the surgery used to be – right across the road from the surgery. There was no one living there. It was vacant property. We cut the grass, dug out trees, everything else. And we made a soccer stadium. We made goal posts. We went to the dump – the scrapyard in the white area, aka the 'White Dump'. This would have been in the late sixties. We picked up planks – timber. I would gather the boys and off we go to the 'White Dumps' to collect timber, old scrap metal, broken nets that the white people used to throw away. We took the valuable stuff we wanted. And then we would make goal posts and erect them. There were no soccer grounds in our area at the time . . . so we made our own. That's where we used to play our league games; our little soccer tournaments.

Keshwar named the ground 'Mole Stadium'

> . . . because whenever we arrived to play there, we would find all these mole humps all over the bloody field. So we had to clean up before we could play – otherwise, the ball hits the mole hill and goes all over the place. I wanted to make my soccer stadium a place where people could come together. I think it was because of the childhood thing that I was captivated by my first experience of a soccer match.

Keshwar played for a number of teams and also started one of his own:

> I owned a soccer team myself. With me and my younger brothers, we made a team called Saints. I managed it and played for it. It was a good team, too. Ferrell, Elvis Singh's younger brother played

> for us. My younger brothers Kenneth, Hylton and Craig also played for the team. A lot of good young guys from Wentworth played for the team: Brian Pretorius, Jappo Walljee, Brian 'Mo' Paulus, the late Malvery Rodganger and his brother Quinton, Rehmans, Captiuex, Spy Walljee, Steven and Kevin Sanders, and Jeff Williams. We had quite a big following in Wentworth. But we were just amateurs and never reached professional status.

Keshwar readily admits that he was no more than an average soccer player. But this did not quench his passion for the game. Weekends see him going to watch the professional teams of the Premier Soccer League and his local team Young Cavaliers. Keshwar believes that Young Cavaliers 'has the potential to be as great as Leeds, if not greater. I love watching live soccer. I got no time for watching Liverpool on TV. That's not so exciting. The TV had nothing to do with my generation. I love being at a live football game . . .'

Keshwar follows the game with the thirst of the five-year-old who first accompanied his brother to Hoy Park. He also does good things for the game, like the boy who was just not quite good enough to be the legend himself but then dedicates his life to allowing others to grow and become legends.

He travels across the country and overseas but cannot wait to return to Elm Street, Happy Valley. It's the familiarity of the landscape, the people, born of a lifetime.

Success in soccer encouraged him to try his hand at other sports. He turned his energy to cricket as part of a group that founded a Wentworth side and included Dennis Petersen, Steven Sanders, Kevin Sanders and Crain Dickson.

> We took that team from the ninth division to the first division. I was the manager of the club. Dennis was the chairman. Crain was treasurer, Steven secretary. Gary Goldstone was our wicketkeeper. Eventually, we grew apart and handed over the reins to the younger generation. I'm not sure what the status is now but I think it fell apart. But we ran it for over ten years, successfully. We won trophies for Wentworth – playing cricket. Eventually in later

years, I ran an under-16 team. I really did it out of support for the youngsters – to give them something to do. Anyway, there was this youngster that was playing and when I asked him his name, he said it was McKnight. So I said to him, 'McKnight?' I asked him who Eddie was to him. He said that Eddie was his father. I said, 'If you are a McKnight, then you're our wicketkeeper.' And I gave him the gloves. You should have seen that kid. He was a natural. For the first time, they were hitting the balls and he was catching them. He got that from his father's genes. I made him a wicketkeeper simply because he said he was a McKnight. I hadn't even seen him play cricket. Nothing. I made the decision based on DNA – that he was a McKnight. That's a fact.

Unfortunately, cricket got lost – simply because there was no one there to nurture it. Loss of interest. Money. People going their separate ways. People get jobs, they move away, and the team weakens. Eventually, it fell. Cricket, as Keshwar reminds me, demands much more resources than soccer.

It is men like Keshwar and a whole coterie of others who facilitated the 'grounds' to capture soccer's growing popularity in Wentworth, removing one mole hill at a time. It was somewhat of a thankless task. And, in the society in which Keshwar lived, with Wentworth labouring under the social and economic disadvantages it did, some might see it also as a fool's errand. But it is a task undertaken by one of those eternally spritely, optimistic, naive and generous souls who actually do make a difference, no matter the odds.

But Keshwar is more than a soccer fan. He is a walking encyclopaedia of Wentworth's history. In a place where there are no museums or societies to chronicle what went before, it is to people like him that Wentworth turns, for its past. The fact that there is no 'one' history siphoned into a museum might be a blessing. It has released Wentworth storytellers everywhere who mix fact and fiction, myth and truth, tomorrow with yesterday. It is simultaneously a researcher's nightmare and nirvana.

If Lloyd Keshwar is the walking encyclopaedia of Wentworth's history, then Wellington Meth, alongside Bennie Whitby, the founder of Leeds, is a fundamental part of its making. Born on 4 December 1945, Wellington is still involved in soccer, a commitment of some 60 years.

Wellington recruited some of Wentworth's best players, such as Elvis Singh and Gary Goldstone.

> What actually happened in those days in Wentworth, the rightful owner of Leeds was Bennie Whitby. Him and I were very close. We worked together. But we wouldn't join together. We wouldn't make one club – because we had that thing in Wentworth with rivalry. So I started going looking for talent. Going to Adams flats. Getting Wilfred 'Kaapie' Phillips and Preston Julius. So we had our own team. And here in Wentworth, we had no team where you could say this is a walkover team. We started . . . There was Cavaliers – and then there was Gay Cavaliers. And we were Young Cavaliers. See, the Cavaliers that they talk about now, I was the rightful owner of it. Then I went and played pro. Dennis [Petersen] and Gary [Goldstone], they played for me before they played for Leeds. I formed the original Young Cavaliers in the seventies. Then I had to make a choice because they wanted me in pro – Golden Arrows, located in the nearby African township of Lamontville. I was the only Coloured who played for Golden Arrows at that time. I was a centre-half.

Meanwhile, as the apartheid local state focused on turning the South Basin into an industrial locale, jobs beyond the petrochemical firms started to afford themselves. Wellington Meth was one of those beneficiaries. He spent his whole working life at the Toyota car plant located down the road from Wentworth:

> I dropped out of school in 1960. I started at Toyota in 1963. That's when it was still Motor Assemblies in Jacobs. If you haven't got an interest in something like school, and your parents can force you, you can write matric and matric and matric and fail and fail and fail. I can strip a car – seats, doors, panels, boot, lining, everything. That's when the welding came in. My dad said, 'You're not gonna stay here if you're not working. I'm the only one working here. Your mother is not working. So we've got to make sure.' And you know what mothers are like . . . You're not at home until your father sleeps. And she throws the blankets

> through the window. You sleep on the side of the wall. Get up before your father gets up. There by the washing stones, you hide the blankets – and make sure you're gone early in the morning before your father goes. The moment he's gone, you know mothers . . . They give you tea. They give you something to eat. They tell you, 'Hey don't make your father see you and catch you here.' I worked for Toyota Assemblies for 45 years.

As Meth sadly, and with some anger, recalls, many of his contemporaries refused to make a career out of working for one company. When new opportunities opened, such as Sasolburg and Newcastle, they were quick to jump ship. But this was intermittent employment and did not afford them in their autumn years the kind of security that Wellington has.

The centre-forward

> This Elvis does not have an electric guitar, but he has an electric pair of boots.
>
> — headline in *The Post*

Elvis Singh's goal-scoring ability is talked about in reverential tones. As Gregory Baptist reflects, 'Put the ball in the box and Elvis will put it in the net.' Elvis joined Leeds from Wentworth Park in 1977 with the likes of Denzil Bull. To tell the story of Elvis is to tell the story of Wentworth, about enduring *braskap* [friendship] and love of the game.

> My parents are both from Newcastle. My father is Indian and my mother is Coloured, but I consider myself Coloured. I talk like my father. My sisters sound more Coloured – also because they talk like their husbands and boyfriends. I've got seven sisters and four brothers.

Elvis's family moved to Durban and lived in Melbourne Road in Umbilo. In 1963, they took advantage of the accommodation on offer in Wentworth. Elvis was six years old. He stopped school after passing Standard 8. It is a refrain one hears often in Wentworth. A son leaves school to earn a wage to support the family. Elvis's first team was an under-13 side called Ramblers:

The manager, Pat Gabriel, told me, 'You're gonna go professional.' At the time I was just playing locally – mostly in Till's Crescent in Sydenham, in Springfield, and here in Wentworth – on those same Wentworth grounds near the church. Father Carey of the Catholic Church used to complain that 'the grounds were full and the church was empty'. Pat Gabriel used to say to me, 'I can see that you're a diamond,' meaning that I shone out. When Gabriel left, George Lansberg took over. He came over from England to manage us in the under 15s and under 17s. He's originally from Wentworth. He used to live just here up the road from me . . . He was a very good coach . . . He gave different types of exercise – not like the training that the young clubs do these days. For two years, I played for under 15 and then I went senior after that. I then went to Wentworth Park – a family team – owned by Duncan Joshua, who is married to my dad's sister. Seven or eight of my cousins played for that team.

Elvis's family were immersed in the game. His brothers Leonard and Ferrell also played soccer – as well as his sister, Arlene.

Elvis laughs as he remembers the only time his mother Joyce came to watch a game: 'My mother watched me play one time – and one time only. The very first time I played professionally in a Clover Cup tournament against Port Shepstone United. I scored a goal and the score was 2-1. The Port Shepstone United players were so upset about losing that they smashed our team bus. My mother said, 'This is the first time, and the last time, that I am ever watching you play.'

His father, on the other hand, never missed a game:

When I played for Leeds, my father came to every single game. He even used to bring my girlfriends with him. He cheered me on and shouted for me at the games. He was very supportive. Then Leeds turned pro in 1980. Before that, we played amateur with Gary Goldstone and Dennis Petersen. We entered the pro league because we won the amateur league three consecutive years in succession. That's how we turned pro. We were the only team that could beat Cape Town Spurs. I was the youngest player with the highest goals scored. I loved my soccer. I can't boast, but all my friends tell me how good I was. They even tell my son Ashley, who now plays for Young Cavaliers, when he misses the goal, 'If that was your dad, that goal would have gone in.' They called us the Green Mambas. There was a newspaper headline once that said, 'This Elvis does not have an electric guitar, but he has an electric pair of boots'. Elvis Presley was big at the time. My nickname is Jerry because my mother loved Jerry Lee Lewis and she wanted to name me Jerry. But, my father named me Elvis – after his music idol.

Elvis was part of the team that turned pro in 1980:

> With Leeds we played most of our games at Curries Fountain. In the first season that Leeds went pro, they were fourth in the league. Selling the team to Errol Hughes was a big and bad mistake. They did it behind our backs and behind closed doors. Errol knew nothing about soccer. All he had was money. We had no money. For that Knockout Cup we won, we only got paid R90. Sometimes we got paid R75 a match. Sometimes we hardly got paid. When Errol bought the team, I can't tell you how shocked we were. And he was our friend. We knew him. He had a lot of money. Still, I don't know why he bought that team. Maybe he wanted to be on top. You know how these businessmen are? They want to make themselves feel big; feel good. I don't even think he paid for the team. He just took it over at a time when it was becoming defunct. John 'Cocoon' Williams was our manager. In 1980/81, Glen Manning was our manager – but he played a purely administrative role.

When asked about his most memorable goal, Elvis's eyes twinkle:

> A memorable goal in my career happened one evening when I was twenty years old. Gary Goldstone and his manager, Don Moodley, came to my house and hooted. Gary was playing for Berea at the time. They parked outside and I heard the hooter and when I saw who it was, I came outside. They told me to jump in the back seat. They said they needed a striker. I was playing for

Left to right: Patrick Moodley, Elvis Singh, Brian Fynn, Gregory Baptist, Clement Tucker, Phillip Peters. Front: Kirk Dutlow.

Leeds at the time. I said I couldn't do it. They asked if they can just loan me for three or four months. It was December. There was a cup game coming up. Then they pulled out about R4 000 or R5 000. I said yes to the money. It was for me to join Berea. Berea was scheduled to play the semi-final against Cape Town Spurs the next week. When the game came, I was on the bench – me and their original striker, Peter Pillay – until half-time. At half-time, the score was 0-0. People were saying, 'Don, we need some goals here.' Don told me to get up and warm up. While I was warming up, the crowd booed. As I got on to the field, in the first two minutes I scored a goal. Then the score was 1-0. It was raining. We won the match.

Glenville then beat Berea in the finals. Elvis returned to Leeds after four months.

At that time, Leeds was playing against Berea. Berea supporters were heavy supporters. They called me a traitor when I went back to Leeds. To make matters worse, in the first game that I played when I returned to Leeds, we beat Berea 5-2. I scored a hat-trick. We finished them.

The Post newspaper headline read 'Elvis sings a different tune'.
Elvis and the team were young, famous and not shy of a good time.

After every game, we went to a supper club where they had karaoke. And we used to go to Blitz nightclub. After we played, we danced the night away. I love dancing. We used to have some nice times there. There was one Saturday night though. Me, Cheesa Baptist, Fuzzy Campbell, Tyrone Bezuidenhout, Putts and I had to play on Sunday against Newcastle Dynamos. We had been to Blitz, and then we went to Durban beachfront. One supporter *speeked* (told on) us, and called John 'Cocoon' Williams. At 4.30 am, Cocoon comes to the beach and catches us in the act. Partying. We were terrible. He says, 'Gentlemen, what's going on here? Y'll have got no discipline! I'm putting all five of you on the bench tomorrow.' He had an old blue VW and drove behind us closely all the way home – with each of us going to our own houses. The next day, all the Leeds players are in the change room and Cocoon is busy writing up his team for the day. He chose me and Cheesa. We won 1-0. I scored a goal, as *babalaas* (hungover) as I was. He was clever enough not to bench his best players.

In between the good times, there was also pain. The death of Cheesa Baptist still hurts. Elvis remembers how they gelled together socially and on the soccer field:

Every day, you are all playing together – and then he's there no more – it's strange. Cheesa was a left-winger. Putts was a right-winger. I was a striker. All their balls came to me. He was my best friend. Putts until today is still my best friend. Then, Cheesa is gone. Mrs Baptist always gave us good luck before a game. She never came to the grounds. Cheesa – that was her angel. Cheesa was her life. When we went to her house after he died, we could see that there was something that was missing.

She wasn't so joyous. She lost her joy after his death. He had galloping cancer. He was gone within a week of us knowing. The same with Cocoon – cancer. He was such a pleasant guy; always smiling. He used to always come to me before a game and ask me, 'How many goals are you gonna score today?' That's how much they trusted me. Even when I was injured, they wanted to play me. Once I had a bad back problem, and I wasn't 100 per cent and Cocoon wanted me to play at a cup final. I scored this goal from the halfway line in Cape Town in 1982. I was so shocked that I celebrated by jumping up and punching my fist up – and throwing my back out.

But the real tragedy in Elvis's life was the death of his wife Sandra:

After my wife died, I cried for one-and-a-half years. She died on 3 August 1997. I am a devil. My wife was 'saved'. She went to the AFM [Apostolic Faith Mission] church. I used to always sit two rows in front of her. She liked to be near a door or a window because she had asthma. One Sunday, I looked back and she wasn't there. I went looking for her. She was by a bin. She couldn't breathe. She was turning blue, pink and mauve. She said she wouldn't be able to cook that day. I told her not to worry about that. We rushed her to Addington Hospital. There were lots of doctors. I just stood there. For half an hour, I just stood there. For a week and a half, she was in hospital. Then she slipped into a coma. That time I was working nightshift in Umlazi. Before two weeks, Addington Hospital calls me at midnight and tells me she has taken a turn for the worse. I go to the hospital. I stay for a while. They ask me if I want to go back to work. I say, 'No.' On the Sunday of the second week, we were all going to visit her – the whole family. When we arrived, they wouldn't allow us in as she had died already.

Elvis fell apart.

I was like a zombie for almost two years. I cried all the time. My wife was an angel. My dad used to shout at me for crying and say, 'Why didn't you go instead?' I wasn't working. The kids were three and seven years old. A year and a half later, I came to my senses. Here's she here. She's always in my wallet. Never mind I don't have money in my wallet, but I have her and my two sons. She was 29 years old when she died. We had been married for five years. I still can't find her replacement since.

Elvis found work at Fidelity Guards for thirteen years. He worked on the road for eight years and then five in the control room. There was a high attrition rate:

> Those eight years were the eight scariest years of my life. I lost a lot of friends from the community in that job. About ten guys died while I was in that job. One Saturday night, we went to one of our guys' bull's party. He was going to get married the following Saturday. On the Thursday night before his wedding, he was shot. I was in the control room. He was 25 years old. It was a cash-in-transit heist a few kilometres from Wentworth, in Prospecton. It was really painful. They don't just want to take the money, they want to kill. Take the money. It's insured. It was in 1985.

Elvis eventually lost his job. 'Other than losing my wife, losing that job was the lowest point in my life. It took me seven months to find another job after that.'

Elvis joined the famed Orlando Pirates in Johannesburg: 'After Pirates, I never played soccer again. After nine or ten months in Joburg, I drank and I found women. That's when I had my other two children – Brits and Bradley. Then I left Joburg for good.'

In March 2016, when I speak to him, Elvis has been unemployed for nine months. He is not well:

> I suffer with sugar diabetes now. I walk every day and do about twelve different exercises – like they show you on the wall in the hospital. They say that diabetes can make you a bit stiff. Like I said, I love dancing. Every Sunday, I used to go watch Butch (brother-in-law to former Leeds stalwart Eddie McKnight) sing at New Lights at the end of West Street – opposite Shoprite. I go to night racing at Greyville Racecourse. And I watch my son

play soccer. He gets shy when I come, but I give him a lot of support. When my wife was alive, it was a highlight going out as a family.

Amidst the sadness and ruin, a blade of grass has pushed through. There is another football-playing Singh coming through: Elvis's son Ashley plays for Young Cavaliers. We will meet him later. First though, is a woman who carved a pioneering path to play football at the highest level.

Arlene 'Webster' Sherene Singh

> Football remains an overwhelmingly masculine world; that is part of its attraction, its rough-hewn heroics, risk-taking adventurers, sublimated hunters and warriors. However, in even the most liberal zones of the world it exhibits only a narrow range of permissible masculinities and remains a stronghold of publicly acceptable homophobia. The worldwide move towards acceptance of new notions of gender and sexuality can only be glimpsed at the very margins of the football world.
> — Goldblatt, *The Ball is Round*

Arlene Singh, Elvis's sister, is in her mid-fifties. She is arguably the most accomplished and famous woman footballer to come out of Wentworth in the apartheid era. She is one of twelve children:

> I'm the second baby. I was supposed to be the baby, but my sister was a mistake. I keep telling her that. Between me and my sister, there are three years. But, between all us – all twelve of us – there's one year, one year, one year. My mother just loved being pregnant.

Arlene started playing soccer on the street with her brothers. As she remembers, she was the neighbourhood 'tomboy':

> My brother and them used to play on the road. They were raw. There was no soccer field. So one day I said I wanted to play with them. They said, 'Are you sure? You're gonna get hurt.' I said, 'I don't mind.' My mother used to say, 'You're gonna get hurt.' I would say, 'It's fine.' Ay, I used to get hurt.

But this did not put Arlene off. She kept going back. And her skills developed, together with her ability to weather strong tackles: 'Then I became good. I think it was just raw talent. I watched my brothers as well. Growing up and playing soccer against the men gave me a lot of practice. I'm a goalkeeper.'

Arlene lived for all kinds of street games:

> Because I was a tomboy, I wanted to try anything. From twelve or thirteen years old, I used to play everything. I used to play tops with the guys. I used to play marbles. I hated dolls and I found girls' games to be boring. When I was a child, I happily played sports outdoors with the boys. My mother would say, 'Guys, time to bath.' And I would say, 'Do I have to?' I was part of the team. You know how the boys picked sides . . . You're on my side. You're on my side. So now I had my team. And when you were the last one to be picked, it was, 'Oh, you're the bad one.' It was fun. I could handle the boys. So, I thought, why not? Watching my brothers, you know how it is when you're a youngster . . . You always want to try what they are trying. I could do tricks, as well. I was improving all the time.

But the chance to play soccer with other women was limited in Wentworth. Much of Arlene's sporting life would be spent on the white side of the racial divide. It gave her the nickname Webster 'after the TV show – the Coloured girl with all the white people'.

She started playing softball at Queensmead in the Umbilo area:

> We had a softball team here in Wentworth. We started playing in the white league. And then one day, these girls were kicking the ball and the ball came towards me. I did a few tricks and I kicked the ball back to them.

It was an instinctive reaction with skills honed on the streets of Wentworth. But it was to change Arlene's life:

> A lady – Irene Richie, I'll never forget her – came over, after we had played our game of softball, and said, 'I see you've got some skills with the soccer ball.' I said, 'Oh, thanks.' She then said,

'Wouldn't you like to play soccer?' I said, 'Yeah. It sounds like fun.' I was seventeen years old. Then they came to pick me up for training. And that was me.

The team was called Ramblers and it was based in the white suburb of Woodlands. Arlene remembers the first trip:

I was nervous in the car ride. I was quiet. I didn't know what to expect. Then we went to put our boots on. I was a striker at that stage. The white girls were chatting away. You know how white girls like to talk. And I was checking them out. I'm new to this. I never used to be with white people. Irene said, 'Come, let me introduce you to the girls.' She introduced me to all of them. Robbie Perret was the coach at that stage.

Arlene started out as a striker like her brother Elvis. Then the goalkeeper got injured:

Our goalkeeper, Joanne Jordaan, hurt herself. We were playing against one of the teams and we just had enough people. Now the girl that was our reserve goalkeeper could never have made it to play as a goalkeeper. You could see I was the strappy type and could move. So they said to me, 'Arlene, please, we need you. Can you go play goalkeeper?' I said, 'But, I've never ever played goalkeeper.' Irene said, 'Just be yourself and the backs will help you.' I was nervous. I played that game finished. Then we found out that our goalkeeper will be off for three months. Damn. Then they said, 'Well, Arlene, you're gonna have to play goalkeeper until she comes back.' When we went to practice that next Monday and Wednesday, they made me practise goalkeeping.

Arlene found it difficult to adjust to the change in position. As a striker she was always involved: tracking back into midfield, demanding the ball. Training was also difficult to adjust to: 'The coach will take the goalkeeper. He'll throw the ball and you've got to dive this way and dive that way. He kicks the ball. You've got to flick the ball over here and there. I missed the camaraderie of training with the others.' But Arlene soon started to come to grips with the importance of marshalling the defence and getting involved as a leader: 'It was lovely. I enjoyed it. That is why I am a goalkeeper up until today.'

Arlene's reputation soared when she saved two penalties in one game in 1986. It was a major tournament in Durban and they were playing the powerful Southern Transvaal outfit. In order to get into the finals they had to at least conjure up a draw:

> It was five minutes before the final whistle. The penalty went against us. I was so nervous. And I could never, ever play with gloves. I couldn't feel the ball. I had to use my hands. I'm thinking if they score, it's my fault. So now I'm sweating. Everybody is talking to me at once. I've got the coach talking to me. I've the girls talking to me. All I said was, 'Leave me.' And Irene Richie came to me and said, 'Arlene, listen to me. If it goes in, it goes in. It's not your fault. Just do me one favour. As a goalkeeper, you have to choose a spot. If you're gonna dive to the right or dive to the left, then you do it. You can't wait. Because by the time she kicks, you can't still be thinking.'

Arlene listened but it did nothing to ease her fears:

> Now I'm shitting myself. Okay, they put the ball down. And I know this girl. I looked at who was kicking the ball. I knew it was hard for her to kick towards her left. I watch people play. She always kicked towards the right side. So I thought, Arlene, this is it. Time's going now. So whether the ball goes in or it doesn't, either way the whistle is gonna blow. And then we'd be out the tournament or in the finals. So I took a step to the right. I watched. Waiting. Then I saved it. I was blank. All I did was go for it. I just made a decision. And then, do you know what they said? In those days, you couldn't move. You had to be still. That was the ruling. They said I moved before she kicked. So there was a re-kick.

As Arlene prepared for the penalty to be taken, she struggled to refocus:

> Now the question is, is she gonna change and go to the right? Or go to the left? That was the decision I had to make. It was just me

and the kicker. I took a step to my right. I stood. And I saved it again. Oh! The crowd went wild. I was up in the air. They were lifting me up. That was my best moment ever! I will never forget that day.

Arlene was not only to save goals on South African pitches. A highlight of her career was the 1988 tour of Italy. She was selected for 'South Africa', in many ways a pariah team, because the country was excluded from international playing fields:

> We couldn't really travel the world because of apartheid. So when this opportunity came along to go to Italy, we jumped at the chance. I was playing for Umbilo at the time. Umbilo was a breakaway team from Ramblers. So, with the Italy opportunity, there was this Italian guy in the country named Mario.[5] He said he wants to get the South African side together and he wants to take us overseas.

The reality of Arlene's economic situation took hold. She was not working and had no money to speak of. She told Mario that she could not afford to go:

> He said, 'Don't worry.' We were getting sponsored. I said, 'Sure. But I also need money for myself.' When you go overseas, you must have money. He said, 'You can get some pocket money.' I said, 'But I'm not working.' I had my passport at that stage. At the back of my passport, you had to stamp how much money you are taking overseas. Now he took our passports because he was organising this whole club that was going overseas. We only get our passports when we are getting on the international flight. Now he gives us all our passports. We look in the back. There it was stamped. Ten thousand rand. Every girl got ten thousand on their passport. No money was given to us. But that was the amount of money that we were taking out of the country. In those years, it was a lot of money.

---

5. A pseudonym.

However, Mario was involved in a scam:

> It was probably the way that he could take money out of the country. There was even an investigation when we came back. Cops came to my house and my mother started getting nervous. She said, 'Detectives were here! Some detectives came looking for you. They were asking something about soccer and money you took overseas.' I said, 'But I didn't even have much money. The money you gave me is the money I went with.' This was 1988. We weren't even thinking. We were too happy to travel. We still thought we were going to get the money.

Back on the streets of Wentworth, when Arlene is mentioned by male soccer players, her talent is recognised in the same breath as her sexuality:

> I'm gay. All my life I knew I was gay. I just knew. I knew I was different. Apart from being a tomboy, I like looking at girls. I didn't like looking at boys. My sisters wanted to play dolly house and I wanted to play with cars and guns. And I always played with the boys. I never played with the girls. Never with the girls. I think my mother knew from when I was still small. But, she never, ever said anything to me. And I never, ever said anything to her. She died. She knew. She told my baby sister. But she never told me.

Early on, Arlene started to distinguish herself in terms of what she wore:

> You have no idea how much I hated dresses. My sister is one year and one month older than me. And you know when you are that close, they tend to buy you the same clothes and dress you alike. You gotta wear the same clothes. Okay now, my sister was like the model. She loved dresses and high heels. She was older than me, so what she chooses, I've got to have too. Until one day. Christmas Day. We used to always dress up for Christmas. She wanted this dress and I hated this dress. I hated it with a passion. My mother says, 'You *will* wear it.' I said, 'I'm telling you now. I won't wear it. You are buying it for nothing.' I was twelve years old.

Odette (left) with Arlene.

For a long time, Arlene kept her sexuality 'undercover', as she puts it. Prejudice stalked the streets and made her open to violence and ridicule. It also put pressure on those she associated with. As Andrew Merrifield warns: 'A place can offer shelter, warmth, protection, be a hearth in a heartless (and heartless) world, a site of resistance, a starting point for survival. Yet places can also imprison, condemn, prevent, keep people in as well as out' (2012: 156).

In Arlene's case, soccer allowed her to escape racial and sexual cages.

Today, Arlene has found love with a woman from Wentworth, Odette. They are open about their lives. There are tensions with Odette's son. But they are happy.

Arlene wants to go on a cruise with her partner: 'I said to her, maybe you and I should get married on a ship out at sea. I said the captain can marry us. I'd love to do that. I'd really love to take her on that cruise. All over the world.'

The pain Arlene endured, the exclusions she remembers, the places she travelled in order to escape the strictures and straitjacket of her community have left wounds, but she still has a deep sense of belonging, epitomised by her parting shot: 'I've always been a Wentworth girl.'

5

The Leftover Years

> There was no farewell game. There was nothing. It just petered out. In fact, we didn't even know that it was folding. We didn't think it was the last game. We were still thinking that we would have got the franchise and that we would have re-opened it in the next season. So, there was no 'last game'; there was no farewell. No ending. In that pro season period, the franchise was sold to this team from Newcastle because they had the money and that was it. There was no official ending. The last game would have been in that same year – 1987. In the new season we never came back with a new team. There was no team to come back with because the team was gone. It was terrible. It was like a death. For me, I didn't know what to do with myself on Sundays. I was supporting this team all my life. All of a sudden this thing is gone. After twenty years that was taken away from us.
>
> — Lloyd Keshwar

Picking up on the theme of ownership, for people like Gary Goldstone, at Leeds, everybody was 'like shareholders. Even if we didn't get a cent.' Like Bennie Whitby, he remains bitter at how the club was sold. Much of the story remains lost in the mists of time. But none of the 'shareholders' got any money. It was sold on to a business person, Errol Hughes. It appears that one of the former players, Patrick 'Putts' Moodley, was part of the deal. According to Goldstone:

> Something went on. All of a sudden it became Errol Hughes's club. Errol Hughes then sold it to whom – I'm not quite sure. Putts will know exactly what happened. But I know there's still a Leeds team in KwaMashu. I'm not saying it's the original. I don't

know where they got their name from. But this club was sold to somebody.

For a while, Leeds hung on as a semi-professional outfit. For Goldstone, the last hurrah was winning 'a top four knockout cup against Cape Town Spurs'. The Cape sides dominated those from Natal and local teams would often be on the wrong end of a trouncing. The final on Sunday ended in a 1-1 draw, even after extra time. The game was replayed on a Monday. Leeds prevailed 3-1. 'I always tell the Kaapie (Cape) *ous* about fitness. We proved to you. We beat you. We played you Sunday and we played you Monday.'

The outstanding Cape Town Spurs. Top row (left to right): Erol Naik, Brian Mendell, Cyril Murrigan, Farook Abrahams, Philip Luiters, Boobie Solomons, Shaiem Jacobs, Gollin Solomons, Pettie Dollie (manager).
Bottom row (left to right): Robin Delcarme, Alex Arends, Salie Adams, Keith America, Calvin Petersen.

Goldstone recalls that the high point of Leeds's attention to organising and looking after records was during the time of Bennie Whitby. After that, they kept going but from 1977 the wheels slowly started to come off. There was little attention paid to record clerks and day-to-day administration. He thinks wistfully of teams such as Bluff Rangers, which had a solid management core and made sure that they were represented at meetings of the professional federation. Goldstone feels that without the 'backroom' Leeds was prevented from transitioning from a good side to 'a great, great side'.

For Goldstone, the other reason for Leeds's demise was the bringing in of players from outside Wentworth:

> You had the whole of Wentworth to breed from – like what we were doing all the years. But that seemed to have been taken away and they were bringing guys from all over the show – and that's where they lost their support in Wentworth. Wentworth people don't know these people here. You're losing now. People want to know, 'Where's that local *ou*? Where's that local *ou*?' Now you are coming with these guys from Port Elizabeth and these *ous* from Joburg.

For Moodley, it was the lack of sponsorship in the South African Soccer Federation and trying to compete with the lucrative National Professional Soccer League (NPSL) that arose in the early 1980s and threatened teams such as Leeds United. Moodley moved to the NPSL, playing for AmaZulu in 1982. Playing in front of huge crowds brought out the best in him.

Ironically, Goldstone, reaching the autumn of his career, moved on, also trying to take advantage of the rich pickings on offer:

> I came to Leeds for two years, and then I got an offer from AmaZulu. I went to AmaZulu in 1981. In 1982, Manning Rangers was my last club. I want to photocopy a nice piece where they interviewed me where father and son played for the same team.

Meanwhile, Errol Hughes, owner of a big-bus fleet, was pumping money into Leeds. By now, the NPSL had been superseded by the National Soccer League. Money flowed in from South African Breweries and television deals (Alegi 2004: 144). Hughes saw Leeds taking advantage of this sea change, and towards the end of the 1980s he approached Moodley to come back. Moodley remembers how

> Errol approached me when he owned the team and asked me to help him out. I said I would as player-coach – and he had to pay

the same wages that I was getting at AmaZulu. Then we got top guys: Gordon Igesund (who went on to coach Bafana Bafana), Owen da Gama (sometime assistant coach for Bafana Bafana). We got him and three guys from Ireland. Now we are talking big-league soccer. I made an agreement with AmaZulu that I was just gonna stay there with Leeds for the first stretch to help them get on their feet – and then I would come back. Now, Errol starts pumping money into the team. Remember he had 32 buses. We played against Chiefs, Pirates – all the top teams. This is the new Leeds now. They just got promoted into the upper league. Now you have to pay your players because you're getting a stipend from the association that we're playing in – this new league. And you get a certain percentage from government and the gate. We once played Pirates in front of tens of thousands of people in Joburg. By now we got all top players. Even white players from top teams, we've got them playing in our Leeds set-up. Players from Maritzburg. We had a few players from our old Leeds structure. We still had one or two good players in that Leeds team. Then the trouble starts. Players' wages go up, star players demand more, Hughes is struggling to keep the team going . . .

Lloyd Keshwar takes up the story:

Leeds became professional in the eighties and they operated in the Federation for a few years. In 1982, they left the Federation and joined the NPSL second division. They won the play-offs and entered the first division – now the Premier Soccer League. So, in order to play professional soccer in that league, they needed funds. They needed money. And, nobody had money. Errol had access to funding. The Hughes brothers were very wealthy businessmen at the time. Generally, they also helped Wentworth. Yes, they saw a business opportunity, but they also helped Wentworth. At the end of the day, they were investing their money. Surely, they were due a return on their money, if one was to be fair. A lot of people talk bad about Errol Hughes. I don't share that sentiment. I don't share it simply because he gave us a team. If it wasn't for his money, we wouldn't have had a team. Leeds would not have existed. At the end of the day, I look at it from the holistic point of view. The big picture is that we had a team. We had a team called Wentworth Leeds. And that is what we wanted. It was a gentleman's agreement to keep the team afloat.

The memories of those years in the professional ranks still remain. Many in Wentworth will never forget the 1985 game against South Africa's pre-eminent soccer team, Kaizer Chiefs. People like Keshwar gave Leeds no chance:

It was a big thing because Chiefs was a big team. Leeds was little Wentworth boytjies from here. The boys said, 'Don't *vaai* [go] there. You're gonna catch a six-pack.' We played them at Glebelands Stadium. Leeds won 3-1. For me, that was the greatest. For me, that was like the Second Coming. Little Wentworth team whipped the top boys. This was a great team. They could do great things.

Football, as Eduardo Galeano writes, often throws up the unexpected, 'the impossible occurs, the dwarf teaches the giant a lesson . . .' (2004: 204). And the newcomers, the minnows, slayed a giant.

In 1986, the team reached the lucrative Mainstay Cup semi-final, playing the mighty Orlando Pirates. Gordon Igesund was player/manager. Igesund missed a penalty and the game was lost.

But despite their successes, the team was costing more and more money. Hughes found it increasingly difficult. Patrick Moodley approached Keshwar and said:

'Lloyd, let's put money together and let's buy this team.' But, to be honest, we didn't have the funding. We didn't have the money. We were artisans and boilermakers. We were two *ous* who didn't have a vision, quite frankly. The entrepreneurial vision. The vision to say, yes, it was a good investment and to raise money. I talk of myself there, but I think there were a lot of people in the same boat. We wanted to try and buy it back from Errol but we couldn't raise money to buy it. That day it was probably about R300k or R400k, but that was a shitload of money. A house used to cost R30 000. Errol rescued the club. You have to give him credit for that. He put his money into it – until eventually it was waning. The team wasn't winning. The players were gone. The Gary Goldstones had got old. And there was no succession plan in place. If you look at Liverpool and Manchester United, they've got a school; an academy. Youngsters are coming through on a bloody conveyor belt. One player pulls out now, you put another player in. The team won't collapse. We never had that type of plan. This was towards the end of the eighties – in 1987. Errol sold the team then to a group of people in Newcastle – Chippa Dynamos. He sold the franchise off. He did so to recover his money. He had invested money from 1983/84 or so to bring it into the higher professional status. Errol had pumped a lot of money into that club.

Hughes sold the team. Leeds had now truly left Wentworth behind. Keshwar believes that Hughes did his best to keep the club afloat:

Errol spent a fair amount of money on Leeds in that time. For that period, he took it over and he sponsored it. That's why I say, give him his due. I'm not saying Errol was a saint. But don't be casting stones when your backyard is not clean. The club had fallen after '87. The support was lacking. The team had been relegated. The team didn't have money to continue. Errol didn't have money to continue. He came and he offered us to buy it back from him. Not me, per se. He made the offer to Wentworth people. I regret not showing an interest at the time. I regret that big time. I really should have sold my house and bought that team. That is one of the big regrets of my life.

Lloyd Keshwar lived those Leeds years with an incredible fanaticism and his memories remain fresh some three decades later. There were many others who played a part in that history. None more than the enduring legacy of Cherrians and the Petersen family.

6

Nurturing New Talent

Cherrians, this is our seventieth year now. We started in the late 1940s. We were originally from Clairwood. We have always been progressive in whatever we did. I've been with Cherrians my entire life. I played, I managed, I coached, I trained, I administrated, I funded. The club today is still in existence. Vibrantly in existence. And we are consistent. Most clubs have come and then folded. We've survived apartheid forced removals, lack of facilities, but have competed at the highest level while being rooted deeply within the community. It's been hard but it laid the foundation of my life and many others.

— Bugsy Singh

Beyond Wellington Meth's instinctive passion for the game, he was also motivated by the social conditions that haunted Wentworth:

Flat life is a sad life to live. If you're staying in a flat – and say you live upstairs and you come down – the first thing you see that's happening on the floor is either gambling or smoking dagga or drinking. So I was so much into football that I thought I could make a change here in Wentworth by getting these players off the street. It's God's gift – like how some people take up priesthood. I've had it my whole life. I was talented with football from young. When I came back from Golden Arrows, I played for Wentworth Park and then joined Cherrians. My family came from Sydenham. When we came to Wentworth, we stayed opposite the garage in Percy Johnson Road – where Dennis Petersen is staying now, that was our house. From there, we moved to Olive Grove. We grew up very hard. And I was the eldest and had to leave school. I was told by my father, 'You leaving school? Well then you can't stay at home until you get a job.' There were fourteen of us and then my father and my mother. So you had to make do for yourself.

A fortuitous thing happened for the Meths after renting at 154 Assegai Road in Wentworth – the family bought a house at No. 41 Olive Grove. All fourteen children and parents finally had a patch of garden to ease the madness inside the house. This was opposite the soccer-crazy Linderbooms, who through the generations have played a part in developing Wentworth soccer. They were integrally Cherrians Football Club, a team formed in 1948 in the nearby area of Clairwood, which was slowly destroyed through the machinations of the Group Areas Act. As the current vice chairperson of the club, George Yusuf Moses, remembers:

> Cherrians are originally from Cherry Road in Clairwood. It came to Wentworth because a guy named Steven Pusher, a schoolteacher, was living in Clairwood. The guy who is also part of us now, the key man in Cherrians, is a doctor named Professor Bhugwan 'Bugsy' Singh. Steven schooled here in Wentworth. Through Steven's links with the players from Wentworth, they took over Cherrians. With Steven coming to school here and meeting the players, he was instrumental in getting them linked between the Clairwood people and the Wentworth people. And then we grew from there. Eventually, Cherrians became a Wentworth team. But because the original team is from Cherry Road in Clairwood, the name remains.

If Leeds United took all before them in the 1970s, then Cherrians kept Wentworth's flag flying as apartheid crumbled. In 1989, the club won the pre-eminent knock-out competition for amateurs. In the amalgamated Southern Natal structure – the highest football structure in the province – over three successive years (1995–97), Cherrians Football Club won the league.

During this remarkable period, Cherrians also won other competitions, such as the Coca-Cola Cup in 1996. In the same year, Southern Natal

Cherrians with the Maize Power Cup.

Association Football awarded Cherrians the hugely coveted Team of the Year. And then, in arguably the biggest moment in the club's history, they won a national tournament against all comers. As Bugsy Singh recounts:

> We won the Maize Power Cup [1997]. And that hasn't been paralleled. Who else has won, at that level, a competition like that? It was a national thing. It was open to all the communities throughout the country – a national tournament, SAFA-run. In that generation when everything is open. Not saying, 'I'm a lahnee in Wentworth, I'm a lahnee in Newlands, and I'm a lahnee in Clairwood and Berea.' Here, it's open to everyone. We had to go to somewhere in the middle of KwaZulu-Natal – there in Stanger. We had to go to Mthatha. We had to go to Port Shepstone. We played our semi-finals in Mthatha at the Independence Stadium. An all-SAFA competition. From there, they flew us to play in Northern Gauteng – the Rustenburg area – and we won ... We came on television. I got the video. At that time, it was a video cassette. But I converted it into a CD. These *laaities* appeared on national television. No other team has done that. This was in

the new South Africa – where we had to compete. Against past
resources. Against well-resourced communities. All those things.
Norman Steenkamp was our coach. The fact that they allowed
you to come onto that runway to take a photograph of the plane
. . . Big officials coming to meet you . . . What does it tells you?
No other club achieved that. Today the *ous* are talking. That
achievement has not been matched.

Speaking to Bugsy Singh in 2018, marking Cherrians' 70th year, he takes special pride in their ability to just keep going, surviving forced removal from Clairwood as well as a lack of resources:

And, we've continued – in spite of . . . all the challenges . . . no
grounds. No funding. No resources. On threadbare budgets.
With hostile corporates. These big companies. I remember going
with Paddy [Patrick] Africa [now in Johannesburg] and a few
other guys . . . We made an appointment with – and saw – the
guys at Engen. I told them, 'You know what . . .' At that time,
apartheid was still buzzing. 'You have a responsibility to this
community. You take all these people here on shutdowns and
everything . . . Apart from . . . I don't want to go into the angle of
community destruction . . . Give us something like this . . . Not
this club . . . But give this community.' But this club wasn't about
the community. By then I had evolved and said, 'Hey, this is more
than Cherrians.' In fact, most of my life, my friends that I made
are from outside Cherrians – because I saw the community. I
didn't see my club. And this is what our club was about. I said,
'You know what? You guys in Engen. Y'll are doing all of this.
Y'll are taking these guys for shutdowns and everything. Put
something back there. Don't give it to this club. Give it to the
community. Do up Ogle Road grounds. Put change rooms over
there. Get some coaches over there. The community can actually
benefit.' Nothing. Nothing happened.

Vaughn Linderboom is the quintessential community man. A former player, Vaughn has become a successful business person and, together with his family and old-time residents of Olive Grove, provides an opening in his company for local young men to get jobs. The club also acts as a catalyst for providing hampers to the old and infirm. And, on the field of play, as Meth attests, they are intent on creating opportunities:

> We took the Cherrians under 17s to the USA in 2012. We took them to Ohio. We help the kids. Cherrians have just sent that youngster, Quade Roskruge, to Chelsea in the UK. He just went for trials there. Cherrians paid for that. Then he came back and just left now last week to go to Australia. This was facilitated by an old Wentworth person living in Australia, Ricardo Fynn. My involvement with Cherrians goes way back. Everybody wanted me to come give them a hand and I wasn't the kind of person to say no. I will die on the soccer field. Clinton Larsen, the Bafana player, also came through us. Clinton stayed just down the road here – across the road from the Linderbooms. They sponsor people. They uplift people. They even give Christmas hampers to the poor at the local church.

Moses emphasises the role of Bugsy Singh and his son Mikhail:

> Somehow Cherrians has always been alive. From 1948 to 2018, it has not died – not once. Whether it is in the lower league, whatever, it has always been alive. This guy, Bugsy Singh . . . I have never seen a person like this. Any one of us can call him right now – whether it is a relative or an auntie – he will drop everything and come to assist you from a medical perspective. He is that type of person. He has that type of heart. We actually had . . . About two or three years ago, we had a thing for him to honour him . . . The whole of Wentworth . . . Everybody who has ever been linked . . . And it didn't really matter if you were a Cherrians man . . . Even if you were involved in soccer . . . Because we soccer people know each other . . . He would assist you. Hands down. People who never even played for Cherrians were at that event – just to honour him. At the event were all the Cherrians from even the Clairwood days. People spoke. His son, Mikhail, is part of our current Cherrians management team. Same heart.

Bugsy Singh, a brilliant doctor (head of surgery at the local medical school), emphasises the ethos of Cherrians and his own growth as a person through his involvement in local soccer:

> ... we always had good people coming through. Great people. And that spirit of looking after people – not exploiting their talents – but looking at them as people ... I've got guys who played for us as juniors, and now their sons are playing for Cherrians. There are many of them. There is Irwin Sass. His son is now playing. He is gonna be going to the UK to train with Chelsea. He won the Diski competition. This year this other boy Ryan has won it. His father played for us as a junior. When his father was fifteen years old, he played for Cherrians. His father is still part of the structure. Guys who play for us always have an affiliation with us. Because we look after them. That's been my philosophy ... We never saw those people as talents ... I got to know Wentworth ... I got to grow up in that community. Know people through the generations. Take Wellington Meth. I know Wellington Meth's wife and daughters and son-in-law as family ... I grew up with them. My values were refined by them. I became a better human being with them. And I am part of that community. I identify with them because I never see them as ... You know, we've done so much ... Wentworth is a community that I found so much value in. I got so much joy working with that community. I have got so much respect for that community because it is a really brutalised community. Because I didn't see them as good football players. I got to know them as people. They got to know me. Leeds great, Tyrone Bezuidenhout's brother Ralton came to see me this morning after 25/30 years. He sprained his knee. Tyrone sent him. It happens like this all the time. All the time. It is a community that I have come to be very close to. Family. This is what our club has nurtured.

For Wellington, one of the grand men of soccer, the emphasis on paper qualifications for coaching is over-rated:

> You've got to be able to read the game. There are some guys who go for those courses and they are good in training. And you, who

The talent spotter, Wellington Meth.

is a good coach, you haven't got those certificates. They'll say, 'Look at that one and that one and him. That one's a Level 1, Level 2, Level 3 . . .' We've tried them and they've failed. Then I have to come in. I call them moles. They come out of the ground and go back into the same hole that they came out of . . . Just digging there. A rat can come out. When you're a good coach, you're a rat – you can see your way out. Now a mole can't. We had teachers here. Sometimes I would reckon, 'Hey, you're only fucken good for marking papers. That's all man. You can't even fucken think. I must keep on coming here.' Sometimes you get fed up because you can see the simple things and they make the wrong changes. You have to be able to sit and say what we are going to do. Small things.

In a place like Wentworth, you have to be a psychologist:

> We had a youngster now – Andrew. They were not playing him at Cherrians. I found out this youngster is easily influenced. If you don't psych him up during the week and tell him that he's playing on the weekend, he's got that air of being maybe on the

bench, he drinks and does funny things. Then when it comes to the grounds, and they are short, they play him. They reckoned he was drunk. So I used to psych him up. The last seven games he played. Top games. I told him, 'Andrew, you are playing. Don't let me down. I'm putting my head on the block for you.' So he is psyched up the whole time. He won't drink. He won't do nothing. He was happy throughout the whole seven games he played. They were saying that Andrew is not the same player that he was before. And that's because he was not man-managed. You manage the individual. You talk to them. You get them to buy into what you want them to do and they will do it for you.

And coaches must accept that they will be proved wrong:

Sometimes when you are a coach, you can put out something. Once we were playing a team that was second. And they had one good player. I said, 'Andrew, I need you to do a job for me.' He said, 'Uncle Wells, what you want now?' I told him, 'I want you to mark that player wherever he goes. Don't give him a chance. He's the one that's gonna kill us. He's killing all the other teams.' He said, 'Don't worry, Uncle Wells.' So I sat on the bank there. He was leading this player. Giving him a gap. He wasn't staying close. I said, 'Andrew, tight marking. Tight marking.' He gave me the 'hold it' sign – 'I know what I'm gonna do.' He had a top game. This player never scored. I told him, 'You are the first player that beat me. That didn't listen to instructions that I gave them. Had we lost, I would have blamed you had that guy scored.' He reckons, 'Uncle Wells, I had him under cover.' I didn't see this thing that he saw. He's got speed. He said he was letting them give him the ball. 'When they put it in the air, I run and I head it away. If they give him the ball, I run and intercept that. He wasn't getting the ball because I know I'm quicker than him. So he waits for the ball to do things.' I said, 'You know what, Andrew? You fucken got me. I thought I knew everything.' And I admired him. That player didn't move. He paid me back for man-managing him. For making sure he doesn't get taken off. That they don't make him a reserve.

It is Wellington's eye for spotting talent that is his main attribute. As the legendary Blondie Campbell reputedly put it: 'If you want a player, go to Wellington and he'll find that player.'

Today he dedicates his time to Cherrians: not only the soccer side but the off-field work: helping youngsters secure jobs and organising hampers for the aged.

In the early 1970s, the ageing Young Cavaliers got a fillip with the energy of Christopher Francis Anderson, who was born on 20 January 1957. He spent on a lot of his time and money on soccer in Wentworth, attending meetings and doing paperwork from the mid-1970s. One of Anderson's central reasons for getting involved in soccer was ironically a physical affliction:

> I was born with a heart with a hole in it almost the size of a R5 coin. I couldn't even walk. When I went to school, every 100 metres, I had to sit down. But, at the age of ten, I had an operation here in Wentworth Hospital and it had never been achieved before. It was the first of its kind. They tried to fatten me up while they were trying to perfect things. There were a whole lot of other operation attempts. They had a whole lot of animals there – mostly sheep – and try it out on them and then try it out on this patient, and don't make it. Those type of learning curves. And when they got to me . . . Yoh! My mother was strong. She prayed everyday – and she has got a lot of children (thirteen), so she made the whole lot of them pray.

Anderson's family moved to Wentworth from Greenwood Park in 1970. He soon earned a reputation as a hard tackler on the dusty streets of Wentworth.

> In Wentworth we stayed across the road from the police station. That road was just ash before they put tar. We used that road as a soccer pitch. Every day we make our rules . . . I made sure nobody dribbles past me. After every game the guys came and showed me all their lumps. They said I kicked them. I was playing soccer and nobody was going to get past me.

Anderson avoided the gangsters and spent his time building the structures of the Young Cavaliers:

> We started an under-18 side. We weren't so much governed by our management. We got another management team in, but we used their name and held functions together. As we went along, we built up a stronger and a stronger team. We had many talented players. Rodney Charles. He is in Swaziland now. He made it to professional. He played for Kaizer Chiefs. Brian 'Pondo' Robinson is still running Wentworth soccer administration. He played for Leeds for quite some time. There were a lot of stronger players like Eddie Daniels. He just died last year.

There was internal bickering and Anderson moved on:

> I built a side called Barcelona at the age of nineteen. And we ran for two or three years. You form a side and you start in the D league. Then you go to the C league. Before you can jump up – I was just about to jump up to the B league – and I had to go work in Swaziland. Because I ran a lot of the administration of Barcelona – going to meetings, walking from Wentworth, Assegai, all the way to Merebank, and find out where is this meeting place and who we are playing next, who are the refs . . . So when I left in 1979, I went for three years and by the end of six months, they sold the franchise to a team in the Barracks [Rainbow Chicken].

Young Cavaliers, though, refused to die and into the present is one of the pre-eminent teams of Wentworth.

Young Cavaliers

> Generations of people are like leaves. The wind casts leaves to the ground, but the fertile forest brings forth others, and spring comes round again.
> — Homer, *The Iliad*

Lorna Richardson (Petersen), sister of Dennis Petersen, is owner of Young Cavaliers and former chairperson of the Leeds Supporters' Club. She is one of the most dedicated soccer supporters in Wentworth. Born on 24 April 1954 in Overport, Lorna moved to Wentworth at the age of fifteen:

> I went to Melbourne Road School and to Sydenham for primary. I also went to Umbilo Road school and then to Bechet. From Bechet, I quit school in Standard 7. I never went to school in Wentworth. My mother couldn't cope anymore. She was falling apart. I went to work when I wasn't even menstruating yet and didn't wear a bra. This was before I even turned fifteen. It was the beginning of the year. I started working just after fourteen.

Lorna's father had deserted her mother, leaving her with six children.

> She was a clothing and factory worker and rent was difficult to pay. Because we were renting, she applied to the department for a house, and she got a house in Wentworth. What was my father thinking? She's got six children and she's a factory worker. My father was a big player. He was a drinker, but not an alcoholic; a gambler, but not serious. And, I think the relationship just broke down along the way. The strains of raising six children and he was a very spoilt, hard person. But she was practically raising us – I'm talking about the physical part – on her own. My father, he just sat and read the paper. My mother had to do everything. It forced me to grow up before my time. Of the girls, I am the oldest – that is why I had to assume such responsibility at a young age. At age twelve, I played the leading role in the family, while my mother was the man. My father actually went to jail for non-support [maintenance] and still didn't pay. My mother eventually gave up.

The family's first abode in Wentworth was

> ... at Number 44 Drake Road, here in Austerville – just mum and six kids. My mother was a seamstress and also a shop steward in the trade union. It was different living in Wentworth because it was a communal type of living. We had to share bathrooms, toilets and the scullery. You never had a kitchen in the house.

You had a scullery, and attached to the scullery was the bathroom and the toilet. A certain number of people living in the house, sharing the house. That's how it was initially. And it was a good couple of houses. You'd only get hot water at four o'clock in the afternoon. The caretaker would burn whatever and switch on the steam room to give us hot water. Once it's finished, that's it. Your dishes, every night, you take them to the scullery, you wash up there. You just go and do your thing. It was two bedrooms and a lounge, which we kind of used as a kitchen to cook in.

Lorna's first job was at a company called Sondor.

It dealt with extractors, rubber and foam. This was off Berea Road in Turner Avenue. While I was working, the younger kids were still schooling. I earned R5 a week. A joke. That was my starting salary. That's why I left that job because my granny got me a job with her at Van Dyck Carpets. I will never forget the two salaries – the carpet factory and that one. I knew nothing, so I went in there as an assistant to everybody. At Van Dyck Carpets, I earned R8.75 a week. All of my salary I gave to my mom, and I kept the change. The change was 68 cents because they took off 7 cents deduction for UIF. That I remember so well. I worked there for many years. In total, it must have been about eleven years. Then I went off on maternity leave.

Lorna met her first husband, Morris Richards, at the soccer fields.

He was also from Austerville and supporting All Blacks soccer team. I was also supporting All Blacks. He sent a message saying that he'd like to talk to me. He sent a message to me via somebody – and I had my eye on *him* at the same time. But, you know girls never said a word – no matter how we felt. We kept it to ourselves. And then he came over in the evening. We had a chat and it developed from there. We courted from 1969 and then we got married in 1974. We got divorced in 1978. It was a two-year marriage; two years apart. I think it was because I saw what happened to my mother, and he was very much like my father in that sense of the child is my responsibility and he wasn't a hands-on father. Everything had to be done for him – up to putting toothpaste on his toothbrush in the morning. For me, I saw myself going down the same road. And, of course, he was a womaniser as well. And very good-looking. We only had one son together – the one that's late; the one that what was murdered – Clint. He died on 11 August 2007. Nadine is from my second husband.

While Morris was extremely hard-working and brought all his money into the home, Lorna wanted more than that:

> That's not good enough. I need a husband. And divorce in the seventies! Wow. My one auntie didn't talk to me for one and a half years. I was a disgrace to the family. She loved me to bits. I was her pet from small. But, she just turned away from me. And she was very, very Catholic. We are staunch Catholics. We can't do that. I said, 'Am I gonna wait until I have six children like mother?' I knew I deserved better. I was very stable. I was hard-working. I was committed in the relationship. I was full of good qualities. Why do I need to put up with someone who's not meeting me halfway? Thank God then I had the sense to see. We had Clint in 1975. I filed for divorce in '76. My mother too wasn't happy with it, but she didn't cast me aside. But they kept their distance from me. All my mother kept on saying was, 'Oh, but he's a good provider. Oh, but he's a good provider.' Good provider? That's not good enough. In those days, if you were a good provider, you were a good husband. I knew what I wanted. I just got my lawyer, got my appointments with him, got my dates, we went to court. Morris didn't show up, so it was uncontested. He didn't even show up.

Lorna went back to work at Van Dyck Carpets.

> Being a single mother, it was very, very difficult; very challenging, but we got through. We never ever had situations where we had rent not paid, lights cut and no food on the table. We had food on the table; just the basic necessities. I coped. I worked a lot of overtime to cope. I worked seven days a week at times.

Lorna (fourth from left) in the local hockey team, c.1982/83.

Sport gave Lorna a momentary outlet, whether it was soccer or hockey. Feelings that women were warned by elders to keep bottled up could be screamed out loud from the stands, usually at the opposing team. Lorna's family was always involved in sport:

> We are a very sporting family. My uncle, Basil Petersen, was a professional soccer player. He played for Berea – among other teams. My uncle Cyril also played soccer for Celtic. My other late uncle Jeffery also played soccer, for Leeds and All Blacks. My mother was a hockey player. My mother's sister who ostracised me was also a hockey player. My grandfather played soccer. So we are born into a sports family. Jeffery and Cyril played for All Blacks at the same time. These are all my mom's brothers – the Petersens. My mother was serious about her hockey. She was an athlete and a hockey player. From school I played hockey. I played for Umbilo. I played for Sydenham and Melbourne. I played for all my school teams. And Bechet.

In 1981, Lorna met Cedric Richardson.

He was playing for a male hockey team. My brother, Dean, played for the team as well. We met on the grounds – Ogle Road grounds – at training, because we used to all train together.

They had a daughter, Nadine, born in 1982.

Cedric and I got married in 1988. Nadine was about six or seven years old when we got married. The reason for that is because I wanted to live with him – even though my family were against it – but I wanted to be certain that, in time, I can live with this person. So, he wanted to get married, and I kept on saying, 'Stop asking me' – and one day, I'll get up and I'll say, 'Okay, I'm ready.' That's why we had such a long relationship – met in '81 and married in '89. Then I knew it was time. And then we got married. We just went to court. We were living in Joburg at the time.

Lorna came back to Durban. Cedric stayed in Johannesburg:

Oh! And then . . . He meets somebody . . . There. And he has a daughter. This was in early '86. Nadine is three years old at this time. Okay, he came down. He spoke about it. He accepted full responsibility. He apologised for his mistake and said it was loneliness that drove him, more than anything else. He doesn't want to be with this person. Blah, blah, blah . . . I didn't want to hear nothing – at first. But, I made a call – a very important call – to London. I spoke to my uncle there and I told him about my situation. He was my confidante. He was my everything. He was like my father. And then he told me . . . He said, 'Look. If this happened with Cedric when he was an apprentice . . . Now, he's out of his time and he's making decent money. He is a good man. I know him personally. He's made a mistake. Can you find it in your heart to forgive him? Because you may call it off, and have regrets. However, if you forgive him, and come together again, the one thing you must not do is throw it in his face. You have to accept the child and accept the responsibility that comes with it. Think it through. I think I'm giving you the right advice.'

Lorna was hurting badly, but she took his advice.

> Cedric kept calling back, I eventually took his calls. And then he said, 'Well, move to Joburg. It's the only way we can stop this kind of thing from ruining us.' I actually looked after the child, after a while. Her mother went to work. Initially, there was tension and problems. But, we ended up playing in the same hockey team in Joburg. She was in the team already. The girls from Durban who knew me, asked me to come and play, and I said, 'I can't because of her.' And they said, 'Don't give up without trying because she's a really nice person. It's just that this thing happened. It doesn't make her a bad person.' So I tried. And it worked. And her and I ended up running the team together. Aztec Hockey Club. It was a team made up of Durbanites based in Joburg. Everybody thought I was mad. The child called me 'mum'. The child died. She had a brain tumour at the age of fourteen. It was terrible, devastating for everyone.

Lorna has been a lifelong Leeds supporter. She has invested thousands of hours and kilojoules in the club:

> It wasn't just an obsession for Leeds. For hockey, I gave it all. For soccer, I gave it all – which we are still doing to this present day. I enjoy the game. I love winning. But, I can take a beating. I bused the people to Curries Fountain. I was chairlady of the Supporters' Club. Initially, my mother was voted as chairlady of the Supporters' Club. But, along the way – I can't remember the reason she fizzled out – and then I was voted in.

A lot of time was spent fund-raising, which involved

> ... hosting events. We organised cheese and wine parties. We did picnics at Easter and New Year; ran buses to make a little bit of money. We ran buses for family picnics. I remember us having a cheese and wine party at the Silver Tree community hall. I hired the buses and saw to everything. The love. The unity. The pride. It was the first time Wentworth brought out a team of that

calibre. Apart from running your family and going to work, it was the next thing that you lived for. Doing things for Leeds, and being there to support them, and getting everybody to support them on a Sunday. We used to make things like cushions. We would get cushions, get the covering, get the foam cut, and have 'Leeds' printed on them. Green Leeds cushions with the felt.

If Lorna is known for her ownership of Young Cavaliers, she is more famous for her catering company called Lornay's:

My cooking started because of having to grow up so early at the age of twelve when my father left. I had to assume that responsibility. I did all the family cooking. My mother had to work seven days a week. I had to supplement the family income. So I became a relatively good cook. And, I just got better with the years. And that is where my cooking started because people would ask me to cook for their baby showers and their kitchen teas and for their little home lunches. I think that's where my cooking became known. This was from the seventies.

In Joburg I supervised OK's canteen for a while. And, I left there to open a takeaway with one of my managers who was white. Boer [Afrikaner]. We had a takeaway in the main street in Hillbrow. I gave up that business because he was so terrible towards the employees. Towards black people. He would frisk the women. And make them open their legs to see that they've got nothing tucked in-between. I split with him. This was in the eighties – '88 or '89 or thereabouts.

Returning to Wentworth, Lorna was approached by a local business person, Martin James:

King Goodwill Zwelithini's son, the Prince, and a whole lot of other dignitaries, were coming to the ICC [International Convention Centre]. And lunch had to be provided for them for three days . . . And I said, 'I don't have a plate. I don't have a spoon. I don't have a thing. How do I go in and just do this thing?'

> Many people then helped me, including a big businessman, Fred Petersen ... I went to Edna Burgess who was the known local caterer, but who was kind of not doing it anymore. I told her my dilemma. She gave me some sound advice and she hired me some stuff, and lent me some stuff. And Martin James provided me with transport for the three days. The rest is history.

Lorna's daughter Nadine, who qualified as a chef, joined the business:

> When she made her decision to come into the business, she said, 'I'm not gonna be a fly-by-night like you, I'm going to study this thing. So, I will work with you in this year.' And that's where the name was born. We're thinking of a name now. Now we need to register. Now we're serious. Because she's going to become a chef. I thought about the name. 'Lorna.' It's got my full name. And the 'Nay' is what Nadine is called. We call her 'Nay.' So then 'Lornay' – the business name.

Nadine's husband Kerwin Kast, who studied hospitality, also became part of the business.

Lorna has had much to grieve about over the years and the wounds are still raw. Her darling brother Skiddo Joseph shot and killed himself ...

> He was terminally ill with emphysema. But he also felt let down by the ANC, of which he was a loyalist. He wasn't dealing well with that, and he wasn't working. What happened on that day, we don't know. We last saw him the day before. He was fine. He was always running to me for food – catering – to see what I got left over from the functions. That for us was devastating. He had a legal brain. He was brilliant. If anybody in our family had problems dealing with government departments, Skiddo would just take charge. For us, as well as being just a loving brother, it was such a great loss.

The other overwhelming tragedy in Lorna's life was the murder of her son, Clint Richardson:

Clint was born on 6 February 1975. Our take as a family is that he was becoming a handful for the police. He hated the police. Let me recount one incident, prior to the shooting. He was watching a soccer game at Pool City. And the guys from the Barracks were attacking this one guy he knew, Hornby. In the incident, they took his eye out and they stabbed him mercilessly. And, Clint – with his three or four friends that were there with him – were trying to stop these guys attacking. A policeman, who was selling drugs in the Barracks, was on the side of Barracks guys, and was saying to Clint and them, 'If y'll get involved, I'll shoot.' So, Clint and them took this guy up to hospital to get him attended to. The policeman followed them because this guy that got stabbed, I think also stabbed one of their guys. Again, this policeman was issuing this threat about shooting Clint and them. So, the guy that lost his eye asked Clint to give a statement. When the incident happened, Clint came home that morning and shook me up and said, 'Ma, this is what happened.' I calmed him down. He went to sleep and went to work the next day. What I didn't know – is that Clint had gone and given a statement at Brighton Beach police station . . .

In the weeks leading up to Clint's shooting, she was uneasy:

We were at a sixteenth birthday party. Then Clint said it is ten o'clock, he's going home to sleep. He was seeing a girl in Burgess Road. So he didn't come straight home to sleep. He went past there. This is like fifteen to twenty minutes after he left us. We get a call to say he's shot. His girlfriend's family called us. He was sitting on the steps and she was sitting between his legs. And this guy walked up past him, walked down the corridor, and within a minute or two came back, and asked Clint, 'Is that your Golf 4 parked outside?' That is how this guy was able to identify Clint as the owner of the car . . . he shot him. He just wanted to confirm that that was Clint, the owner of the car – the Golf 4. Then this guy got in his car and sped away. Clint died on 11 August 2007. It had all the hallmarks of a hit.

Lorna took up the case with the zealousness of a broken mother:

> We didn't know who he was; neither did the girl know who he was. Never seen him before. A month later, there was no response from the cops. That's how we suspected the cops were involved. I became a pain to the police – the CIDs. I was almost there on a daily basis. I've lost my son. I'm going mad. I want something. They're not doing anything about it. So anyway, the girl that Clint was seeing at the time he dies, this girl goes to the grounds to watch a soccer match with her friend. At the grounds, she just freezes. There she sees this guy. And the shock. He realised that she recognised him. He got in his car and he was gone. But, she was smart. She took down his car registration number.

The suspect stood trial but was eventually acquitted:

> The first week after we buried Clint, I couldn't get out of my room. My house. I just felt like I could stay there, sleep forever, not wake up, not carry on living . . . I had stopped smoking for nine years and I went back to smoking after that. And then, I spoke to myself. I said, 'I've still got Nadine. I need to run the business. I've got to get up. I've got my husband. I've got other family. I've got to fight.' I made up my mind the Monday after that. I said to myself, 'As soon as I walk in here, whether I'm doing nothing – just walking around and fiddling – but, I just gotta get back.' And that's how I pulled myself up to carry on going. I went to the cemetery quite a lot. Initially, I was just sitting on the next grave, because he didn't have a tombstone at that time. And I just talked. They all just sat in the car while I sat there talking to Clint. Just crying. And then I would come home. It probably helped – as well as getting back to work, slowly.

Lorna not only turned her energies into her business but also into arguably Wentworth's most successful soccer club of recent times.

Lorna Richardson's passion is Young Cavaliers, an old Wentworth club, which, while never reaching the same heights as Leeds or Cherrians, nurtured a number of young players in the early 1970s. They now play in the South African Breweries (SAB) League, three leagues off from the Premier League.

The whole family is involved:

> In 2012, we just got on board as supporters of Young Cavaliers. We only had supporter status. In 2013, we started seeing where to help – and Nadine and Kerwin, being so passionate about the team, got to know the boys well; loving the boys, loving the team. For us, Cavaliers is not just about the soccer. Yes, we're passionate about soccer. But, it's also about the upliftment of these young boys with so much potential, who are from dysfunctional homes, families – a lot of them. Poverty – a lot of them. And just giving them love. We help them in their personal lives as well. We try to find jobs for them. We help some of them to get their driver's licences. One of them, we got him a job as a sheriff's assistant. Things like that. In little ways. We are not wealthy, but wherever we can, we try to improve their lives. We help a few players in their homes. I pay rent for the two Ghanaian players every month. I've been doing so for over a year. And I give them a little stipend every month. We look after their daily needs. And the Ghanaians, we see to their food completely – their groceries, their meat and their vegetables.

Many a young footballer desires to play for Young Cavaliers:

> Because of the way we run the team and the love we have for the boys, they are our marketing. The way the boys are happy, people are drawn to us – even from outside of Wentworth. We've got players from Bonela, Newlands, Sydenham, Umlazi . . . Without boasting, Young Cavaliers is the best team in Wentworth. I love the game and I love the boys.

In the years that the team started rising up the ranks, they were helped by an experienced coach, Falcon Rose, who has since moved on. The celebrated Delron Buckley, now 42 years old, replaced him in 2019. Buckley himself is a remarkable story of growing up in Sydenham near

Young Cavaliers, 2019.

Ettie Abrahams's Sparks Estate and rising to play at the highest level in Germany, while earning 76 national caps for Bafana Bafana (Subrayan 2017).

For Lorna, like so many people in Wentworth, soccer is inextricably connected to loss. The kind of loss so severe that it either crushes you, or when you stand up again in its aftermath, you find yourself seeking out opportunities to lessen the loads that other people carry. The loss of Clint is difficult to bear but she has not allowed it to wear her down. It's a story of her life.

Leeds is now part of history. They were of a time and a place. But what of the post-1994 generation? The children of those who played the game?

Ashley Singh makes his mark

> Your children are not your children. They are sons and daughters of life's longing for itself.
>
> — Sousanis, *Unflattening*

Ashley Mark Singh is 22 years old, born on 13 November 1993. The year 2016 was a milestone year for him:

> We won the league for the 2015/16 season. We won the Easter tournament. I started a new job this year. I'm working for the sheriff of Chatsworth. So, 2015/2016 has been a big part of my life because we won the league for Young Cavaliers and we won the Easter tournament – and I scored in the finals for the Easter tournament. I play striker. Like my dad. My life has changed. I moved in life. I succeeded. I progressed in life in 2015/16.

Ashley is known for his shyness:

> Growing up for me, I was a very quiet boy. I was shy. I'm still shy, but not shy like that – like how I was before – because of Aunty Lorna. I think I was just born shy. I used to just stay inside. I never used to go out. The only time I used to go outside was for school and soccer training. I wish I had known my mother. I was only one or two years old when she died. I think she was maybe like me. Quiet. People say I take after her. A lot of people say I've got her laugh. Only after my matric in 2013 – that's when I used to come outside.

Lorna Richardson has been central to Ashley's life:

> She's done a lot for me. It's not only about soccer. She looks after our lives. Because of her I got my driver's licence. Without her, I would have never have got my licence. She helped me push towards getting a job. And now, I'm happy.

Ashley is aware that he comes from Leeds 'stock' but is slightly ambivalent about the impact on his career:

> A lot of people talk about my father [Elvis Singh], that he was a good soccer player. A striker. But, I've never seen that. A lot of people tell me, but I wish I could see back in the days because a lot of people say he was one of the best strikers in Wentworth, so I have to believe that. But, I don't believe that. I've never seen that. If there was video footage, well then . . . But, there's nothing. He kept some newspaper articles for me to read. I wish I could see

it for myself so I can judge on my own. Leeds was a big team, I heard, back in the days, and they made it pro. There are a few big players that came out of there. My father, Dennis Petersen, Greg Baptist, Cheesa Baptist and my uncle Jerry 'Rat'. That's who I know from Leeds.

Ashley, though, is more effusive about the influence of his aunt Arlene: 'Arlene had a big impact on my soccer career. She played professional. And people heard about my family. Now the pressure comes towards me.'

Despite the ongoing disappointment of the play-offs, Ashley is confident about the team:

> Young Cavaliers is going to progress a lot. We've got a good side. Two times we went to play-offs and we missed it. I think the third time we will get promoted. I plan to stay with Cavies . . . I really enjoy playing for Young Cavaliers. The team has got good vibes. We gel together. Every time after the game, we have team building. We have food together. We eat. We joke. I really enjoy it over here. It's a family. Everybody loves it here. All the players. It feels like the family I never had.

Ashley made a home at Lorna's:

> When I started working here at Lornay's Catering, she used to tell me that at weekends we start early in the morning, like at 5 am. She used to tell me to sleep here for the night. And every week I used to do that. Then, I just started like living. It's like I feel comfortable living here. There's love in this house. For me, in Ogle Road, where I used to stay, I used to just sleep and watch TV. There was no love there. I really suffered a lot in my life. Sometimes our lights used to get cut for about four or five months. No water. Then they would come back again. Switch off again. And there's no food. Sometimes I had to go to school with creased clothes because I've got no electricity to iron them.

Besides the job and the soccer, Ashley is in a relationship: 'Her name is Kiara James. We've been dating for three months. This is serious. This is the girl that I'm going to marry.'

Rumpshakers to Barcelona

> You are the bows from which your children as living arrows are set forth.
>
> — Gibran, *The Prophet*

In Wentworth, the Schreibers are a well-known football-playing family. Brothers Edgar, Vernon, Albert and Ian all played for the top teams in Wentworth. And there is a new Schreiber coming through. Edgar's daughter Adrienne is on the fringes of the national women's team and plays for the local team Barcelona. Born in 1992, she is a child of democracy and the new structures of soccer that come with it. Whereas people like her father had to negotiate their footballing lives outside state support, somebody like Adrienne has benefited from the new soccer set-up, travelling to high-performance centres and playing for her country.

Adrienne started playing the game early:

> I've lived in Wentworth all my life. One day, I think I was five years old, I started kicking a ball around. From watching my family play soccer . . . I had always watched the family soccer on the grounds – Ogle Road, Bayview – wherever they played. There was a team called Wiestham from here in Wiest Road and I said I wanted to join them when I was five years old. I just said to my father one day, 'Daddy, I want to play soccer.'

Edgar, a lover of the game, took up his daughter's plaintive plea:

> He said, 'On Tuesday I will take you down to the grounds.' The training sessions were on Tuesdays and Thursdays. That Tuesday, we went to Ogle Road grounds and we spoke to the coach at that time. That was Uncle Collin. My father said to him, 'Ay, she wants to join.' The coach asked me if I was sure and that, if I was sure, it was fine – I can join. Then I started with the under 7s. I was the only girl on the team. So, I started with them. Then, on the Thursday, I was told to come with particulars – my birth certificate, photos, and my parents had to sign a form. At first they were sceptical because I was a girl and I was only five years old. The coach said to my father, 'Can she play?' and my father

said, 'Look, I wouldn't waste my time bringing her if I did not think she was good enough.'

Edgar left Adrienne to train with his own team. When he came back, the coach told him that he was impressed:

> My father left me alone on the grounds when I was five year old, but it was okay. My cousins were playing with me. Also, because I was a tomboy, a lot of my male friends were also playing in the same team. That was also why I wanted to play. I was always hearing them tell me all the time, 'Ah, training was so nice.' Things like that. And then in primary school, when I was like that age, there wasn't soccer for me to play. Uncle Collin was the coach of this Wiestham team. I played with him up until under 13, because I was told I could only play with him until under 13. From there, I had to join a female team because it started getting rough at that age. So, from the age of five, I carried on playing with the boys up until the age of twelve. I was still the only girl on the team. I used to go to tournaments all over and play for Wiestham. At the age of twelve, I joined a ladies club called Bayview. Even there, I also had a problem. They said I was too small – I didn't own an ID book yet – and that I was too small to play senior ball. They said I was too young on the whole.
> But then, when I played, they made a plan. They made a plan for me to play with my birth certificate . . . from twelve to sixteen, I played with Bayview.

However, Bayview started to break up:

> Everybody had other important things to do. Plus, the ladies felt they were getting too old, so they stopped playing. I was much younger compared to the others, because now the ladies I was playing with were almost 40 years old. So that's why I was too small to start playing with them – because they were so much older. And then, that's when the manager spotted me. Brendon Brown. He was the manager of Rumpshakers at that time. And he asked me to play for them. And then in January 2009, I joined Rumpshakers from Newlands. I was fifteen.

The team had a successful run in 2009. In one tournament, they came up against Barcelona in the finals. The Barcelona coach, Lewis Donnelly, was impressed and approached her to join. Barcelona is a Wentworth-based club. She joined. From then on, it was a roller-coaster ride. Through the schools networks, she was selected to represent KwaZulu-Natal Province. More was to follow. She was selected for South Africa's under-17 squad, Amaglug-glug.

> I came back home. I told them the news. Everybody was excited. By this time, Mrs Anderson, my teacher, did not know that I had been selected. So, on the Monday before assembly, I said to her, 'Hey, Miss. I've been selected to play for the country.' She was excited and just before assembly could start, she wrote something on a piece of paper and she called the principal. And then he called me up in assembly in front of the school. The whole school. He said that this is the kind of person to look up to.

In-between, injury struck and home life deteriorated.

Adrienne speaks of a troubled relationship with her mom, of arguments, late-night parties and alcohol abuse in the home. Her bond with her mother is not strong. She decided to stay with her father at the age of seven. For a brief period as a nineteen-year-old, she went back to her mother but it was not a success. All of this prompted her to move back in with her dad and granny.

* * *

Ashley and Adrienne are the new generation of soccer talent. But, it is not only soccer skills that are handed down. In Wentworth, new generations also get sucked into old feuds and wounds that refuse to heal.

7

The Field of Relations

> Places are fragmentary and inward-turning histories, pasts that others are not allowed to read, accumulated times that can be unfolded but like stories held in reserve, remaining in an enigmatic state . . .
>
> — De Certeau, *The Practice of Everyday Life*

For a time, I kept my focus on tracking down soccer stalwarts. In this kind of research, the pace can be slow and then suddenly quickens as word gets around. It was in that period of acceleration, when photographs were rescued and supporters and players of Leeds and other clubs like Cherrians provided new sources of information, that my gaze happened on a front-page newspaper story:

> A packed church was petrol-bombed, a man shot dead and a 71-year-old hit in the arm by a stray bullet as gang war gripped Wentworth. Religious leaders and residents believe the violence, over a 48-hour period, was sparked by the murder of a former gangster outside a Florida Road nightclub two weeks ago (*Daily News*, 31 May 2016).

It is one thing to wax lyrical about the power of soccer to create opportunities for young people. But what about those young men with hoods pulled low, hanging on the corners of flats and streets. I had developed enough presence in the area to feel encouraged to try to understand what was driving this latest spurt of violence.

The bare outlines were easy enough to trace. The man shot dead in Florida Road in central Durban was 32-year-old Kyle Morrow. Morrow was allegedly a member of the Destroyer gang, or one section of it. He became embroiled in conflict with the Young Destroyers. The irony is that Morrow was killed by an off-duty policeman who instinctively reacted to the shootings in a nightclub as rival groupings squared up.

The killing was swiftly followed later that night with the drive-by shooting of a house in Wentworth belonging to people allied to Morrow (*Daily News*, 31 May 2016). And then on 28 May 2016, Kyle Sewell, 25, who was at the Florida Road shooting, was killed. He was allegedly part of the Destroyer gang opposed to Morrow's part of the gang. On 4 June 2016, Sewell's funeral was held amidst strong police presence. For good reason. At Morrow's funeral on Friday 21 May, a man was arrested for spitting on his coffin.

With a bit of digging, it emerged that the conflict had a longer history. As the story goes, one of the leading members of the Destroyer gang at the beginning of the new millennium was Michael 'Bumpers' Edwards. He was shot in the back of the head on 17 July 2005. He was 39 years old. The assassins, it is alleged, were also from the Destroyers, who at the time were known as Naughty Youngsters. The killing led to a split. The alleged assassins got bigger and more powerful. Only a rump was left of those loyal to Edwards's memory. But then a new generation of (Young) Destroyers arose, grouped around Edwards's son, Llewellyn 'Doogoo' Edwards.

While full of bravado, the killing of Kyle Sewell clearly rattled the Young Destroyers: 'Our friend got shot 23 times like a dog.'

One of them, George,[6] tells me that tensions were so bad that a lot of people refused to come to his wedding:

> The other Destroyers knew where the wedding was going to be. They knew everything. People in my wedding party were scared for their lives. They want us dead because they want this area.

Despite this, for George and his crew, knowledge of place is vital for survival, even if that means the constant threat of death:

> You see how it's going here in Wentworth? We stay here by the oil refinery. We're surrounded by factories. We've got Island View,

---

6. A pseudonym.

Treasure Beach, Engen, Mondi, Sappi and Jacobs at the bottom. This is our life. We live here. We work here. When job finish here, we jump back. We know who's sniffing. The foreman is sniffing. So, when we are on the job, we are connected. But, we don't know outside there – because we are not connected there.

For one of George's crew, the way of life in Wentworth has been honed through the generations and has become almost genetic:

It's evolution that makes them that way. It's like if you put people in a cave and you make them walk around hunched in the cave, and they have children in the cave and live in that cave. Over a period of 50 or 100 years – a 150 years the most – over that cycle, those children's children's children's children's children will never stand up straight when you bring them out of that cave. Your body ends ups adapting to that cave of bending like that. Your genes will end up like that. So, our children, way down the bloodline, will have adapted to their surroundings and end up just that – like their fathers and mothers. Even if you take them in the open, they'll still have it in their blood to be like that. No matter where you go, you can just tell, 'This one's from Wentworth.'

Listening to George, one is reminded of Pierre Bourdieu's concept of habitus, which allows us to explore why individuals act in a certain way and the strategies they use to manage everyday life. Bourdieu's long-time collaborator, Loïc Wacquant, defined habitus as

. . . the system of durable and transposable dispositions through which we perceive, judge and act in the world . . . acquired through lasting exposure to particular social conditions and conditioning via internalising of external constraints and possibilities (Wacquant 1998: 220–1).

As I talk to these young men I think about a photograph of Tony Bowes, who was shot twice in the head at the beginning of December 1982. It's juxtaposed to a photograph of him as a child.

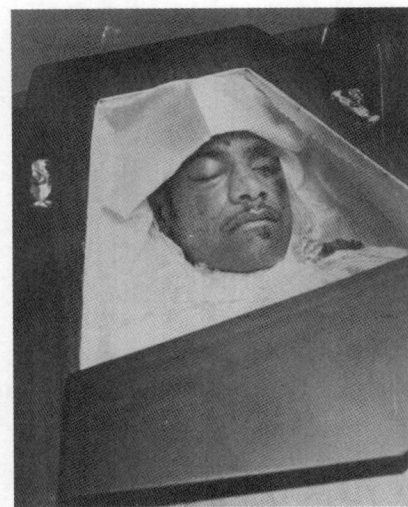

Tony Bowes, shot twice in the head, 1982.

Bowes immediately after he was confirmed. His parents thought he could escape the gangs by sending him to a private school.

Some of the young men I talk to in 2016 will die in the next few months. There are no jobs here, drugs consume bodies and lives. Dignity and respect come from defending a narrow piece of turf and settling the scores of one's fathers.

This posturing, hardness is

> undoubtedly just one of the ways of making a virtue out of necessity . . . the obligation to be tough with oneself and others . . . are ways of resigning oneself to a world with no way out, dominated by poverty and the law of the jungle, discrimination and violence, where morality and sensitivity bring no benefit whatsoever (Bourdieu 1991: 96).

In listening to the young men who hug the bottom of stairways of the flatlands one is reminded of Walter Benjamin's destructive character who is perpetually standing

> . . . at the crossroads. No moment can know what the next will bring. What exists he reduces to rubble – not for the sake of rubble, but for that of the way leading through it. The destructive character lives from the feeling not that life is worth living, but that suicide is not worth the trouble (1978: 303).

For Benjamin, the destructive character is a positive force, someone related to the epic hero. The destructive character clears away and destroys current and inherited commonplaces, making them open to the new. He simplifies social and architectural space by deciding what deserves destruction. It seems that in Wentworth, this decision has come to settle on him, himself. What comes next is of no import, there will always be uses for a street corner or a tavern, maybe better uses like a crèche or soccer club, but he does not burden himself with building. He is incapable of that. His sole gift is knowing what needs to be destroyed. A certain kind of street-level gangsterism is passé. It's old, embarrassing and spent. It must go. And to do that properly, the Destroyers have to be swift, strong and ruthless. It is not suicide in which rival factions of Destroyers are engaged. It is something far more profound: it is erasure.

On Kyle Sewell's arm was tattooed, 'I'd rather live like a man than die like a coward.' The reality is actually an inversion: 'I'd rather die like a man than live like a coward' (Desai 2016).

At the end of 2017, Llewellyn 'Doogoo' Edwards was shot dead. The gang members that promise to talk clam up.

I walk on.

A place to call my own

> Because of their precarious existence at the margins of urban life, the urban poor are forced into a constant struggle to be less excluded. Exclusionary practices are effective precisely because they operate partially and differentially for different categories of the urban poor, thereby turning the struggles of displaced persons into a competition to be less excluded than someone else.
>
> — Murray, *Taming the Disorderly City*

Walking Wentworth's streets, talking, one gets a sense of the impact of changing social relations. The occupations that were once the niche markets of the Coloureds – sheet metal, boilermaker, welder, fitter and turner – were opened up to African labour. Many of the trade schools that produced these workers have closed shop. Where these trade schools exist, they are no longer the sole preserve of the Coloured and Indian working and lower-middle classes.

As Coloureds compete with Africans in these former niche areas, so the lack of opportunities are exacerbated. All over Wentworth, Coloured youth hang around the bottom of stairs that lead to cramped apartments. Coloured women, too, who once worked in the clothing and textile factories in nearby Clairwood have seen jobs disappear as South Africa has opened its doors to Chinese imports. Niche racial labour markets, such as retail outlets that were the preserve of Coloured women, now have to compete with African labour. The reality for many is that the only way to survive is on social welfare, pensions and state grants. Census data reveals that a third of Wentworth's population (15–65) is unemployed, and monthly individual incomes range from R1 600–R3 200; 'Austerville (a neighbourhood in Wentworth) has a substantially large population of individuals with no income' (Chari 2006: 439).

The issue of housing simmers and boils. No substantial housing developments have taken place in Wentworth since the early 1960s, and in many two-bedroom flats in the area four generations are forced to share space. A document by the Coloured People's Development Project in 2012 points to the fact that:

> MSGW [MSGW stands for the 'Coloured' areas of Marian Ridge, Sydenham, Greenwood Park and Wentworth] are communities . . . their families have grown and expanded over the years. There has been no housing allocated to accommodate these growing families. This has led to overcrowding with its many pitfalls. Besides low-cost housing that needs to be provided, there is a growing number of young people and families that want to purchase their own homes. As there is no development for this group of people, they are forced to buy old homes at exorbitant prices and then still take out further loans to make those homes habitable. This is very difficult for this group and they are forced to rent outbuildings at high prices, which will be the equivalent of a normal home loan without the renovations, or at the very worse live with parents and that sort of living has its own significant effect on family life (Coloured People's Development Project 2012).

When a series of confrontations did occur over housing in early 2016, the irony was that it came in the context of a government service delivery project. Some R140-million was allocated to refurbish 1 148 dilapidated and crumbling flats in Wentworth. In addition, eighteen new flats would be built and twelve decanting (holding) units to house people while the flats were being upgraded. Instead of galvanising the community, however, the project lead to divisions and tensions over how exactly government money should be spent.

On 18 February 2016, gunshots rang out in Alabama Road. This was not the usual drive-by shooting or gang members letting off steam. The spark for the conflict was the upgrading of flats. After a period of many years, during which there had been neither improvements to housing in the area by government, nor any commitments for future construction,

Conflict over the upgrades.

government finally agreed to a programme that would involve local labour and be overseen by a local committee.

Just as the programme was taking off, locals turned themselves into 'battering rams', as one bystander put it, and invaded the flats and decanting units. Armed security and police pushed them out and the upgrading ground to a halt.

The second assault on the flats took place on the weekend of Friday 4 March 2016. It was more co-ordinated and bloodier. The 'trespassers' managed to enter the flats but private security and then the police moved in with teargas and rubber bullets. Six people were arrested.

The community, who at first celebrated the upgrading, was now torn apart. The project pitted the Austerville Project Steering Committee (APSC), which was mandated by the community to oversee the refurbishment, against those who argue that the money spent on upgrading should be rather used to build new houses. Those who support the invasions and seek to stop the refurbishment, in the hope this will translate into a commitment to build new houses, have come together in what has come to be known as the War Room.

A member of the War Room pointed out the stark commonality of interests and differences that lie at the heart of this conflict:

> The APSC wants the flats to be refurbished. The War Room also wants the flat to be refurbished. We want the same thing; the identical thing we want. We are saying that alongside the refurbishment there must be housing development – because it's reasoned this way: Okay, fine. They're gonna redo our flats. Four generations are living in the flat. They're gonna be taken out of the flat into the decanting units, while their flat is done up. When the flat is done? They're still 21 people living in one flat ... while the refurbishment is gonna refurbish flats, it doesn't alleviate the overcrowding.

Those who stand to benefit from the refurbishments see their last opportunity to hand over something worthwhile to the next generation. On the other side, while there are opportunists who see a chance to grab a place to rent or 'sell', it is also true that the human battering rams have spent much of their adult lives without a room of their own and face no prospect of obtaining one. There are flats in Alabama Road where four generations live in two rooms. According to the local city councillor, Aubrey Snyman, out of the approximately 30 000 people in the area, some 4 000 are on waiting lists (*Daily News*, 29 February 2016). But the list is, in fact, a myth. Government does not keep track of how long someone has been without a home, and thus prioritising their claims first. The list is malleable, local, able to be gamed. And no new houses will be built, so the mythical list is for something that does not, will not, exist. The list will shorten when someone dies and lengthen when teenagers become adults. But still people queue to put their names on the list. And in scenes out of a Kafka novel, bureaucrats with all the decorum of officialdom take down their details.

These perpetual 'waiters' now feel that the R140 million should be used to build new dwellings rather than refurbish old ones. The persistent refrain is that the flats are overcrowded (Desai 2017). I talk to some flat residents about everyday life and space in their flats.

Berenice Goodman[7] is 34 years old and lives in a two-bedroom flat in Alabama Road that she shares with her mother Mary, her three children, and her boyfriend:

> My mother is in the one room with my two girls. In the second room, it is me and my boyfriend and the baby [two years old]. The flat is small. There is not enough space to live in. But what can we do? We don't have anywhere to go. We just have to live here. The bathroom is very small.

Berenice knows as the children grow, space will increasingly become an issue:

> When they reach puberty, we are just going to live with it. That's what happens in a lot of places. You find in these flats, there are adults living with their parents, as well – still, to this day. There are girls living here that are 30. Some are 40. They are not married, living with their children, in the same two-bedroom flat. It is harder for girls, but we don't have a choice. And when girls get to puberty, they want their privacy. But this is the only place we have to live.

There is a constant worry, a panic almost, about children getting kidnapped. Parents tend to keep their children indoors and even though I could not confirm a kidnapping it had become a 'fact' in the flats.

Space is also a constant refrain for Darryl Anthony. He is 66 years old and married to Dorothy, who is 64. They have three children, Mike (39), Esther (35) and Emma (29):

> With three children and two grandchildren, it is seven people living in a two-bedroom flat. Three generations. Our children never moved out the house. They are not married. They just got spoilt. That adds more problems to the list. It is noise. We need a break from time to time to sleep. We are pensioners. Now and then you get noise through the night. That's the bigger boys.

---

7. I have used pseudonyms for the residents of the flats.

Coming up and down the stairs. Mike has got a child, but that child is not with us. Esther and Emma have got children – a three-year-old and an eleven-year-old.

Darryl bemoans the lack of space:

> Our major problem we are having at the moment, right now, is the allocation of space. If Mike works nightshift, then we all have our beds for that period. But, if he is not working nightshift, then one of us has to sleep in the lounge. Just make yourself at home on the two-seater couch. If you feel you are uncomfortable, then you can take the little small mattress and put it on the floor. That's the difficult part – when he is not working nightshift.

Darryl and Dorothy have their own room:

> The children are in this bigger room. That is why we changed the room. Normally, the bigger room was the parents' room and the smaller room was the children's room. But, because they grow up so tall and big, we had to swap the rooms to give more space for them. So, we took the smaller room. There are times when they spend weekends away when they go out with their friends. We had a double bunk, but then we brought it down to open it out because the one can't sleep upstairs [on top bunk] – or they are fighting to be upstairs. They say they are going to fall off the bed. I say, 'Oh my God.' So I said let me be on the safe side and just put it down flat.

Darryl worries about privacy, especially with men and women sharing a room.

> Up until now, it's still not right. But I tell them, any changing that needs to go on, you go to the bathroom and change behind the door. You don't have to be in the room. If you are by yourself, then sure. Fine. Close the door to the room and then you can change there. That is it.

As the children grew older, Darryl worried even more:

> The age brackets, now. The explanations. That was hard. When we came into that phase... When they turned eleven, twelve, thirteen... When they became young ladies, I said, 'Dorothy, you got a job, here. You need to explain.' At least the girls learn about puberty in school now. It makes it much easier for the parents. That will cut out a lot of things around explanations because that is a very sensitive issue. You've got to get the girls to talk to the girls. The changes... But we have to do it, because they have to know it. Somewhere along the line, you've got to figure out, how am I going to do this? The wording has to be correct. That's number one. You've got to use the right words for these things. That is very important – and the way we address the issue itself. It musn't cause embarrassment. But it takes time to get to that stage. There are certain places where you have got to pray for guidance from above – to guide you on the right path, to say the right words – so that the person is more content afterwards. If you just say it roughly, you will hurt the person's feelings and they will rebel against you and tell you off. That can cause massive problems.

Berenice's flat is one of those recently upgraded:

> This flat was just newly renovated, but it doesn't look like it was renovated. It's terribly done. It was just done to say well we done it. They were given R90 000 for each unit to do our flats and this is the result. My floors are terribly damaged. When I came, the pipes were leaking. A friend fixed my pipes. He fixed my geyser. Underneath my bath was leaking. He fixed all that for me. Out of my own pocket. It's terrible. This is the type of pain we were given. And yet we were given R90k per unit. They were supposed to put ceramic tiles on the floor. They were supposed to do it decently, but this is the result. We have got to live with it. They said they are not coming back. My bath. You will swear I don't wash my bath. They were supposed to enamel it, but it

An upgraded block of flats.

was painted over with paint. Now the paint is peeling, so it is yellow. And then the top ceiling in the bathroom, I think the top people's bath is leaking, so it is damp. I am just afraid that one day it will cave in on us. God willing, nobody will be bathing at that time because we will die.

Darryl is constantly aware of violence breaking out and the upgrades have not helped:

Now, there are no lights on the staircase, so you can't just go out. You don't know who is on the steps. It's dark. You don't know who is outside. From the time that we came back from the decanting units, in this area, there are no lights since the upgrades. No lighting. The outside and the staircase. So it's not easy to just go outside. You don't know what will happen. You might end up getting into trouble.

And, there is always danger lurking outside. What are the stories of the young men who hang on the stairwells?

The stair boys

> The flats stole my life. Alabama Road is the most dangerous road in Wentworth.
>
> — Henry,[8] born 1990, dressed in an ANC T-shirt

Three young men stand at the bottom of the stairwell. It's Monday 22 February 2016. The night after the battle to occupy the newly built flats in Alabama Road. There are signs all over of a war. Blood. Blankets. Mattresses. They are jocular, as if this was just another night in the hood. As Bourdieu reminds us:

> The joke . . . is the art of making fun without raising anger, by means of ritual mockery or insult . . . tokens of attention of affection, ways of building up while seeming to run down, of accepting while seeming to condemn . . . (1984: 183).

They are keen for a chat.

For Henry, the pace of upgrading has been painfully slow:

> Starting in 2014 they've only upgraded two units – one unit with six three-bedroom flats; one unit with six two-bedroom flats. There's that one unit in Quality Street and the one on the corner of Austerville Drive near Jonas Road. After those two units got built, the project just stopped. They used all the Coloured men to do the heavy lifting – digging the foundation, carrying rocks, laying the foundation – and then the contract got given to blacks. How does that happen when we have got builders here? Artisans. We've got plumbers, ceiling guys, painters, window guys, welders, bricklayers, guys who do plastering, pipefitters and boilermakers, but we didn't get the jobs for this new housing project.

There is resentment that the promises of using local labour have not been upheld, and also a sense that the upgrades are really about local government elections, a sop to the community to garner ANC votes.

There are many stair boys hanging out with little to do. In a rudimentary survey conducted in the course of the research, of 11

---

8. I have used pseudonyms for the stair boys.

The corner of flats is where people socialise.

blocks of flats there were some 62 people between the ages of 18 and 35. Of those, 27 were in full-time jobs; an unemployment rate of nearly 45%. Another 12 were intermittently employed, mainly in what the petrochemical industry refers to as shutdowns, which last for about six weeks every six or so months. I ask the stair boys about jobs in the area. Peter, still laughing at Henry's T-shirt, pipes up:

> It's hard to find work here. Indians, Pakistanis and Asians don't want to stop working. They want to work until 10 pm – and not worry about being paid overtime. We've got papers. We paid for these qualifications . . . We are hustling here for R1 and R2. Police harass us here on the corners because we are not in uniform. A Coloured man in a uniform is not a threat. A Coloured man not in a uniform doesn't have a job and has to get searched by cops.

Henry takes up this point with some gusto: 'Black people and the Malaysians [who own a local petrochemical plant] are killing employment and dropping the job rates. A job that is rated at R135 an hour, a black man will do for R70 an hour.'

The life trajectory of many male Wentonians from a generation ago is on the decline, if not largely extinct. Take the case of Arthur Cyril Stokes, son of Papa Stokes. Arthur joined the building trade at the age of seventeen.

> My first job was at Rorvick & Bruce – I worked as a bricklayer. I learnt [the] trade on-site. They used to send us to building sites. The company had a lot of building jobs. They would take us onto the sites and give you on-the-job training.

After almost two years in the job, the company closed down.

> The Apprentice Board sent us to Murray & Roberts to finish our apprenticeships in 1971. We worked for Murray & Roberts for a year and half, we finished our apprenticeships, and then we qualified in 1972. Then I was a real bricklayer. Then I worked for Dura Construction. And then I worked a long time for Alexander Hamilton as a bricklayer. Then I spent nineteen years with Grant Mathee Builders. I retired there. When I turned 60, they were forced to put us off. The owner didn't want to let us go because he couldn't get people to replace us. He even cried. They wanted him to hire black people and more black people.

The days when Wentonians could rely on family connections to secure their children part-time jobs and take advantage of opportunities in the building trade is fast on the decline, accelerated by deracialisation and erosion of the apprenticeship system.

Alabama Road is the only life Henry knows. Will only know. A young Master's student from the University of Vienna accompanying me asks me later why Henry did not leave? To where? With what? He has no skills, no formal qualifications, no networks. As Bourdieu et al. put it, 'the lack of capital intensifies the experience of finitude; it chains one to a place' (1999: 124). But at the same time, the street offers Henry a way to survive, to get by. The street, as the events taking place over February and March 2016 indicate, is 'not a closed space, not a static place but the ground on which space and place, and that means also agency and power, are negotiated' (Goetschel 2009: 242).

There are those who do get out. Comet Harban grew up in Cycas Road in the first half of the 1990s. His name has a twist:

> My father was very old when he had me. He was 46. Hence my name, Comet. My mom was very young. What happened was she had nausea and stuff and they took her to the family doctor. And the doctor made a joke and said, 'Hey, maybe she is pregnant.' My father said, 'Ha, no. If she is, though, we can name him Comet', because just like a comet it comes once every 46 years. The tests came back positive.

Growing up was tough.

> Growing up in Wentworth is like survival mode. The area that I grew up in as a boy . . . Wentworth was quite rough at that time. I remember there was a time when I was at church and I was getting confirmed. I was twelve. And, walking up the road, the guys would come up to you and literally try to rob you for whatever you had – and actually hit me for being from a certain area. It came to a point where I couldn't even go to the grounds to play soccer. That is what I used to have to do back in the day. You go and play, and they would ask you, 'Where you from?' – and because they had issues with the bigger boys in the area – because you are from the area, you are associated with them, with that gang or that crew – and a lot of time I couldn't go play soccer. It got to a point where I used to go back and tell the boys, 'Hey, listen, this is what happened . . .' And they told me, 'We can't do anything. There is nothing we can do. You have to actually *be* one of us.' And it got to point where I decided to do that and to do all that stuff. Not to glorify it, but for survival tactics, I needed some kind of protection and I didn't have it. I didn't have any brothers or stuff like that. Our gang was the Rasta 7s. This happened for a while.

But for Comet it was music that was his first love.

Comet Harban.

I used to always be rapping from quite young. I found it as a way out – just to get off the streets, in a sense. I was in a group called TYB [The Young Bruinous].

He played soccer for Cherrians but kept returning to music. Getting married with children, he refused to throw in his ambitions. At age 37 he is still

> ... enjoying the ride and putting the music out there. Even the younger generation feels like they can vibe to this. I try to tell a story with my songs. The older generation loves it. I'm working on my second album. Ironically, the one I did was called *Steady But Sure*. Steady, in terms of the discipline and focus – and 'sure' that I knew it was going to come. And I've learnt now to like block out the noise. I got a lot of good reviews. Past the failure and ridicule is success. I am rapping because I want to. Now, I am saying: this is my purpose. This is what I am supposed to be doing. I have never believed that more now than ever before in my life. Music. Writing it. Rapping it. The book, *The Alchemist*, tells you that if you put yourself out there, the universe will meet you halfway. And, in the beginning, I didn't have any beat-makers. I didn't have any contacts. But when I dropped that *Steady But Sure* album, everything opened up.

Through all the rapping, Comet kept his day job in construction that now sees him working in Ghana as a safety manager. He returns for visits but insists he will never come back permanently. He rues all the talented people from Wenties who cannot leave:

> This is the thing about Wentworth people. People from Wentworth never want to leave. But those that always leave never want to come back. Even now that I am down in Wentworth for four days, I want to go home now. Same thing. Same boys. Same ways. Same corners. It's just the same thing. For me, it's nice to come home. It's nostalgia. I see my friends. I see my family. For three days I hear the same stories. People limit themselves. For me, the best talent – and I have been around and I have seen things – still the most talented people came from this place. Wentworth. Football players. Entertainment. Wentworth for me is it. But the people are so caught in this 'I can't do it. It will never be me' mentality. Or, they have that talent, but it is never matched with the work ethic. Wentworth is a well of talent. Wentworth people are so caught up in daily routines and stuff. I can't put a finger on it, but you have got to go from the outside to look in. I can only make this comparison now because I moved out. I remember back in the day when I was like, 'I am never leaving Wentworth. This is home.' I was scared to go to Joburg. This is the posie [home], bru. Where am I going? But eventually I realised, what the hell was I thinking? Thank God I am out. I actually thanked God that I was out of Wentworth. Not that Wentworth is a bad thing, but I removed myself from the cycle.

In the streets around the flatlands of Wentworth, the cries and demands grow in number and become louder by the day. Tensions are running high. The spectre of housing delivery has created the conditions for a localised civil war in the area. Suddenly, politics drops its pose and reveals a more gang-like character.

There are slender pickings from government. When they do present themselves, Wentonians turn on each other to grab what they can. The tensions accumulate inwards not outwards when there is something on offer. It is an environment

> ... where joblessness and lack of housing force too many to a life that defies the rhythms of a working area and create endless petty irritations: that is, when a people have been produced with no presence in the world apart from the infractious presence in the streets, then the sources of value that characterised the older tradition become meaningless and anachronistic ... (Charlesworth 2003: 173).

And so the posturing and posing.

For poet and entrepreneur Rodney Roskruge, Wentworth exists as a convenient labour reserve, even as the jobs on offer are on the decline or only on offer during the periodic shutdowns:

> Wentworth, for me, is a worker mindset. It's not a creator of work. You don't create work in Wentworth, I think. I think we are more of workers than creators of work. When you are walking on the streets of Wentworth, you will hear a person say, I want to do this course and go to Secunda (Sasol). Why must we all go to Secunda? And maybe it's because of how Wentworth was built. I think that the way we are positioned, with all the business happening around us, and townships, in their nature, is to create reserves for the factories and the companies. Hence we have reserves created and located to reserve a labour force for the Engens and the Saprefs. So, we are not stopping that. We are continuing to produce labour. Hence, we can sit down for five, six months. When there is a shutdown, we get to go to work and get excited and then wait again. The mentality is that of a worker – not a mentality to create work for workers. Not many people in Wentworth talk about creating work. Go outside Wentworth and you will meet people who talk about creating work. And in some spaces, many people are worker mentality. Largely, we are workers in Wentworth. It's a township thing. It's a reserve thing. Umlazi is a reserve. It will reserve you for work. It will keep you for work.

The boys that hug the walls, through the generations (photo: Cedric Nunn).

You are there on the reserve bench waiting for a shutdown. That is what you do in the townships.

The young men at the bottom of the stairs are always willing for a chat and friendly barbs. Many a time somebody arrives with a couple of quarts of beer; some meat for a braai. The fact that there could be a drive-by shooting or an ambush by a rival gang is suspended in the immediacy of enjoying life. One gets the sense that

> there is still a sort of economic calculation in the unwillingness to subject existence to human calculation. The hedonism which seizes day by day, the rare satisfactions ('good times') of the immediate present is the only philosophy conceivable to those who 'have no future' and in any case, little to expect from the future (Bourdieu 1984: 183).

Despite the years of violence that ran through Wentworth in the 1970s and '80s, 59-year-old Kevin Alexander (who we will meet later) sums up the sense of nostalgia:

> Wentworth is a funny place. It is a place that is no more like the old Wentworth that it was when we were small. A place where we would help you out if you needed sugar. Your mother could ask you to 'go get some soap there'. Now, even the children are too scared to go ask. You can't go tell them to go 'Mrs So-and-so because Mommy wants that'. No, you can't. It is because people no more have that heart. Like at Christmas time. We used to invite people for lunch. You could come sit here – even if I don't know you. Now, they will only come if there is alcohol. You can't tell people, 'Do you want to come have lunch with me?' You can't. The first thing they think is if there is any booze there. Like me ... I had so many friends – who used to come sit with me and drink with me. But they are not saved. It's not like before. On Christmas Day we used to sit by Austerville. It wasn't a thing about dressing and drinking. It was about sharing.

Some accept the idea of being forgotten in the new South Africa with a degree of resignation, if not bitterness. Others try to push themselves up the queue by highlighting their Colouredness, their liberation history and links to the soil of Africa.

Mourning and melancholy mix with militancy in this township. Mourning for a time past. For talents gone to waste. And melancholy that the end of apartheid brought no redemption. Flats get refurbished, but no new ones (a paltry eighteen) are built. Jobs are advertised, but there is a sense that Coloureds need not apply. One evening, while tracking some photographs, I meet a woman whose brother once played for Leeds. Bucking the trend, she obtained a doctorate in education. She lectured for a while at a local tertiary institution. When her job was advertised for a longer period, it was written as a transformation post limited to black Africans. She waits in the street in which she grew up. Finally a call comes. She is offered a temporary job. A temporary reprieve.

The kind ministry

> I could have been killed how many times. If you look at my back you will get a shock. If I were to tell you how many times I have been in intensive care, you will get a shock. It even came over the radio that I was dead. I flatlined. Kevin Alexander died. But I was

still alive. Dr Whitehead at Addington Hospital came by, tested my pulse, and said, 'Get this man to theatre. He is still alive.' They had already covered me with the white sheet and thought I was dead. She came by to certify that I was really dead and realised that the pulse was light. They gave me nine pints of blood after they had poked me and shot me. It was 1986 and the guys in town poked me and shot me. We were fighting and all that, so they got me. They made me a tea strainer. You must see my back. [Removes shirt.] Right on top I've got two big ones.

— Kevin Alexander

But if there is melancholia and mourning, there is also belligerence, anger and large doses of philanthropy.

People like Rodney Roskruge, aged 29, are not just hanging around street corners. He is deeply involved in encouraging a culture of writing and publishing:

'Publish My Work.' It is work as in what you write. Our plan is to go to schools. Have as many workshops at the schools. Inspire them. Package your book. Using what you have. Use hashtags. And then after hosting these workshops at all the schools, we are going to start collecting that work . . . It could be poems. It could be novels. When we collect throughout Wentworth, every school will have its own book per year. Fairvale High School will have its own book . . . So, every year, like you have trophies for football, and you are at school reading and writing every day, but reading and writing is not catered for, so we are going to collect all those books. Then at the end of the year we are going to do this huge festival in Durban where we launch every school we are visiting.

For Rodney, it is not just about writing but about escaping the mentality of the labour reserve:

We teach them entrepreneurship. How to sell a book. What is a book? How to package a book – you are selling what is inside. This portion goes to the school we visited. This portion comes back to the company. It's business. It's entrepreneurship. It's publishing.

Rodney Roskruge, storyteller.

It's your voice. It's stories. It's your history being documented. It's your commentary. Unbottling. All the librarians are already excited about that. There is interest from Microsoft – they want to come with us. And other guys. Many people are excited about the project. Just starting with the three schools – Wentworth High, Umbilo and Fairvale. It will tell a different story.

Amidst the 'trouble', I notice a flat that is surrounded by flower pots. It is hard to attract the occupant's attention. Somebody has disconnected the bell. Eighty-four-year-old Doreen Houghton points to a little garden she had on the hill behind the flats:

> I've started this whole garden. On the one side, I was planting all the stuff that we need in the kitchen – like beans, potatoes and onions. But then the neighbour's children kept on picking vegetables and herbs from my garden for their grannies. So, I changed my tune. I planted trees. Here is a curry leaf tree – that big – with seeds and all. Next to it is an avocado pear tree. It was

Doreen Houghton's garden.

> much bigger. It was ready to give food. Then the neighbour from the other side of this block came to cut them right down to the bottom. I gave part of the garden to my neighbour downstairs. Now they are stealing from one another. The one neighbour went and hashed a place [local slang for appropriating something without asking for permission, often backed up with the threat of force] in the garden. She hashed it. So I had to move more to the one side so that we can make little gardens and then spread them out when they get big enough to spread out.

Her daughter insisted that Doreen stop working in the garden because of the potential for trouble from the neighbours. But her mother did not throw in the spade. She made flower beds in front of the flats. When they were interfered with, she took them to the back of her flat.

> And my flowers came up. Here, I've got St Bernards, which gets a beautiful red bell flower. On this side, I've planted St Joseph lilies. Some in white. Some in yellow. I've got Ten Commandments. Here's my Bleeding Heart. I've got genuine stuff. That's my garden on my windowsill.

Doreen's green patch creeps up the hill.

Listening to Doreen talk about her attempts to build and nurture a garden reminds one of the oft-quoted phrase of a person living in the *favelas* of Rio de Janeiro: 'One has to be an artist to survive as a poor person . . . you have to imagine space where there is none' (in Ramphele 1993: 23).

Kevin Alexander turned 59 on 11 April 2019. He is a ubiquitous presence in Alabama Road where he has lived for 30 years. He runs Maureen's Tuck Shop, which was started by his wife and has been going for seven years. Kevin is a man of male trades: carpenter, boilermaking, engineer. Maureen worked at St Augustine's Hospital:

> I worked all over. I just finished off now at LTN, a company that works in the petrochemical field. I was eleven years with them. I'm still with them, just off the books now. They call me for shuts. The shop works because what I did it for was my wife. I was on the road all the time. KM [Kevin/Maureen] Contractors was mine. We used to do roofing and building. Then I stopped because of age.

Kevin worries about the upheaval caused by the upgrades:

> My mother [Queenie Alexander], in Major Calvert, passed away last year. Just when they had finished renovating her flat. She never even moved in. She came in for two days and she passed away the next day. It was too much stress for her. They moved her and moved her. Old people, you can't just throw them around. You've got to let them know in advance. An old woman does not like you to come and do your own thing in her house. When she came back, they had put in a shower? How can an old woman get in the shower to take a bath? Old people . . . They do the same thing here with us. They sweet talk you. I've been watching them. They tell you move out and tell you not to move back in until you are happy with everything, but it's not like that. The truck comes. You've got to move your things. You don't get to inspect your place. You don't know what's going on. So when you get back there, you can get a heart attack. Old people are like that. If they are not happy with that, they can get upset. My old lady got a heart attack. They started her upgrade in 2017 and she moved back in and died in September 2018.

Kevin spent a total of twelve years in jail for murder (seven years) and attempted murder (five years) in the 1990s.

Kevin is one of so many people interviewed who was 'saved' late in life:

> I drank for twenty years. I partied. After I stopped drinking, my head opened up. So, in my marriage, I am married for 36 years, but twenty years was a waste. I just stopped drinking. Stopped smoking. And I went to church. I got saved. I'm with Grace Tabernacle. I was Roman Catholic before that. So, it was Christmas Eve – after my wedding anniversary – we bought all our liquor and we were going up to Anstey's Beach on the Bluff to have a party there. Just the men. My sister and my wife were going for lunch at the Elangeni Hotel. And then, as they were going, I said, 'No. Y'll carry on. I'll meet y'll there. I'm going with my wife and the ladies.' And I went with them to the Elangeni. We sat at the table. My sister and all of them had wine. My wife doesn't drink and smoke. She's saved, too. The waiter asked me

what I was having. I said I was having a Coke. From that day, up until now, I have had Coke. I was going to church for two weeks before that day. That's all it took.

He was a member of the notorious KI gang in Wentworth. But today he is a successful business person and community builder:

> I hold classes here for six boys twice a week. I teach them piping and technical drawing. I teach piping in the bedroom. I teach them how to read drawings. In the tests they are going to give you, you should know these things. Free classes. Just to help them. Many have already found jobs. Kind Ministry is actually a business. KM Contractors. We started it once we got saved. We just prayed about it. I've got signs up all around Wentworth saying 'KM Ministry'. I got a sign on the Bluff. We don't do for everybody – only pensioners, people that have no income, and people that someone in the church tells us about someone whose heart is broken – not where there is family working and there is drinking.

Being 'saved' had an effect on his business acumen:

> The growth of the inner businessman in me happened only when I just got saved. I understood the value of investing, saving, purchasing property only when I got saved. I think that when you get saved, things change. God blesses your life. God changes your life.

The shop is a centre for charitable acts:

> My wife has about five kids that she buys uniforms and school books for. She like sponsors them. The children at the back will come tell you their needs. There are three old ladies that I buy groceries for. And there are two ladies who I pay rent for. I help them with their rent. Pensioners. They have no sons. No daughters to help them. I also put in toilets and paint the house. Put new doors. A lot of small jobs. KM Contractors . . . The KM

is for Kevin and Maureen. When I prayed on it, I just got KM in my mind. I never thought. Only afterwards I realised that it was Kind Ministry Contractors. I opened that business to help pensioners pay their rent. Those that can't afford it. I do my job, but I take the money from there and I go do what needs seeing to. Fix your house. Then I will find out about another old lady in church: that lady is suffering. She's got no roof – or it's leaking. I go there on a Saturday to go patch it up. I do things like that. That is my business: Kind Ministry. Running for seven years and still going. We are also in Zululand. We are busy there. We are building a school and a hospital. When I'm finished, I come back here again. My heart has changed. Fireworks. I buy a whole lot of those 100-shooters. Other children have got – and some haven't. Nothing to hurt them – just something to hold during a celebration. For fun. To have something. To be part of the celebration. And they all say thank you. They know: Here, it's God's house.

Kevin will never leave:

I want to be here. Why must I go live in a big house on the Bluff? God put me here for a reason. I can talk to the drug addicts. It's better me living here than there where I can't talk to anybody. Like here, the mothers here next door want to go to the Bluff. This old man that stands here ... He drives for us. He works for us. We took him off the road. Gave him a house. Pay for his board. Buy him food. Buy him clothes. That's how God works. Still, he drives the car. If the old ladies want to go to the Bluff, he takes them there, no charge. That's what Kind Ministry is here for. It's to help. And I've still got a lot more to learn.

There are always possibilities to change the environment and touch people's lives:

If we can help one another, I think we can have a nice place. Even if the businessmen got together ... Look at how many businessmen we have got in Wentworth? We don't have to battle.

Even R1 000 a month. With 60 businessmen, that's R60 000. How many homes can you fix with R60 000? Pensioners – especially now when people are living longer. I know a lot of old people. I love old people because I grew up hard. My father used to drink. I look after everyone old. I just love old people because I have seen too many of them suffering. I've seen my friends neglect their mothers. Some of them just talk any how to old people. I think that's why. There are two Kevins. The old Kevin is dead. The new Kevin is something else.

All over Wentworth, affirmative action goes by another name, a feeling of marginalisation, of once more being pushed to the end of the queue. Despair alternates with anger and creativity, like that of Doreen Houghton.

In Wentworth, one gets a sense that 'community has become both an emotional withdrawal from society and a territorial barricade within the city' (Sennett 1974: 301). This is allied to a deep sense that in contemporary South Africa, the Coloured community has been pushed to the end of the queue, waiting for leftovers. As Zoë Wicomb has contended, 'not everyone wishes to abandon racial naming: black groups jealously guard their blackness, coloured groups cling to their colouredness' (1998: 363). In Wentworth, this is tied to feelings of belonging and place nurtured from the early 1960s.

8

Living History

> People who don't follow football think of it just as a game, something that can be packed away when it is finished and forgotten about. But the game, played out by twenty-two men in an hour and a half, is only the kernel of something greater. The game is the core, you might say, of the Game.
> — Pearson, *The Far Corner*

In the mid-1970s, Leeds United captured the imagination of Wentworth. When they played at Curries Fountain, buses took full loads of family and supporters to watch. Gangs united for the day. This was remarkable given the level of violent confrontations during this period:

> ... territorial wars were fought with guns, knives, stones and broken bottles. Every weekend there were murders. Funerals were held on Mondays and Tuesdays, when the solemn line of hearses would make its way to the cemetery on the other side of Quality Street. The cemetery is the largest expanse of green in Wentworth and it is littered with the graves of young men. Occasionally a knifing would take place in broad daylight; some had their stomachs slit open or organs sliced off ... (Rostron 1991: 37).

And victory on the field of play meant more than the cup. It settled scores with other areas that fancied themselves as more worthy than the Wentonians. Especially sweet was victory against teams from Sydenham, the 'other' Coloured area that produced top outfits such as Spearman Lads, who had in their ranks top defenders like Phillip Frank.

Phillip Frank (left) and Terrence Reddy of Motherwell, June 1980.

As the heavy levels of pollution make the asthma pump one of the most ubiquitous aids in Wentworth, and drugs and gangs strike at the social fabric of everyday life in the area, so people have also come together by creating forms of social life. Leeds United played a major role, not just for its success on the field, but for what it came to mean, contributing to a collective communal identity, even if was for 90 minutes on a Sunday, which could easily unravel on a Monday.

For Dennis Petersen, looking around the neighbourhood he has lived in for the past 50 years, the challenge in forging a soccer culture has many heads but the main one is gangs and drugs:

> There's a lot that brought soccer down in Wentworth. But in the main it's the drugs. Guys feel that they don't need to train to play. We used to enjoy training. We even had our own floodlights. The club bought it. Now, when there's no lights, they stop training. Even when it rains, we'd train during the rain. The drugs are a big problem. You see, there's a lot of youngsters that are selling drugs, because that's their only source of income. Selling for the big guns – big guns from Wentworth and from elsewhere.

A park in bad repair that was used to play pick-up games of soccer in the mid-1980s.

Of course, the gangs have always been there. But there were other outlets for solidarity and expressions of youthful ability that brought a sense of self-respect and even dignity to young men. Leeds United embodied much of that. It is reflected in the way the gangs united behind the club, laying down weapons and staunching deep wounds for 90 minutes. Success on the field was seen as an affirmation of the whole community. And everyone who lived there knew Wentworth was not only about gangs; there were fearsome characters on the field of play, too.

Patrick Moodley points out that today the weapons are deadlier and the stakes higher:

> Compared to the gangs of our days . . . these youngsters are carrying guns. They're killing each other. In our days, it was bush knives, knives, and fair fights. There's none of that now. Now it's just killing. Guns are the order of the day now. With these drug lords supplying the youngsters. The shootings by these drug lords wanting to own the areas; to own nightclubs. People were getting shot in these guy's clubs.

Here and there, soccer has made an impact. In Patrick 'Boa' Wiseman's immediate neighbourhood:

> We had all the fighters and the fighting types. Gangsters. I sat them down and reckoned, 'See here now, I'm gonna give y'll jerseys. But, every one of y'll are gonna play. The whole lot of y'll as y'll sitting here. Whether you can play ball or you can't play ball. Win, lose or draw. Y'll are all going to the grounds together. And if you don't want to play, you are gonna get left in the gully by yourself. The rest are going to play.' That's how they formed. Now, the amazing part is that we didn't see the hidden talent in the area. That's where now it has become a hunting ground for us. For talent. For the youngsters.

Today, Wentworth leaks as much as it congeals.

There are those who have made it. Their first reaction to wealth is to flee Wentworth for the nearby hills of the Bluff. And once there, they 'fit' into a white society, which for decades rejected their mothers and fathers. Many are in construction and see the importance of networking with white people and sponsoring teams from the area.

Of those who have made it economically, besides a few notable exceptions, very few give back. According to David Stanley, one of the walking, talking encyclopaedias of Wentworth's soccer history:

> So, the role models and successful businessmen from our community are keeping stuff to themselves. They're not developing the community. We can do so much development. If you can see the youngsters from Wentworth and see the potential that they've got with soccer, you will be shocked.

This transition of richer Wentonians to the Bluff, literally around the corner, has only served to reinforce the distance between the two areas.

The very talented players that Wentworth still has the capacity to produce ineluctably move to professional clubs. Clinton Larsen, the Bafana Bafana player whose father Bull played for Leeds, is one example. Retired, he now coaches a Premier division professional team. Gary Goldstone's son, Gary Junior, went on to play for Kaizer Chiefs.

The heady days of Leeds United travelling across the country, winning trophies and defeating local professional teams is part of a distant past. A number of processes conspired to work against successful clubs, such as Leeds United, in sustaining their form.

Still, there are signs that soccer is on the up. There are six teams in the NSL Castle League, three below the Premier. Young Cavaliers, owned by Dennis Petersen's sister, Lorna, consistently makes the play-offs for promotion from the SAB League to the Motsepe League.

Mobility does not mean that a sense of place has completely dissipated. As opportunities for working-class employment close down, the old feelings of a minority 'not white enough during apartheid, not black enough now' re-surface, leading to Mohamed Adhikari's summation of 'coloured people's perennial predicament of marginality' (2005: 110). The reaction is to cling more closely to Wentworth and a Coloured identity: to shut out the 'hostile' outside world.

Conflicts and tensions are also reflected inwards. Gangs fight each other for territory and trade, street by street. Truces seldom cohere any more. Non-governmental organisations (NGOs) that feed off and against the local petrochemical industry vie for funding. And when the state occasionally makes an attempt to upgrade local apartments, which are, quite literally, falling apart, low-intensity warfare breaks out.

The three to four years spent talking to soccer players and lovers of the game leaves one with an indelible impression of a continuing love affair with the beautiful game. Listening to the Green Mambas gathered in Gregory Baptist's lounge, exchanging banter, knowing every detail of the lives of those who left to go to Cape Town and across the oceans to New Zealand and Australia, one is reminded of Michael Herzfeld's evocative phrase 'the poetics of manhood' (2005: 192).

Dennis Petersen never left Wentworth. He still lives in the same street and is surrounded by family. The family bonds that survived the forced relocation from Cato Manor to Wentworth persist into the present. He is integral to the running of Young Cavaliers.

Gary Goldstone lives in the formerly white, upmarket suburb of Westville. His wife Ursula is manager of the Umhlanga Plaza. She has been there for 38 years. Before that, they were in northern KwaZulu-Natal. Gary says of that time:

I did not work. All I did was use my van. I was connected to a catering company. That's why I practically know the whole of northern Zululand, catering for a mainly Zulu clientele for weddings and funerals. So every single weekend I was making my money with my bakkie.

Then I got a Hilux. I bought it for a song in an auction – R31 000. I did it up. It cost me another two/three thousand. Seven years later, I sold it for R33 000. I should not have sold it. I should have still had that bakkie. And I had my own shop down in Austerville called Sunshine Amusement Centre. It was near Adams shop [K1 Section], but facing Tifflin Road – where the carpark is. I was there for eleven years. I got into trouble for that 'entertainment' because they made a mistake at the licencing office and put 'Entertainment Centre', so when it's 'entertainment' you're entitled to sell liquor. Then I get a call – from the captain at C.R. Swart police station in that division. He said, 'Goldstone! Listen, you have to come see us concerning your licence.' I said okay. So I go there. It's a white woman. She says, 'I'll tell you something, Mr Goldstone. You're never gonna get a licence because you have a conviction list as long as the bottom part of my arm.' I said, 'What is this about? I've rehabilitated a long time ago.' But, I got away because I always went with a lawyer.

In many ways, this sums up Goldstone's life. Full of roadblocks, some self-created, but always managing to charm or bluff his way out of trouble.

Patrick Moodley, after teaching at Fairvale High, tried his hand at business:

I had a nightclub in Wentworth, it was called The Rainbow. It was a big restaurant. A nightclub. Mine was a pub, restaurant and a nightclub. But there were absolutely no fights by my place – no fights; not a single fight. I only closed it because one night we got held up. They robbed the garage across the road and then the other three came up to me. Whoa! I thought, Lord, why tonight? And I was just about closing up. I'm standing here behind my bar – near the panic button. They said, 'Do you want to move

> your hand, or do you want to die?' I said, 'I haven't got the keys here.' Two guys are raiding the machines; they're raiding the restaurants; they're raiding the bar tills. We used to sell top chow – crayfish, prawns . . . This was between 1998 and 2001. I owned it for three years – until that night when I saw my life flashing before my eyes. I was saved because the *kerels* [cops] were chasing them because they had robbed someone there on the Bluff in Bluff Road. Everywhere there was a big noise from their sirens. These guys ran down my stairs. Their car was waiting downstairs. The police shot three of them in the head. Dead. Their second car got away. That car had my stuff. They got away with that. Now, I was scared, because these *ous* normally come for revenge.

Moodley closed the club:

> I went into financial management for five or six years . . . I worked for Liberty Life for about seven or eight years. I took a year's rest before I came into teaching. That was around 2008/2009. Then I filled in at two schools – New Forest in Montclair and an interfellowship school. I'm Catholic. I came to Umbilo School in 2011. They said, 'Hey. There's a *graf* [job] here.' My old mate Dale Seidel was the deputy principal of Umbilo. When I left Fairvale, he left there as well. Now, it's alright here at Umbilo.

Gregory Baptist works at Engen and still lives in Wentworth. He is a keeper of Leeds's history, collecting photographs and articles and was a driving force in the reunion of 2014. Elvis Singh lives close by. One-time captain Barry Duschene made the move to Australia. One of the 'wild ones', Raymond Mentor, now a pastor, made a life in Cape Town as the principal of a Bible college, but in more recent times has set up a ministry in Merebank. Raymond and Graham Birch (former captain of Leeds) were joined together at the hip:

> He came in from Cavaliers and came into Leeds as well. We were all together. Most of the players who were in his team. We were drugging together. Living together. Doing everything together. We

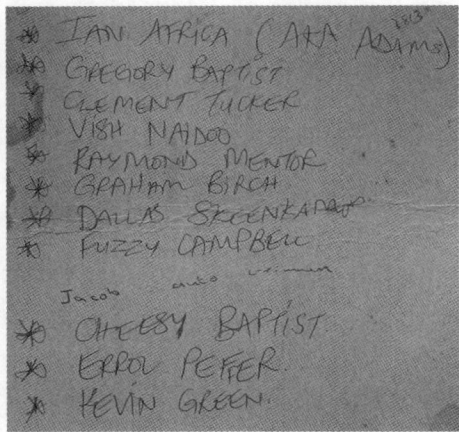

The Leeds team sheet.

met and married our wives together. We had children together. Wherever we went, these two families were together.

Birch regales me with stories of the life of Raymond and his three brothers, Edward, Charlie and Leon.

All were in the reformatory. The youngest one, Charlie, was in Tokai. He got twenty years for stabbing and killing someone. All those brothers were naughty. Raymond and Leon went first. They went to Cape Town and they used to come back on holiday. In the reformatory you do not drink and you don't smoke. You only eat and train. And you have to learn a trade. They teach you. You get up early. You work. There's no lounging around. You go to school. And Raymond was very, very clever. He's a year older than his brother. So the brother was in Standard 6 at Wentworth High and Raymond was in Standard 8. Raymond was short and he was the same height as his brother. They said, 'What, Bushman, please. Hottentot, you are Standard 6. Don't tell us you are in Standard 8.' So he had to go right back with his brother to Standard 6. Anyway, they saw how he was just flying through the exams.

Raymond was also a fighter, having learnt the art of boxing while at the reformatory. He and Birch were wild, taking on all comers. While Raymond used his deadly fists, Birch's weapon of choice was a metal pipe. Two of Raymond's brothers went to prison; Edward got eighteen years, Charlie twenty years.

Gangsterism and soccer joined them but these days, it's all about being 'born again'. Birch, after moving around a bit, is back living in Wentworth. He was one of the original members of the Sinners gang. Today, he is a man of God and family. It is a road that so many have followed, often forsaking the traditional churches for the relatively new Pentecostal churches. For most, it is mystical vision that pushed them to belief, but it is also life's journey. As Ludwig Wittgenstein wrote:

> Life can educate one to a belief in God. And *experiences* too are what being this is about; but I don't mean visions and other forms of sense experience which show up as the 'existence of this being', but, e.g., suffering of various sorts. Experiences, thoughts, – life can force the concept upon us (1984: 86; my emphasis).

Boa lives right opposite a major school. He is waiting to turn his coaching certificate and knowledge into getting the young ones together. Things move slowly.

And remember Terrence Smith, the pioneer entrepreneur and breakdancer? Conversations take surprising turns. Talking about his family, Terrence Smith (aka Cele, Singh) remembers his father:

> I was five years old . . . One day I was playing outside and they [the family] called me inside. He [the father – John Cele] was sitting on the couch and said, 'I am your father,' and then he gave me 50 cents. When I was 35 years old, I took a road trip to Richards Bay to look for him – my father. I went to all the areas and spoke to all the chiefs. They tried to help me and pointed me in various directions, and I followed the trail, but I couldn't find him. I spent two weeks in Richards Bay looking for him. Two weeks later, I came back home. Exactly two weeks after my return, he was murdered. This was in 2004. He died by being bludgeoned to death with a hammer to the head. It was a man and a woman

who killed him. They killed him for a R300 pension. Then, when he was dead, they loaded him into a wheelbarrow and put him into his bed like he was sleeping – to avoid murder charges. So I never really met my father . . .

Terrence and his wife moved around KwaZulu-Natal but have found a home once more in Wentworth. Trained as a boilermaker and welder, he works in the ship repair industry. Because he works night shift, Terrence says that he knows what's causing the sickness among people in Wentworth, and it is the words of a man who has moved in and out of the area:

> When we go to Kokstad for a weekend, on the way back, as soon as we hit Toti [Amanzimtoti], you get an instant headache because of the pollution. Welcome to Durban. I am asthmatic. I feel it hard. The oil refinery flares every day at 3 am – that's when they push high pressure hot air into the valves through the pipes to clear the pipes. This process lasts for twenty minutes. When I moved back to Wentworth I developed a heartbeat that was too slow. My mother died of cancer. My neighbour is 36 years old and has an irregular heartbeat condition. You know, saying, 'I have cancer' around here is like saying, 'I have the flu.' That's how widespread and common it is.

Life is more settled now:

> I'm such a family man these days. People here remember me as a fighter. I used to fight with my family and kick the door down. Swearing and shouting. Most people here have domestic fights because they are struggling and take it out on spouses or families. It's just frustration of being faced with not knowing what to do. And also another thing is living in cramped conditions; a lot of people under one roof. These days I've changed so much. I'm cool. I'm gentle. I'm a father. My street-thug name was 'T-Bones' and I was uncontrollable . . . I am a family man now.

But still, Terrence sees the need to get out:

If you keep to yourself, you are fine. You are 'at home'. A flat can never feel like a home. If I come home from work and I feel like I want to stand by my gate . . . My fence . . . Then I am at home. I want to sit outside. I want to feel free. Without anybody walking past you and throwing their cigarette stompies at your feet or spitting in front of you. It boils down to being a space thing. I would love to move into a yard. When they upgrade these flats and hand them over to us, my plan is to rent out my place and go live in a house. I'm planning to move to Joburg. I won't give up this flat. That, I won't do. I have lived here for too long to give it up. I grew up in this place. As far as it being a 'home', it's not really a home if you don't have yard. If I say to kids, 'Go play outside', I want to know that they are secure and safe.

Terrence has watched boys growing up in front of him turn into drug lords who are the instigators of a turf war that sees people stabbed and shot on a weekly basis. As Terrence reflects, the market for drug-selling is congested and so drug lords defend their territory even if it means killing people from across the street who they knew since they were children. 'People think it's a gang war. It's not. It's a drug war. Last year somebody died every week. We were just burying people. It all boils down to money and geography. Either you move – or you're dead.'

The flats above Alabama Road in Wentworth, in which the fight for territory is intense.

In 2009, the United Musicians' Benefit Association paid tribute to Sonny Pretorius for his 51-year contribution to the music and dance fraternity. Into his eighties, Sonny was performing in a one-man band. In February 2018, he died at the age of 88.

Abdul Adams was always looking for new challenges and

> ... was made an offer to join Orlando Pirates. I had a trial there and was about to sign when I met Abdul Bhamjee at a mosque in Johannesburg and he persuaded me to join Dynamos. I spent three years there but picked up a serious knee injury. When I returned to Durban I was approached by Tongaat Crusaders to coach their outstanding young team, which included Dhanpal Naidoo and his brothers. It reminded me a bit of Leeds because the team was young, talented and very community-oriented. After a few years, work and family commitments resulted in me leaving professional soccer.

Today, Adams manages the Orient High School astro turf soccer facilities in Durban.

Bugsy Singh is still with Cherrians. But he always sees beyond the field of play. He is in touch with an old Cherrians' stalwart Marlon Burgess, a successful business person in the medical services industry in Johannesburg. Singh's

> ... view is that there is Wentworth Hospital. It's totally compromised. You have to accept that state resources are depleted and our community is suffering. What we can do is that we can set up this facility – in conjunction with the local clinic. Augment them. Support them. And do like minor things. So, for example, someone needs a circumcision ... Someone needs an endoscope. They've got a lump to be taken out. I get the human resource from King Edward Hospital and other networks ... Spend twice a week, thrice a week ... Three, four hours ... Sort problems out. You got a problem. You don't need to go to Wentworth Hospital ... we will expedite the care. What often happens is that these patients get lost in the bureaucracy. Even though health care is taking a big hammering, we underestimate

the number of good people in the system. There are good people who will come: Marlon, because he's in the industry, will provide the technology and equipment and so on.

By February 2019, Arlene Singh is back in Wentworth. When both Odette's daughters came to live with them on the Bluff, the landlord threatened to put up the rent. Arlene heard that you could borrow money on your pension and saw this as a way to obtain a home of their own.

> What I actually wanted to do is I wanted to build on my mother's place [Ogle Road house]. But when I spoke to the builder across the road, I asked him how much it would cost me to build on top of my mother's house? He says, 'Oh, about R500 000.'

The loan only amounted to R275 000.

> So, I've got the money now. I'm getting the loan. What do I do? Within a week the loan was processed. Odette came home and I told her the money is in the bank. She was so excited. She was so happy. Now, we've got the money, but we've got nowhere to live. We are homeless. So I am thinking . . . I'm wracking my brain. I said, 'You know what, at the back of my mother's house there is space.' But, when you looked at it, it didn't look that big. I was talking to my niece, Tracy. I told her we need to get a place. And then my boss, Edwina, said, 'Hey, why don't you do one of those log cabin kind of things in the back?' I said 'That is actually a bloody good idea.? A lot of people can't believe how spacious it is. You must see us party in the kitchen. With margaritas. We've partied hard in this kitchen.

There were extra perks to having a log cabin:

> This whole thing took six weeks to erect. Another reason we did this is that you need plans for brick structures, but you don't need plans for this. You know how much it costs for plans. The best part of it is that if I want to go stay in Johannesburg, I can take my house with. Pick it up, put it on a flatbed truck and you go.

Arlene is effusive: 'It was like heaven coming to my own place.' The old family habit has come to bite Arlene. Her new sport is sitting in front of the TV and watching horse racing.

> Channel 239. I'm addicted. We were always a gambling family. We grew up gambling. When the big people were playing cards and dice, the children were also playing beside them, as well. We were always gamblers. Aunties. Uncles. Everyone.

With gambling has come a belief in the mysterious workings of God:

> With my back, I used to suffer every day. I used to take tablets every day. One Saturday I fell on the floor with pain. Odette couldn't get me onto the bed. Pain like you cannot believe. I cried. The next night I was sleeping. Our bedroom door was closed. When somebody sits on your bed and then gets up, and you feel that depression, that's exactly what I felt. Our bed was near the door and I was facing the door. This thing, whatever it was, got up. And because we have wooden floors, I could hear the footsteps going towards the door. I didn't want to look. My eyes opened. My arm couldn't move. I couldn't wake up. I heard the door handle click, but the door didn't open. The next minute it was quiet – like this person went out. It wasn't a scary feeling. I knew it wasn't human. And since that day in September 2018 I haven't had a back problem. A lot of people say it's my mom. I don't believe them. I say it's God. Only God can take my pain away. My mother can't take the pain away. Overnight my pain vanished.

Arlene is up for a promotion, but, as usual, there are hurdles in the way:

> I'm 55 this year. I've got five more years to work. My company's retirement age is 62, but I don't think I'm going to do seven more years. I want to retire now. It's hectic at work. The pressure. I went now for an interview for a supervisor's position – they call it a warehouse manager. So now I'm waiting . . . But because I haven't got my matric . . . they are debating because one of the

requirements is that you've got to have your matric. But I've been doing this job for a long time. I know the job. I got the highest marks in the interview. They haven't appointed a person yet, but that is what they are debating about . . . I'm going to be ten years with the company and they can't overlook something like that. The last president didn't pass matric and he was running the country. In the next two or three years, I will be retiring, so what must I be studying further for? I'm just leaving everything in God's hands.

How are things with Odette?

Our anniversary is on 17 May. We've been together for eight years. My sister says we must just stay engaged – for my mother's sake because that would have killed her. We are planning a wedding, but we are not sure when. We want to just have a little something outside and a dinner. I asked about the priest – and he is not saying anything, so I'm also just keeping quiet. I don't know how to go about it. We are both Anglican. They allow it now. My cousin Mervyn can marry us because there are priests that don't do it. Mervyn is a full-on Anglican priest. The only thing that is holding us back is a priest and a budget. I was thinking of a spit braai and salad. At John Dunne, you can pay R10 000 for food, décor, everything. But, let's get the promotion at work first. I didn't even know that the priest could marry us. Father Brian is in cahoots with both of us.

By November 2018, Ashley Singh was working for the sheriff's office and is involved in a serious relationship. He is 25. Ashley is still haunted by his upbringing:

Whatever I have said about my family, maybe they will deny the facts. But I was there and I suffered. It is hurtful. Families can turn . . . That's why I used to play soccer – because soccer used to keep me away from the things that were happening at home. Sometimes I used to go to school not eating for like two or three days. When your stomach makes a noise. That's how it was in school. And at that time it was exams. So that was the one reason that I just wanted to move away from that house. Thank God that Lorna came through for me because from there on onwards, my life just turned around.

Like many households in Wentworth, the Singhs were held together by their granny:

When my granny passed away, that's when everything went wrong. She was the core of the house. She held everything together. With her passing, everything dropped down and we went apart. She was like a breadwinner. Old people know how to organise a home. At that time, people used to give her money for rent and food. Why couldn't they do the same when she wasn't there?

Ashley has left Cavaliers and plays for a team called Beacon Park, which is in a league just below Cavaliers. He has been approached by a revived Leeds that is based in Ogle Road, his old stomping ground. But this is a Leeds only in name, not in substance. What are the plans for the future?

I am doing a course in occupational health and safety. I'm working and studying. I wasn't planning to, but one lady in our office always said just study. Just in case. So I'm studying. It's a one-year course through College SA. I'm studying online. Whatever happens there, I am not guaranteed that I will get a job in that field.

Ashley is certain about the role soccer played in his life:

I just know when someone's got a bad background. A lot of people nowadays are on that drug Sugars. I thank God that I never ended up like that. And thanks to soccer. When I used to go to soccer, it used to keep me off everything at home. I used to play soccer every day – even when there was no training. I used to play with my friends. Every day. Even on a Saturday.

Gary Goldstone (right), late in his career.

How to capture a life? Gary Goldstone. Sometimes spoken about loudly, sometimes in hushed tones, Goldstone's soccer was not just about his immense ball-playing skills. It was about the way he conducted himself on and off the pitch. On the field he wanted to win, throwing incredible energy into motivating his own side to greater heights, even to the extent of slapping his own centre-forward for missing a goal. In the change room, he would show his anger if Leeds lost, sometimes even demanding his goals back. And off the field, he lived life his way; he got into trouble with the law, entered a mental home and partied hard. In Argentinian football, there is the image of the *pibe*, born in the ghetto, who starts life playing on patches of land, with Diego Maradona as the most obvious example:

> The image of the typical *pibe* player is based on exuberance of skill, cunning, individual creativity, artistic feeling and improvisation . . . a lot of disorder is expected . . . There is a tendency to disregard boundaries, to play games even in private life (life is experienced as a permanent game or gamble if necessary);

> additionally there is a capacity of recompense, penalise or forgive others in an exaggerated way; to convey arbitrary judgements and choices; to display irrational and stupid heroism, and a capacity of 'die' (by being imprisoned, a drug addict or alcoholic) and to be resurrected; and a special talent in critical games to make the unexpected move, ensuring victory for the team ... The *pibes* serve as mirrors and, at the same time, operate as models defining the ideal of a style, a way of playing (Archetti 1997: 38).

As Lloyd Keshwar remembers and those who played alongside and against Goldstone attest, his way of playing, of living, of the sheer will to win changed Leeds and those around him. As was said of the *pibe* Maradona, 'the teams that Diego played for were transformed by his aroma' (quoted in Archetti 1997: 42). And that is what Goldstone gave to Leeds in its heyday, changing it into a team that played with style but also a winning mentality. Goldstone epitomises the epigraph that began the journey of this book; 'It is for winning, and winning in style ... Because, when it came to it on the pitch, when the whistle blew and money, power, status, reputation and history were all sent to the bench, you wanted it more' (Goldblatt 2006: xii).

Wentworth's history-keeper, Keshwar, who never played for Leeds but wore it close to his heart, captures this love affair of a team and its ethos:

> I was the MC for the Leeds United reunion. I loved Leeds. I supported them. All of them are my friends. They were good players – Putts [Moodley] and Elvis [Singh] and them. They were bloody good players. Today we are still as thick as thieves. If you see us on Sunday on the grounds, you will see all the Leeds guys. Under a pole, y'll see us sitting there – having a beer and talking and teasing one another. Sunday afternoon the game is at three o'clock. Young Cavvies are playing. Ogle Road grounds. We came from an era where we survived. Look at these photos. On a Sunday afternoon, y'll see all the boys there – well, not all, but by and large most of them. We are all good friends.

David Stanley fervently believes,

> had it not been for apartheid, Wentworth and Leeds could have turned out the best international soccer players of all time: Elvis Singh. Cheesa Baptist. Patrick Moodley. Gary Goldstone in his prime back then. Bully Larsen. It was a joy to watch. They could beat the best teams comfortably. I was just a puppy. For us, they were our inspiration. For a community that could easily get swayed from the path of right, soccer was our life. Sunday, after church, was 'get ready and get to the grounds'. Even if we squashed in the car, eight of us, we were there. Curries Fountain was our entertainment.

In thinking through the lives of those associated with soccer and culture more broadly in Wentworth, one is struck by how important place is to them; then and now. As Charles Wright Mills keeps reminding me, 'the biographies of men and women, the kind of individuals they variously become, cannot be understood without reference to the historical structures in which the milieu of their everyday life is organised' (1970: 161).

Old timers/new times

> I think about equal opportunities now. If we all had equal opportunities ... But then again maybe nobody would have watched me play football. A lot of people knew me in Wentworth because the community was still so small then. It was only the brown government houses. And we wanted to rise above the houses, above everything that was thrown at us. This gave us passion. A winning mentality. When we played we were more than Leeds, we were Wentworth.
> — Gary Goldstone, June 2018

Seeing the Leeds stalwarts sitting under a tree, watching a new generation in new circumstances, one is struck by the bonhomie and camaraderie. Somehow, despite the years that have passed and different paths taken, what Raymond Pahl and Liz Spencer call 'personal communities' (2004) come together even if just for some Sunday afternoon banter. But the longer you socialise and hang around, you come to realise that the bonds are much deeper.

Sociologist Richard Sennett bemoaned the 'fugitive quality of friendship and local community', in which 'no one becomes a long-term witness to another person's life' and people have 'no deep reason to care about one another' (2008: 148). In Wentworth, among these men and their families, there are long-held bonds and deep care. Goldstone still makes a turn in Wentworth, popping in to visit Boa and spending quality time with Dennis Petersen. News of the death of a stalwart or the sickness of a spouse spreads quickly. In the midst of my research, Eddie McKnight's wife took seriously ill. Every Leeds player I met was already in the know, their worry and care palpable.

Some have done better than others economically, moving to more middle-class areas. But even here, there is what Mary Richmond at the end of the nineteenth century called 'friendly visiting', which involves an 'intimate and continuing knowledge of and sympathy' with a friend's 'joys, sorrows, opinions, feelings, and entire outlook upon life' ([1899] 1969: 180). In June 2018, Everton Football Club had a get-together. There were former players who came from as far afield as Australia. More reunions are planned. Preparations are afoot for Wentworth soccer legends to play a few games in Australia against old teammates who emigrated. Wentworth, whether in actual bodily form or in the heart, draws people back.

Sitting under a tree, Leeds legends watch Young Cavs. Much banter. Much concentration on the field of play. In investing their hopes in this new generation on the ground where their own lives were turned into legend, these old Leeds stalwarts find joy. Janelle Wilson (2005: 26) tells us: 'What we are nostalgic for reveals what we value.' And the values that animated the past, the building of a collective, the style of play, the desire to win, not only for the team but a whole community, the quest for dignity, are all still here, under the tree.

There once was a team called Leeds, uniting a township in common purpose, taking on all comers and winning. In Afrikaans, *leed* means suffering, affliction and grief. In dumping Coloured people in places like Wentworth all those decades ago, the architects of the Coloured condition ensured that years of suffering would unite those it dispossessed. The collective suffering eventually pushed the white minority from power through struggle. But in Wentworth, some of them responded with more than just suffering and struggle. They responded with a devotion to building a soccer culture and style of play that at once imagined a community and captured the imagination (Anderson 1991).

For Lorna, dreams of a soccer team reaching the top bubble up in her mind once more:

> Young Cavies are a semi-professional club. If they win the league – which they are six points clear of . . . with five more games to play – they go to play-offs, to which we've been before. We've won regional play-offs. And we lost by one goal in the provincial play-offs. That would have taken us to the next level . . . And then we would be one away from PSL. And then we go pro. If all goes well, by 2018 we could have a professional team. Out of Wentworth.

It is 2019 and Young Cavaliers fail at the final hurdle. Still. Faith runs deep. Others might well call it a 'cruel optimism', the persistently unsatisfied hopes that you can never give up on (Berlant 2011).

Young Cavaliers under 13, 2019.

There is an eerie similarity between Young Cavaliers and Leeds of yesteryear. Not only because of the Leeds legends that come to watch them play and get involved in the club. But because of the way the club and place come together. As Lorna puts it:

> Soccer was almost done in Wentworth. Then, when Young Cavies came back – and the way in which we handle things and the way in which we support . . . We brand. We sing. We chant. We encourage and motivate our team. We are a family unit. We are not just a soccer team. Our home is where the boys feel comfortable. They get a meal after the games. A lot of players feel some sort of loyalty and attachment to us. A lot of other teams don't have that.

Leeds reached incredible heights and then fell. The connection to Young Cavaliers is about the past and the present. As John Berger reminds us, it is often 'on the site of loss that hopes are born' (1984: 55).

Is it still possible for a community team to make it to the heights of the professional league? Already, Young Cavaliers leak some of their best players to bigger clubs. And like the Leeds of old, will not the very success of Young Cavaliers lead to its demise as a community team? 'Community' – that easily abused word which divides and unites only to divide again, as illustrated by Goldstone's reflections:

> There's so much talent in that place. And they are all divided. Each team has got three or four good players. In those years, we had the benefit of the whole league supplying Leeds players. If that goes on, it could come about again. It would take a long time. But, with proper management and a good structure, it can be done. If you are looking at getting into each and every Wentworth school, and you have Wednesdays from Grade 1 football, and after two weeks, playing five-a-sides. No running. No training. Nothing. Just playing five-a-side. I would have still been doing it today if I didn't get sick. After three weeks, with seven-year-olds you can see the above-average. He's not brilliant. He's not great. But these three are better than the other sixty. So you look at that and you take those three – maybe seven or eight of them – and then you do them every Saturday continuously for

years and years and years. We've got gems growing up and dying and we don't even know it.

And, as Wellington Meth points out, the very success of Wentworth's soccer teams can also act as its Achilles heel:

> We've got a problem now. In the old days, we could play whatever age players. Now the new rule is that you will start with five under-21 players. Those who are seventeen, eighteen, nineteen, too. Where the problem comes in is that we've got five teams in Wentworth in the Castle League. Now we are all fighting over these players. For talent. Cherrians, Cavaliers, Aces, Suburbs and Celtic. So we are all fighting for youngsters now. It has got so bad that even if you can't play football, we put you there. Five minutes later, we take you out and put in a senior player because we can make three changes. I can see . . . Never mind he's fourteen. I can put the older guys behind and encourage him.

Obsessed by the game, David Stanley turned his interest to coaching youngsters in the late 1990s:

> I had a phenomenal junior team. Every tournament we played, we won. If I was in trouble with not getting things right – not getting a formula right – I turned to my old mate Kaapie. By 2000, our under 13s could take on under 15s. Any junior team at least two years older than them – and give them a good hiding. They called themselves Silver Stars. They were under 13. People still worry me to coach. I just don't have the zest in me. We can create over here. But, there's no unity. There is just nobody that's willing to drive it. People get involved for three months and then after four months they lose the zest. They don't go any further. There are big companies here. There's Engen. There's Sapref. There are refineries that they can siphon millions out of. But they all just disappeared into life. They went to go get careers. They are all big grown men now.

Stanley, in the style of Wright Mills (1970), is able to link local challenges to wider issues, the local and broader social relations:

For the past 50 years that people have been living in Wentworth, 80 per cent of them are suffering from some kind of health ailment. Asthma. Sinusitis. Babies are born with defects. They are not developing medical illnesses; they are born with health defects. It's put down to one thing and one thing only: we have been polluted over the years. It is so heartbreaking. We allow industries like Engen and Sapref to bluff the community. They pump in R10k here and there. Bang. There you go. I don't want to call it ignorance – because there are a lot of educated people in our community – but maybe we don't put our heads together enough. That's why I am not coaching anymore. These companies make about R400 million an hour. If they can pump a million into soccer – which is small change – and into the development of sport . . . What a difference it would make. Our youngsters are only smoking drugs. You can take them to the grounds. You can try with them. There are just no proper facilities to keep them motivated. This has been like this from the time it was built. Nothing has changed. They tried to do the toilets up; to do up the change rooms that had been ruined by all these Whoonga

A new generation at play (photo: Cedric Nunn).

heads and Sugar heads [cheap drugs that give an instant high but almost immediately let you down]. But no proper strict measures were put in place. That is the whole essence of it.

For the newcomer to Wentworth, the belching smoke and acrid dust manifests in an immediate watering of the eyes and sniffing of the nose. But for Wentonians, it has been normalised: the asthma pump and the story of another person afflicted with cancer, part of everyday life. One is reminded of Rob Nixon's evocative exposition of slow violence:

> Violence is customarily conceived as an event that is immediate in time, explosive and spectacular in space, and as erupting into instant sensational visibility. We need, I believe, to engage a different kind of violence . . . incremental and accretive, its calamitous repercussions playing out across a range of temporal scales (2011: 4).

Environmental organisations make Herculean efforts to expose the transgressions of local petrochemical companies and the culpability of local government in this process, but these are defensive battles largely conducted behind the backs of the community. There is no sense of outrage, as there is no spectacular event such as Chernobyl or Bhopal. Rather, the violence is slower, longer, normalised into the very landscape.

Tensions continue to bubble in Wentworth. The jobs that could once build a career as a fitter and turner, pipe fitter and allied jobs in the shipping and petrochemical industry are on the decline. Where there are jobs, they are mainly temporary, in what the petrochemical industry calls shutdowns. Gangs have become more and more violent, carving out territories and defending them with their lives. When the pathways that defined the immediate previous generation of Wentonians is rapidly eroded,

> . . . when the sense of honour that has characterised the community has been destroyed; when the presence of large gangs of young people cut off from the relations in which an older generation learnt its values, and for whom those values of

> mutual respect can make no sense ... they derive respect from having no respect for others as an instantiation of 'hardness' ... (Charlesworth 2003: 82)

And space is everywhere closed down. There is no money to go into town. Many in the flats live their lives within a few square kilometres and will always do so. While older Wentonians may find God and salvation, young men have learnt that the long walk to freedom

> ... is a road to nowhere; one that never seems to end, and that no matter how far they walk along it, their condition does not seem to alter. There seems only more uncertainty and the resolve of another plan or scam to get through the problems of the immediate pressing future (Charlesworth 2003: 152–3).

There are deep personal histories in this book. At the same time, one is deeply aware

> ... that *the most personal is the most impersonal*, that many of the most intimate dramas, the deepest malaises, the most singular suffering that women and men can experience find their roots in the objective contradictions, constraints and double binds inscribed in the structures of the labour and housing markets, in the merciless sanctions of the school system, or in the mechanisms of economic and social inheritance (Bourdieu and Wacquant 1992: 201; original emphasis).

While residents of the flats complain about lack of space both inside and outside, as well as the violence that accompanies gang life and drug peddling, they see Wentworth as *their* space, a Coloured place. Throughout my research, the community made their feelings clear, that Coloureds have been marginalised politically, both locally and nationally, and that Wentworth is at least a place they can call home and the flats are something to bequeath their children. Long-time resident of Wentworth Helen Kelly, who once felt like an outsider as a 'Transkeian' Coloured, tells me in no uncertain terms:

> We, as a Coloured community, feel like Wentworth belongs to us. Outsiders are not welcome. When the oil refinery wanted us to move, Wentworth refused to move. They said the oil refinery must move. They said, 'We are born here. We are not moving.' And it's not because they love the place. It's the effort of moving. It's cheaper to stay here in Wentworth. And where will we be thrown if we get moved out of here? Oh my God. Hell and gone from everybody. There are also white people living among us in the flats. Cheaper rent. They can't afford to stay on the Bluff. It's not la-di-dah white people. It's these struggling ones. Some of them are married to Coloureds here. Some of them are here just to buy drugs. The moment you move into Wentworth, you stop being white. You become Coloured.

By defending this narrow piece of turf that is at once loathed and valued, walls of identity are constructed as much as they are trespassed by black African children travelling to attend school or whites sliding down the hills of the Bluff and making a home.

The colour lines that colonialism and apartheid invented are still with us. 'Race', as Kwame Anthony Appiah puts it, 'has become a palimpsest, a parchment written upon by successive generations where nothing is ever *entirely* erased (2018: 133; original emphasis). Within this widely held community perception that Coloureds are marginalised, Manual Castells's point about identity becoming 'the most valuable resource to defend their interests, and ultimately their being' (1989: 228) is particularly apposite. The irony is that as Wentworth sees the trespass of more and more black Africans from schools to workers in the contiguous petrochemical industries, the more the idea of Wentworth as 'our' place congeals. As Akhil Gupta and James Ferguson put it, the more 'actual places and localities become . . . blurred and indeterminate, *ideas* of culturally and ethnically distinct places become even more salient' (1992: 10; original emphasis).

The fact that the drive to build new houses by the ANC government has passed Wentworth by does not loosen a sense of place but simply reinforces it. People feel that this is the only space they have and therefore seek to defend it. In this sense, Wentworth is conjured up in 'the memory of living in a securely circumscribed place, with a sense of stable boundaries and a place-bound culture with its regular flow of time and a core of permanent relations' (Huyssen 2003: 24). This cannot be read as simply a yearning for apartheid but rather as a response to the circumstances of the present; the sense of loss of opportunities in the marketplace, of being pushed down the queue by Africanisation, skills handed through the generations no more needed, as well as the state's neglect. In this environment, place becomes a way of protecting the little that one has. And networks of support become even more important.

Although this book is predominantly focused on the local, one cannot ignore the broader political demand for land expropriation (from whites) put forward by some national political parties. While this demand may only have been formulated initially as a populist slogan within internecine ANC battles, it is now firmly on the policy agenda. While land expropriation is focused on farmland in rural areas, it is widely understood by academics that the most pressing land hunger actually exists in urban and peri-urban centres. Government maladministration aside, township development has been severely stymied by the ownership rights of private individuals and government doing very little that is socially productive with their property.

A stone's throw from Wentworth is a disused horse-racing track. It served as an important green lung for the people of the South Basin where pollution is arguably the highest in the country. Despite protests from residents, the land is earmarked for a logistics park to service heavy haulage vehicles and space for additional heavy industry. When it was clear that the race course would be sold, some members of the community put forward proposals for flats that would allow space for vegetable gardens, a place where children could safely play outside while keeping the area as a green lung. This was not considered and the government backed the proposed container park. The logic seems to be that space is preferentially allocated to taxable entities, no matter the social needs. As the struggles around refurbishment in Wentworth have shown, even if some of those taxes are allocated to make living conditions slightly better for some, it cannot be spent for the desperation of others.

The South Durban Community Environmental Alliance is the main organisation in the area and sees something more insidious: a progressive land grab that hems in and presses against the residents, increasing pollution and traffic, making life more and more difficult and forcing people out. This has already happened in nearby Clairwood where trucks and containers have progressively stolen into the residential core (*The Post*, 25 February 2018). Alongside plans to expand the harbour, one gets a sense that with the trucks coming in and out of the oil refineries and container parks and a growth of warehouses, the residents of South Durban will become part of what Nixon calls 'administered invisibility', which results in 'spatial amnesia, as communities, under the banner of development, are physically unsettled and imaginatively removed . . .' (2011: 151).

The NGOs that provide Kimbies (nappies), the neighbour who takes over a child, the church that hands over groceries – all make possible the living of a life that is one step above bare and yet also splitting at the seams.

The contradiction that runs through David Stanley's assertions about the petrochemical companies polluting the area is that they are almost always seen as the 'solution'. It is something that affects the community on many levels; the companies that provide work, that fund NGOs while simultaneously being fingered for the high rates of cancer and asthma. Engen, which figuratively and literally sits inside Wentworth, has set up the Engen Community Stakeholder Forum (ESCF) 'as a forum for Engen to effectively liaise with Engen's fence-line communities in the South Basin . . .' (ESCF 2015).

The founding document delineates different kinds of organisations and sets out their responsibilities. NGOs that want to apply for funding need to register with the ESCF. This means that it has not only the potential to divide community organisations, but registered organisations can potentially act as a Trojan Horse in the community, denuding the possibility of a united front against Engen. Occasionally though, Engen's role is criticised. For example, on 29 May 2018, local activist Frank Alexander wrote to Engen raising a number of issues:

- We want to sit at board level to decide the future of our community.
- We want to be equal partners so we can determine our own destiny as a people.
- We want our 24-hour clinic from all the pollution you have caused over the years.

- We want the companies that maintain the refinery to come from the community.
- We want soccer grounds and the school and soccer stadium to be done up because you sponsor millions of rand in sport yet the grounds opposite the refinery are dilapidated.
- The NGOs and NPOs [non-profit organisations] that sit at your table are treated poorly; we know this. They are at the mercy of your crumbs that you wipe off your table.
- That is why we have no tangible development because they engaged in glorified begging and you as Engen can tap yourself on the back for doing absolutely, totally and completely nothing for the last 50 to 60 years.

Here, once more, we see the ambiguous and even contradictory relationship with Engen: Engen pollutes the community, uses NGOs and NPOs as Trojan Horses but Alexander wants the community to sit on the Board of Engen, to sponsor a 24-hour clinic for the patients that it has made sick. It would be easy to read this as a classic case of militant action that masks a sense of disempowerment. However, the ties that bind the bodies and hopes of Wentonians to Engen have a long history. Rather than see it as contradictory, can it possibly be realpolitik? With the Coloured middle class opting to escape Wentworth, artisans from the area competing in a deracialised market and pervasive unemployment, Engen represents the one place in which resources can be leveraged. At the same time, many Wentonians feel that their parents gave the best years of their lives to Engen and that the community is 'owed' a commitment to uplift the area. In a place where things seem to be falling apart, disappointment looms on every stairwell, and exacerbated by the effects of the Jacob Zuma Presidency with its rampant corruption and advancement of sleazy cronies, pride can come from pioneering a role in building the petrochemical industry, the very thing that is slowing killing you.

There is optimism that things could turn for the better among people like Rodney Roskruge who is busy with a short story. It is provisionally entitled 'In Waiting of the Big Rains', which prophetically is being finished in the midst of Durban's heavy rains that claimed the lives of over 80 people in April/May 2019:

I was trying to imagine the big rains that were coming. Now it feels quite prophetic. It also means 'waiting for the real leaders' because we have a drought of leaders now and they won't be able to take us where we want to go. They are still acting white in black skin. So we are waiting for that big rain that will wash away everything like it is doing now. And maybe some leaders will die. Bless them. But we need fresh ones. Those are rains we are really waiting for.

Others rely on direct political action. A group that included Frank Alexander, Melanie Haines, Allen Holmes, Terrence Ogle and Brandon Manique led a protest on behalf of their demands in June 2018. Engen moved for an urgent court interdict that relied on the apartheid-era National Key Points Act to outlaw protests. The interdict was granted. A return date in court looms. And so it will go on.

The more time you spend on the streets of Wentworth, you begin to also appreciate the existence of what Manuel Torini calls 'intimate activism', which involves the 'capacity to create minimal conditions for ethical and material endurance' (2018: 438).

Torini is instructive in that he attunes us to go beyond the desire to focus on the larger conflicts that occasionally erupt to what happens in everyday life:

> ... in many worlds politics is not about debates and argumentation ... but about ... surviving, coping and resisting ... In many worlds, activism, or the rehearsal of new social projects in the face of suffering, *is* watering plants or putting some ointment on infants' noses, or maybe 'doing nothing' (2018: 452; original emphasis).

We see this in Wentworth: the work of Kind Ministry, Rodney Roskruge's commitment to writing circles and fostering a culture of reading, Doreen Houghton's attempts at a vegetable patch, and Lorna Petersen's 'boarding house'.

Back in the field of play, Lorna bemoans the costs of running a team:

The cost of running a SAB team is about R10k . . . R15k . . . It can go to more . . . A month. We don't play at home all the time. There's home and away. We travel out. There's wear and tear. There's petrol. There's referee fees when we are at home. There's boots . . . Not to mention one or two personal lives where we pay rent and buy food for a household. Plus you must have kit. The list goes on and on and on. What we need is businessmen to come and throw their weight behind us. The Engens – in fact, all the big companies – won't get involved, unless you have an academy. And I don't have the time for all that. People will help you when you have already 'arrived', but they won't help you out along the way.

Still, Lorna's eyes light up when she talks about the new talent that is coming through. It motivates her to never give up.

Nobel literature winner Mario Vargas Llosa tells us that sport and soccer in particular is

> . . . a spectacle which does not transcend the physical, the sensory, the instant emotion, which unlike, for example, a book or a play, scarcely leaves a trace in the memory and does not enrich or impoverish knowledge. And that is its appeal; that it is exciting and empty (1997: 168).

Vargas Llosa is wrong. Memories abound about a team called Leeds. The historic and inspirational links are as clear as a footpath through the veld. The path is a bit overgrown through lack of everyday use but indelible still. Big people walked there and continue to: Lorna, former chair of the Supporters' Club, her brother, Dennis, a star of the mid-1970s' dream team. They lived through 'the best of times' (Leeds winning trophies at the highest level) and 'the worst of times' (memories of apartheid evictions, the violence of the new broken ambitions).

The new season. Will spring come? The youngsters stir renewed hope. The eternal question haunts: will Young Cavaliers escape the lower leagues and finally arrive? And if they do, will they lose their *place*?

References

Abrahams, E. 2009. *Eddy of Time: Rialto FC: 1958–1961*. Self-published.
Adhikari, M. 2005. *Not White Enough: Not Black Enough: Racial Identity in the South African Coloured Community*. Cape Town: Double Storey Books.
Alegi, P. 2004. *Laduma! Soccer, Politics and Society in South Africa*. Pietermaritzburg: University of KwaZulu-Natal Press.
Anderson, B. 1991. *Imagined Communities: Reflections on the Origin and Spread of Nationalism*. London: Verso.
Appiah, K.A. 2018. *The Lies That Bind: Rethinking Identity*. London: Profile Books.
Archetti, E. 1997. '"And Give Joy to My Heart": Ideology and Emotions in the Argentinian Cult of Maradona'. In *Entering the Field: New Perspectives on World Football*, edited by G. Armstrong and R. Giulianotti, pp. 31–52. Oxford: Berg.
Benjamin, W. 1978. *Reflections: Essays, Aphorisms, Autobiographical Writings*, trans. E. Jephcott. New York: Schocken Books.
Berger, J. 1976. *A Fortunate Man: The Story of a Country Doctor*. London: Writers and Readers Cooperative.
———. 1984. *And Our Faces, My Heart, Brief as Photos*. London: Vintage.
Berlant, L. 2011. *Cruel Optimism*. Durham, NC: Duke University Press.
Booth, D. 1998. *The Race Game: Sport and Politics in South Africa*. London: Frank Cass.
Bourdieu, P. 1984. *Distinction: A Social Critique of the Judgment of Taste*. Cambridge, MA: Harvard University Press.
———. 1991. *Language and Symbolic Power*. Cambridge: Polity Press.
Bourdieu, P. and L. Wacquant. 1992. *An Invitation to Reflexive Sociology*. Cambridge: Polity Press.
Bourdieu, P. et al. 1999. *The Weight of the World: Social Suffering in Contemporary Society*. Stanford: Stanford University Press.
Burns, J. 2012. *La Roja: How Soccer Conquered Spain and How Spanish Soccer Conquered the World*. New York: Nation Books.
Caine, B. 2010. *Biography and History*. Houndmills: Palgrave Macmillan.
Casey, E. 1998. *The Fate of Place: A Philosophical History*. Berkeley, CA: University of California Press.

Castells, M. 1989. *The Informational City: Information Technology, Economic Restructuring and the Urban-Regional Process*. Oxford: Blackwell.

Chari, S. 2006. 'Post-Apartheid Livelihood Struggles in Wentworth, South Durban'. In *The Development Decade? Economic and Social Change in South Africa, 1994–2004*, edited by V. Padayachee, pp. 427–43. Pretoria: HSRC Press.

Charlesworth, S. 2003. *A Phenomenology of Working-Class Experience*. Cambridge: Cambridge University Press.

Coloured People's Development Project. 2012. 'Coloured People's Development Project'. Unpublished document in author's possession.

De Certeau, M. 1989. *The Practice of Everyday Life*. Berkeley, CA: University of California Press.

DeLillo, D. 2004. *End Zone*. London: Picador.

Department of Economics, University of Natal. 1952. *The Durban Housing Survey: A Study of Housing in a Multi-Racial Community*. Pietermaritzburg: University of Natal Press.

Derrida, J. 2005. *The Politics of Friendship*, trans. G. Collins. London: Verso.

Desai, A. 2016. 'Die Ou Ballie is net so 'n Naai soos Ons: Race, Place and Gangs in a Durban Township'. *Acta Criminologica* 29(3): 99–109.

———. 2017. 'Service Delivery and the War Within: Wentworth, Durban'. *South African Review of Sociology* 48(1): 85–99.

Engen Community Stakeholder Forum. 2015. 'Terms of Reference for Engen Community Stakeholder Forum [ECSF]'. Engen Petroleum Limited, Durban.

Erasmus, Z. 2013. 'Throwing the Genes: A Renewed Biological Imaginary of "Race", Place and Identification'. *Theoria* 60(3): 38–53.

Frisch, M. 1998. 'Oral History and *Hard Times*: A Review Essay'. In *The Oral History Reader*, edited by R. Perks and A. Thomson, pp. 29–37. London: Routledge.

Fynn, L. 1991. 'The "Coloured" Community of Durban: A Study of Changing Perceptions of Identity'. Master's thesis, University of Natal, Durban.

Gaffney, C. 2008. *Temples of the Earthbound Gods: Stadiums in the Cultural Landscapes of Rio de Janeiro and Buenos Aires*. Austin: University of Texas Press.

Galeano, E. 1998. *Soccer in Sun and Shadow*. London: Verso.

Gibran, K. 2015 [1923]. *The Prophet*. New York: Vintage Books.

Goetschel, W. 2009. 'Street, Life, and other Signs: Heine in the Rue Laffitte'. *City & Society* 21(2): 230–44.

Goldblatt, D. 2006. *The Ball is Round: A Global History of Football*. London: Viking.

Guijt, I. and M.K. Shah (eds). 1998. *The Myth of Community: Gender Issues in Participatory Development*. London: Intermediate Technology Publications.

Gupta, A. and J. Ferguson. 1992. 'Beyond "Culture": Space, Identity and the Politics of Difference'. *Cultural Anthropology* 7(1): 6–23.

Hargreaves, J. 2000. *Freedom for Catalonia? Catalan Nationalism, Spanish Identity and the Barcelona Olympic Games*. Cambridge: Cambridge University Press.

Hayden, D. 1995. *The Power of Place*. Cambridge, MA: MIT Press.

Herzfeld, M. 2005. *Cultural Intimacy: Social Poetics in a Nation-State*. New York. Routledge.

Homer. 2007. *The Iliad*. Ann Arbour: University of Michigan Press.

Houston, G. 2006. Interview with Robert McBride, 26 October. SADET Oral History Project, Johannesburg.

Huyssen, A. 2003. *Present Pasts: Urban Palimpsests and the Politics of Memory*. Stanford: Stanford University Press.

Jameson, F. 2003. 'Pseudo-Couples'. *London Review of Books* 25(22) 20 November: 21–3, https://www.lrb.co.uk/v25/n22/fredric-jameson/pseudo-couples.

Johnson, V. 2017. 'Coloured South Africans: A Middleman Minority of another Kind'. *Social Identities* 23(1): 4–28.

Knowles, C. 2000. *Bedlam on the Streets*. London: Routledge.

———. 2003. *Race and Social Analysis*. London and Thousand Oaks, CA: Sage.

Lippard, L. 1997. *The Lure of the Local: Senses of Place in a Multicentred Society*. New York: The New Press.

Maré, G. 2014. *Declassified: Moving Beyond the Dead End of Race in South Africa*. Johannesburg: Jacana.

Merleau-Ponty, M. 1969. *Humanism and Terror*. Boston: Beacon Press.

Merrifield, A. 2012. *John Berger*. London: Reaktion Books.

Mills, J. 2005. *Subaltern Sports: Politics and Sport in South Asia*. London: Anthem Press.

Murray, M. 2008. *Taming the Disorderly City: The Spatial Landscape of Johannesburg after Apartheid*. Cape Town: UCT Press.

Nauright, J. 1997. *Sport, Cultures and Identities in South Africa*. Cape Town: David Philip.

Ndebele, N. 2006. *Rediscovery of the Ordinary: Essays on South African Literature and Culture*. Pietermaritzburg: University of KwaZulu-Natal Press.

Ngidi, M. 2014. 'Inter-Race Soccer and the 1960 Race Riots in Durban'. *Historia* 59(2): 326–43.

Nixon, R. 2011. *Slow Violence and the Environmentalism of the Poor*. Cambridge, MA: Harvard University Press.

Pahl, R. and L. Spencer. 2004. *Rethinking Friendship: Hidden Solidarities for Today*. Princeton, NJ: Princeton University Press.

Pearson, H. 1994. *The Far Corner: A Mazy Dribble through North-East Football*. London: Little Brown.

Porsfelt, D. 2009. 'Supporter Rock in Sweden: Locality, Resistance and Irony at Play'. In *Sporting Sounds: Relationships between Sport and Music*, edited by A. Bateman and J. Bale, pp. 193-209. London: Routledge.

Ramphele, M. 1993. *A Bed Called Home: Life in the Migrant Labour Hostels of Cape Town*. Cape Town: David Philip.

Ramsamy, S. 2004. *Reflections on a Life in Sport*. Cape Town: Greenhouse.

Richmond, M.E. [1899] 1969. *Friendly Visiting among the Poor: A Handbook for Charity Workers*. Montclair, NJ: Patterson Smith.

Rostron, B. 1991. *Till Babylon Falls*. London: Coronet Books.

Sangster, J. 1998. 'Telling Our Stories: Feminist Debates and the Use of Oral History'. In *The Oral History Reader*, edited by R. Perks and A. Thomson, pp. 87-100. London: Routledge.

Sardica, J. 2013. 'The Content and Form of "Conventional" Historical Biography'. *Rethinking History* 17(3): 383-400.

Sennett, R. 1974. *The Fall of Public Man: On the Social Psychology of Capitalism*. New York: Vintage Books.

———. 2008. *The Corrosion of Character: The Personal Consequences of Work in the New Capitalism*. New York: W.W. Norton.

Sousanis, N. 2015. *Unflattening*. Cambridge, MA: Harvard University Press.

Subrayan, M. 2017. *Delron Buckley: My Life*. Durban: Hope to Overcome.

Torini, M. 2018. 'Hypo-Interventions: Intimate Activism in Toxic Environments'. *Social Studies of Science* 48(3): 438-55.

Tuan, Y-F. 2001. *Space and Place: The Perspective of Experience*. Minneapolis: University of Minnesota Press.

Union of South Africa. 1950. *Population Registration Act, No. 30 of 1950*. Pretoria: Government Printer.

Vargas Llosa, M. 1997. *Making Waves: Essays*. New York: Farrar, Straus and Giroux.

Venter, G. 2018. 'Discord in the Dressing Room: The Ideological Complexities within Non-Racial Football during the late 1970s'. In *Exploring Decolonising Themes in SA Sport History: Issues and Challenges*, edited by F.J. Cleophas, pp. 55-66. Stellenbosch: African Sun Media.

Wacquant, L. 1998. 'Pierre Bourdieu'. In *Key Sociological Thinkers*, edited by R. Stones, pp. 215-29. London: Palgrave Macmillan.

Walsh, S. and J. Soske (eds). 2016. *Ties that Bind: Race and the Politics of Friendship in South Africa*. Johannesburg: Wits University Press.

Wicomb, Z. 1998. 'Five Afrikaner Texts and the Rehabilitation of Whiteness'. *Social Identities* 4(3): 363-83.

Wilson, J. 2005. *Nostalgia: Sanctuary of Meaning*. Pennsylvania: Bucknell Press.
Wittgenstein, L. 1984. *Culture and Value*. Oxford: Basil Blackwell.
Woolf. L. (ed.). 1967. 'Virginia Woolf: "The New Biography"'. In V. Woolf, *Collected Essays, Volume IV*. London: Chatto & Windus.
Wright Mills, C. 1970. *The Sociological Imagination*. Harmondsworth: Penguin.
Young, J. 2016. 'The Lexicon of Love'. *Chronic Books*, Supplement to the *Chimurenga Chronic*, April.

Index

Abrahams, Edward (Ettie) 28, 29
Abrahams, Farook 133
Abrahams, Michael 68
Abrahams, Sydney 68
Aces United (football club) 62, 73, 217
Acts of Parliament
    Group Areas 60, 139
    National Keypoints 225
    Population Registration 22
Adams, Abdul Kader 77, 110–11, 206
Adams, Elijah 13, 74
Adams, Julia 13
Adams, Salie 133
Africa, E. 45
Africa, Patrick (Paddy) 141
alcohol 25, 75–6, 83, 145, 186
Alexander, Mr 34
Alexander, Frank 223–4, 225
Alexander, Kevin 10, 185–7, 190–3
Alexander, Maureen 190, 192–3
Alexander, Queenie 191
Ali, Enver 62
All Blacks (football club) 61, 62, 64, 149, 151
Amaglug-glug (football team) 164
AmaZulu (football club) 95, 100, 102, 105, 134, 135
America, Keith 106, 133
Anderson, Christopher Francis 146–7
apartheid relocation 1, 141, 199
apprenticeship system 180

Aralian Lads (football club) 38, 61, 92
Arends, Alex 133
Austerville Project Steering Committee (APSC) 172, 173
Avalon Athletics (football club) 39, 40, 60
Aztec Hockey Club 153

Bandawe, Tapuwe (Taps) 19
bands *see* music and dance
Baptist, Mrs 122–3
Baptist, Gregory 106–7, 111, 112, 118, 121, 161, 199, 201
Baptist, Trevor (Cheesa) 96, 106, 107, 108–10, 111, 122–3, 161, 213
Barends, Boy 106
Barnes, L. 29
Barracuda (football club) 41
Bayview (football club) 163
Bechet Teacher Training College 105
Berea (football club) 64
Bezuidenhout, C. 45
Bezuidenhout, Keith 39, 54, 74
Bezuidenhout, Ralton 143
Bezuidenhout, Tyrone 108, 122, 143
Bhamjee, Abdul 206
Big Four (band) 15
Bilham, Pat 51, 54, 74
Birch, Graham 45, 70–2, 75–6, 108, 201–2, 203
Bishop, Paul 95, 96

233

Blair, Pat 59, 94
Blankenberg, Neil 96
Blitz (nightclub) 122
Bluff Rangers (football club) 133-4
Bonhomme, S. 29
Bowes, Tony 167-8
Brooks, Philly 85
Brown, Brendon 163
Buckley, Delron 158-9
Bull, Denzil 108, 118
Burgess, Edna 155
Burgess, Marlon 206, 207

Campbell, Fuzzy 122
Campbell, Victor (Blondie) 28, 29, 39, 40, 45, 64, 73, 74, 75, 77, 93, 146
Campbell, W. 29
Cape Town Spurs (football club) 94-5, 105, 119, 121, 133
Captiuex (Saints player) 115
Carey, *Father* 35, 111, 119
Carrelle, Roy 41, 42
Cato Manor 3
Cele, Henry (Black Cat) 96
Cele, John 20, 203-4
Celtic (football club) 217
Cerro (football club) 98
Charles, Rodney 147
Chelin, Lawrence 88
Chelsea (football club) 31
Cherrians (football club) 138, 139-41, 142-3, 144-5, 146, 217
Chockrane, H. 29
Clairwood 139, 141, 223
clothing and textile industry 57, 170
Cockrane, Gerald 50
Coetzee, Dougie 88
Coloured community
    definition 22-3
    employment 112-13, 118, 179, 199;
        see also Wentworth, employment
    housing 9-10, 13; *see also*
        Wentworth, housing
    marginalisation 100, 186, 194, 199, 220
    and Mauritius 10
    middle class 26-7, 224
    other 13, 14
    and Transkei 10-13
    and World War II 32-3
Colouredness 3-4, 10, 186, 194, 199
community and communion (as concepts) 3, 78-9, 216
construction industry 180
Coon Carnival *see* music and dance
Cross, Kevin 89
Curries Fountain 27, 55, 63, 78-81, 100, 105, 120, 213

Da Gama, Owen 135
Daniels, Eddie 147
Dasheen (gang) 63, 80
Davenhill, C. 29
Davids, June 49-50, 54
De Klerk, Marike 23
Deane, E. 29
Delcarme, Robin 133
Destroyer (gang, aka Naughty Youngsters) 165-6, 169
destructive character 169
Dickson, Crain 115
dogs 55
Dollie, Pettie 133
Donnelly, Lewis 164
drugs 25, 67-8, 75, 76, 88, 169, 196, 205, 210, 218-19
Dunn, Derrick 46
Durban
    housing 9-10, 171

industrial development 222-3
map of 4
racial geography 4-5, 6, 22, 26, 27, 56, 60
Durban City (football club) 86, 87-8, 102
Durban Suburbs (football club) 39, 94, 217
Duschene, Barry 105, 108, 110, 201
Dutlow, Kirk 121

Easthorpe, Denzil 40
Edwards, Llewellyn (Doogoo) 166, 170
Edwards, Michael (Bumpers) 166
Egelhof, F. 29
Engen 141, 223-4, 225
Essop, Adam 49, 74
Everton (football club) 31, 214

Fataar brothers 14
Federation Professional League (FPL) 22, 100-1
Flames (band) 14-15
football
　and apartheid 28, 30
　boycott of South Africa 40, 96, 101, 129
　coaching 143-5
　defectors 100
　definition of 195, 226
　identification with clubs 1, 57
　and masculinity 125
　non-racial 39-40
　South African 21-2
　township 87
　white 87-8
　women's 127-30, 131, 162
Francis, George 40
Francis, Gerry 29, 30-1
Frank, Phillip 195-6

Fredericks, Goofy 59
friendship 58
Fynn, Brian 45, 121
Fynn, Godfrey (Zulu) 94
Fynn, Goofy 67
Fynn, Hector 40
Fynn, Ricardo 142

Gabriel, Pat 119
Gama, Kenneth 40
gambling 62, 208
gangs 7-8, 14, 25, 45, 68, 88; *see also* Wentworth, crime, violence and gangs
gardens 15-16, 17, 188-90, 225
gay sexuality 130-1
Gcabashe, Reginald 40
George, Albert 38
George, James 94
Gillot, Gregory 105, 108
Golden Arrows (football club) 117
Goldstone, Christopher 58, 62, 66-7, 70, 83
Goldstone, Cora 43
Goldstone, Dorothy 58, 66, 84
Goldstone, Gary 3, 6, 30, 38, 39, 40-4, 54, 58-64, 65-70, 71, 72, 73, 74-5, 76, 81-5, 86, 87-90, 98, 99, 100, 105, 106, 109, 110, 115, 117, 119, 120, 132-4, 137, 199-200, 211, 212, 213, 214, 216-17
Goldstone, Gary *Junior* 74, 198
Goldstone, Shirley 43
Goldstone, Ursula 30, 68, 69-70, 76, 83-4, 199
Govender, Buddy 105, 108
Govender, Manna 83
Govender, Vish 95, 96
Grand Challenge League 39

Green, A. 45
Green, K. 45
Green Mambas *see* Leeds United
Grey, Bob 41, 42
group biography 2, 3

habitus (concept) 167
Haines, Melanie 225
Happy Valley 8, 9, 115
Harban, Comet 181–3
Hartze, Bernard (Dancing Shoes) 30, 31
Harvey, Butch 45
Harvey, Graham 50, 54
Henry, Zoot 62
Holmes, Allen 225
Homiel, Walla 73
Houghton, Doreen 188–90, 194, 225
Hoy Park (Old Kingsmead) 112, 115
Hughes, Errol 46, 96, 97, 120, 132, 134–6, 137
Hulley, Archie 86
Hulley, C. 29
Hutchinson, Patrick 46

Igesund, Gordon 135, 136
Indian community 26
International Federation of Association Football (FIFA) 40, 96
Isaacs, L. 29

Jackson, Bradley 19
Jacobs, Shaiem 133
Jaffer, J. 29
James, Kiara 161
James, Martin 154, 155
job reservation 33
Johannes, A. 29
Johanneson, Albert (Hurry Hurry, Black Flash) 30–1
Johnson, A. 29

Jonathan, G. 45
Jordaan, Joanne 127
Joseph, Skiddo 55, 56, 155
Joshua, Duncan 119
Julius, Preston 117
Justine, Marshall (Psycho) 36, 38

Kaizer Chiefs (football club) 53, 136
Kast, Kerwin 155, 158
Keshwar, Craig 116
Keshwar, Hylton 116
Keshwar, Kenneth 116
Keshwar, Lloyd 9, 24, 30, 31–2, 44, 52, 53, 66, 77–8, 79–81, 84–5, 108–10, 111, 112–16, 132, 135–7, 212
Khumalo, Given 96
Kind Ministry 192–4, 225
King, Duncan 36
King, Roland (Roley) 61
Kiss (dance group) 16–17

Lamontville Golden Arrows *see* Golden Arrows
land 222
Lansberg, George 119
Larsen, Bull 198, 213
Larsen, Clinton 142, 198
LeCour, Charlie 108
Leeds United (football club)
    colours and kit 31, 36, 37, 54
    demise 2, 51, 132–4, 137, 159, 199
    discord 75–6
    early years 36–47, 48–9
    and families 45–6, 49, 52, 76
    finance 37, 50–1, 53, 153
    mascot 55, 76
    name and nickname 30, 31, 44
    origins 32, 35, 48
    and professionalism 38, 44, 97, 108–10, 120, 135–7

social aspects 27, 45-6, 52, 54, 56-7
squad system 37-8, 45, 53, 54
supporters 55, 76, 77, 83-4, 147, 153-4, 195
training at night 49
transport to matches 77-8, 79
trophies and major victories 64-5, 74-5, 96, 105, 120, 133, 136, 199
and Wentworth identity 22, 94, 196, 197, 214-15, 226
Leeds United Football Club (England) 30
legislation *see* Acts of Parliament
Leicester City Football Club (England) 42-3
Leslie, Desmond 71
Linderboom, Lenny 92
Linderboom, Vaughn 141-2
Lornay's (catering company) 154-5, 161
Luiters, Philip 133

Madida, Fani 96
Manique, Brandon 225
Manning, Glen 120
Manning Rangers (football club) 108-10, 134
Marais, Dingaan 36, 46
Marais, Pinky 36, 46, 50
Marais, W. 45
Mashaba, Shakes 96
Matthews, Ronnie 62
Mayisa, S. 45
Mayville 3, 52, 58, 91, 92
Mbunjutwa, Thembela 12
McAlister, Henry 69
McAllister, J. 29
McBride, Robert 23
McKenzie, Margo 108
McKnight, Eddie 38, 44, 49, 50, 54, 66, 85, 116, 214

Mendell, Brian 133
Mentor, Charlie 202, 203
Mentor, Edward 202, 203
Mentor, Leon 202
Mentor, Raymond 45, 108, 201, 202-3
Meth, Ronald 36
Meth, Wellington 35, 60, 62, 116-18, 138-9, 143-6, 217
Middleton, Norman 86, 87
Mohan, Dharam 40
Moodley, Don 94, 100, 120-1
Moodley, Emily (née Hendricks) 103-4
Moodley, Helen (née Booysen) 104-5
Moodley, Patrick (Putts) 16-17, 98, 103-6, 108, 109, 121, 122, 132, 134-5, 136, 197, 200-1, 202, 213
Moodley, Steven (Crimes) 103, 104
Moonsamy, Dudu 94
Morrow, Kyle 165-6
Moses, George Yusuf 139
Motherwell (football club) 31, 39, 92, 98
Motor Assemblies (later Toyota) 47, 117
Mulheron, Eddie 108
Murray, Iris (née Knock) 11
Murray, Patrick 11
Murrigan, Cyril 133
music and dance 14, 16-19, 181-3, 206
muti 96

Naidoo, Dhanpal 206
Naik, Erol 133
National Professional Soccer League (NPSL) 95, 100, 134
National Soccer League (NSL) 95, 134
Nelson, Keith 39
Newlands East 56
NGI Lads (football club) 59
Ngubane, Lawrence 96
Ngubane, Mlungisa (Professor) 96

Nkabinde, Talfran 40
Nxumalo, Albert 13

Oakley, Ashley 64
Odette (Arlene Singh's partner) 131, 207, 208, 209
Ogle, Terrence 225
Oliver, Mr (Uncle Willy) 77–8
oral history 1–2

Palm Springs Hotel 5
passing for white 23, 24
Paul, Colin (Stormy) 36, 38, 44, 47, 49, 50, 54, 84
Paulus, Brian (Mo) 115
Peppers, Charlie 67
Perret, Robbie 127
Peters, Neville 46
Peters, Paul 36, 38
Peters, Phillip 37, 38, 54, 108, 121
Peters, Wilfred 54
Petersen, Basil 58, 59, 63, 151
Petersen, Calvin 133
Petersen, Cyril 151
Petersen, Dean 152
Petersen, Dennis (Rocky, the Menace) 3, 39, 40, 41, 43, 44, 46, 54, 58–60, 61, 62, 63–5, 66, 85, 86, 87, 89, 98, 105, 109, 115, 117, 119, 138, 161, 196, 199, 214, 226
Petersen, Fred 155
Petersen, Geoff 38
Petersen, Jeffrey 151
Petersen, Joyce 78
Petersen, Obed 39, 98
petrochemical industry 5, 6, 88, 117, 199, 204, 218, 219, 223–4
Phillips, Wilfred (Kaapie) 38, 117
pibes (Argentinian footballers) 211–12
Pillay, Charles 87

Pillay, Peter 121
place and space (as concepts) 1, 6–7, 131, 166–7, 180–1, 190, 213
Pretorius, Brian 115
Pretorius, Luffy 46
Pretorius, Seth Robert (Sonny) 15–16, 206
Price, Chicken 88
Pusher, Steven 139

race classification and racism 4, 20, 22–3, 25, 221
Railway Swallows (football club aka Brazilians) 32, 34–5, 47–8, 61
Ramsamy, Samba 86
Reckless Breakdancers (dance group) 18
Reddy, Terrence 195
Reg Wright Sports 36
Rehmans (Saints player) 115
Rex (dog and Leeds mascot) 55–6, 76
Rialto (football club) 28, 30, 59
Richards, Clint 150, 155–7, 159
Richards, Morris 149–50
Richardson, Cedric 151–2, 153
Richardson, Lorna (née Petersen, formerly Richards) 55–6, 78, 147–56, 157–8, 159, 160, 161, 199, 210, 215–16, 225–6
Richardson, Nadine (later Kast) 152, 155, 158
Richie, Irene 126–7, 128
Riley, Lynette 64
Roach, Ronnie 32, 38, 44, 54
Roberts, Neil 88
Roberts Construction 41–3
Robertson, B. 45
Robinson, Brian (Pondo) 96, 147
Robinson, Gerald 108
Rodganger, Malvery 115
Rodganger, Quinton 115

Rose, Falcon 158
Roskruge, Cornelius 12
Roskruge, Rodney 11-12, 184, 187-8, 224-5
Roskruge, Quade 142
rugby 23
Rumpshakers (football club) 163-4

Saints (football club) 115-16
Samuel, Bernard 71
Sanders, C. 29
Sanders, Kevin 115
Sanders, Steven 115
Sass, Irwin 143
Schreiber, Adrienne 162-4
Schreiber, Edgar 162
security industry 123
Seidel, Dale 201
Sewell, Kyle 166, 170
Silver Stars (football club) 217
Singh, Arlene (Webster) 119, 125-31, 161, 207-9
Singh, Ashley Mark 120, 125, 159-61, 164, 209-10
Singh, Bhugwan (Bugsy) 138, 139-41, 142-3, 206
Singh, Bradley 124
Singh, Brits 124
Singh, Elvis (Jerry) 45, 66, 105, 106, 108, 109, 117, 118-25, 160-1, 201, 212, 213
Singh, Ferrell 114-15, 119
Singh, Jerry (Rat) 161
Singh, Joyce 118, 119, 125, 130
Singh, Leonard 119
Singh, Maniraj 40
Singh, Mikhail 142
Singh, Sandra 123-4
sleeper trains 32, 33, 47
Small, Robbie 44, 50

Smith, C. 45
Smith, Gladys Joan (formerly Singh) 20
Smith, Paul 14
Smith, Quinton 18
Smith, Terrence (T-Bones) 17-20, 203, 204-5
Snyman, Aubrey 173
Solomons, Boobie 133
Solomons, Gollin 133
South African Bantu Football Association 22
South African Breweries (SAB) 134
South African Council on Sport (SACOS) 85-6, 101, 106
South African Football Association (SAFA) 98, 140
South African Railways 32, 33, 35
South African Soccer Federation (SASF) 21, 86, 95, 134
South African Soccer League (SASL) 21-2
South Durban Community Environmental Alliance 222-3
Spearman Lads (football club) 37, 39, 54, 93, 195
Speedy (gang member) 80, 81
sponsorship 53, 134
sport
　and contestation 27
　inter-race and multinational 21, 22, 85
　non-racial 86, 107; *see also* South African Council on Sport
stadiums 112; *see also* specific names
Stainbank, N. 29
Stalls, H. 29
Stanley, David 198, 213, 217-18
Steenkamp, Norman 45, 141
Stokes, Casper (Arthur Cyril) 24-5, 32-3, 34, 180

Stokes, Daphne 32
Stokes, Gertrude 33
Stokes, Maureen 32, 33
Stokes, Neville 24-5
Stokes, Papa (Phillip Gordon) 24-5, 30, 32, 33, 34-5
Stokes family 32-4
Strydom, Moses 40
Swartz, Martin 36, 54

Taps (dance group) 19
Thompson, B. 29
Tills Crescent 59, 91, 119
Titus, Lesley (Fishy) 38, 44
Tongaat Crusaders (football club) 107
Townhill Hospital (Pietermaritzburg) 83
Treasure Beach 6
Trikamjee, Ashwin 100
Trucks (gang, formerly Sinners) 70-1, 82
Tucker, Clement 45, 121
Tucker, H. 45

Ullbricht, James 38, 50
Uncle Willy *see* Oliver, Mr
urban poor 170

Van der Berg, Harold 74
Van Niekerk, Bony 44
Van Niekerk, George 36, 46
violence 204, 219

Wagner, H. 45
Walljee, Jappo 115
Walljee, Spy 115
Wand, Selby 40
War Room (Wentworth) 172-3
Warren, S. 45
Watts, Alan 88

Wentworth
 character and description 5, 7, 9, 21, 52, 69, 88, 183, 220-2
 children 26, 99
 churches 14, 25, 31, 35-6, 111
 cricket 115-16
 crime, violence and gangs 14, 27, 57, 165-9, 170, 171, 177, 195, 196-7, 198, 199, 205, 219-20
 domestic violence 204
 employment 21, 25, 27, 47, 57, 92, 99-100, 117-18, 170, 178-80, 184-5, 199, 219, 224
 extended families 210
 football 20, 22, 25, 30, 47, 88, 92, 105-6, 113-14, 116, 146, 159, 198, 199, 213-14, 215, 216-17, 226; *see also* names of specific clubs
 gardens 15-16, 17, 188-90, 225
 health 218
 history 1, 3, 6, 10, 56, 116
 housing 138, 148-9, 171-8, 183, 184, 199, 222
 identity 25, 194
 pollution 21, 196, 204, 218, 219, 222, 223
 protest and activism 225
 relocation of Wentonians to Bluff 193, 198
 social conditions 138, 143, 148-9, 170, 183-4, 185-6, 220, 223
 sports grounds 35-6, 88, 92, 114, 197, 218, 224
 and writing and publishing 187-8, 225
Wentworth Hospital 206-7
Westridge Park 59-60
Whitby, Bernard (Bennie) 30, 31, 32, 35, 36, 45, 46-54, 57, 116, 117, 132, 133

Whitby, Ignatius 36, 46
Whitby, June *see* Davids, June
Wicks, Dennis 88
Wiestham (football club) 106, 162–3
Williams, Jeff 115
Williams, John R. (Cocoon) 45, 93,
    120, 122, 123
Wiseman, Audrey 91
Wiseman, Chanel 93
Wiseman, Gregory 94, 102
Wiseman, Marice 93
Wiseman, Patrick (Boa) 91–103, 198,
    203, 214
Wiseman, Sharon (née Sharpley) 92–3,
    102
Wiseman, Warren 93, 94, 101–2

Xulu, Cedric (Sugar Ray) 40

Yorkshire (football club) 28, 29, 39
Young Cavaliers (football club) 115,
    117, 120, 125, 146, 147, 154,
    157–8, 159, 160, 161, 199, 215,
    217, 226

Zoy, Timothy 96